The Fearmakers

Other Books By John McCarty:

Hollywood Gangland: The Movies' Love Affair with the Mob

Movie Psychos and Madmen: Film Psychopaths from Jekyll And Hyde to Hannibal Lecter

Thrillers: Seven Decades of Classic Film Suspense

The Modern Horror Film: 50 Contemporary Classics

Deadly Resurrection (a novel)

The Complete Films of John Huston

The Official Splatter Movie Guide, Vols. 1 and 2

Splatter Movies: Breaking the Last Taboo of the Screen

Alfred Hitchcock Presents (with Brian Kelleher)

The Little Shop of Horrors Book (with Mark Thomas McGee)

The Amazing Herschell Gordon Lewis and His World of Exploitation Film (with Daniel Krogh)

You're on Open Line: Inside the Wacky World of Late-Night Talk Radio

The Sleaze Merchants: Adventures in Exploitation Filmmaking (forthcoming)

The FEarMAKers

The Screen's Directorial Masters of Suspense and Terror

Edited by John McCarty

First published in Great Britain in **1995** by
Virgin Books
an imprint of Virgin Publishing Ltd.
332 Ladbroke Grove
London W10 5AH

First published in the USA in 1994 by
St. Martin's Press, New York

A catalogue record for this book is available from the British Library

ISBN 0 86369 869 7

Design by Carol Haralson
Printed in the USA

Title page: From *The Old Dark House* (The John McCarty Collection)
Half title page: From *The Innocents* (The John McCarty Collection)
Contents page: From *Phantom of the Paradise* (Copyright © 1973 American International Pictures)
Facing plate, Acknowledgments: Bela Lugosi and Helen Chandler in *Dracula* (1931), Browning's
most successful talkie, yet a film often pointed to as a missed opportunity for greatness on Browning's
part. (Copyright © 1931 Universal Pictures)
Above: The inimitable William V. Mong as an eccentric, miserly millionaire in Christensen's
The House of Horror (1929). (George Eastman House)

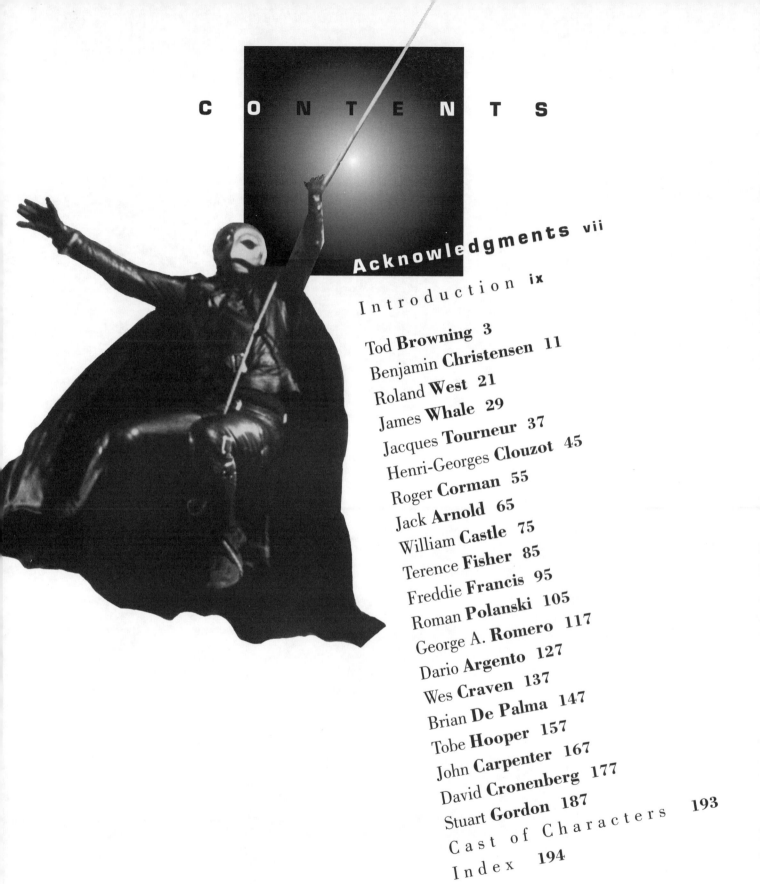

CONTENTS

Acknowledgments vii

Introduction ix

Tod **Browning** 3

Benjamin **Christensen** 11

Roland **West** 21

James **Whale** 29

Jacques **Tourneur** 37

Henri-Georges **Clouzot** 45

Roger **Corman** 55

Jack **Arnold** 65

William **Castle** 75

Terence **Fisher** 85

Freddie **Francis** 95

Roman **Polanski** 105

George A. **Romero** 117

Dario **Argento** 127

Wes **Craven** 137

Brian **De Palma** 147

Tobe **Hooper** 157

John **Carpenter** 167

David **Cronenberg** 177

Stuart **Gordon** 187

Cast of Characters 193

Index 194

A c k n o w l e d g m e n t s

On behalf of myself and my contributors, I would like to **thank** the following individuals and organizations for their respective contributions in bringing this book to light for fearfilm fans everywhere: John Brent; Raymond G. Cabana, Jr.; Michael J. Collins; Walter L. Gay; Bruce G. Hallenbeck; Ken Hanke; Veronica Carlson; Stuart Gordon; Kevin Brownlow; Eric Caidin (Hollywood Book & Poster); Film Favorites (Linda Rauh); George Eastman House (Kaye MacRae and Barbara Puorro Galasso); Roy Skeggs (Hammer Films); Trevor Paul; Canada (Caroline Forcier Holloway); National Archives of (St. Martin's Press); Scott MacQueen; Gordon Van Gelder Gordon; Richard Gordon; Ron Borst; Robert Gitt; Alex Guy; John Foster; Marlene Condon; Val Warren; Gordon R. Michael Dobbs; Jeanine Basinger; James Condon; G. Chmura; John P. Lowe; Jerry Haber; Hal Stanton; Stephen Kathleen Caban; Ken Holmes; Richard Finegan; Patrick Duquette; of Motion Picture Arts and Sciences; the Academy Wisconsin; Lincoln Center Library for the University of Arts; and also the late **Chester Morris, Una Merkel,** and Performing **Frank McHugh.**

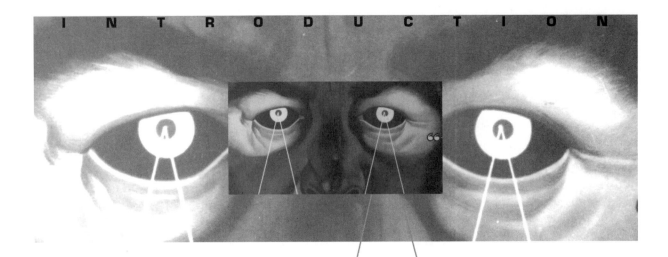

Let's talk about fear: shivery, chills up your spine, hair standing on end, edge of your seat, hands over your eyes, spilled popcorn in your lap *fear.*

Remember the delicious rush of terror you experienced in that dark movie palace or multiplex where you saw your first fearfilm as a youngster, the one you have never been able to get enough of and continue to seek out at the movies to this day?

Whether the first movie that scared you out of your pants or skirt as a youngster—and set your standards as an aficionado from then on—was a silent, F. W. Murnau's *Nosferatu* (1922)—the screen's first incarnation of Dracula—the Lon Chaney *The Phantom of the Opera* (1925), or *London After Midnight* (1927)—director Tod Browning's warm-up for the 1931 Bela Lugosi version of *Dracula*; a classic early talkie like Universal's *Frankenstein* (1931) or *The Mummy* (1932) or Warner Brothers' *Mystery of the Wax Museum* (1933); a ghoulish and graphic fifties Hammer Horror like *The Curse of Frankenstein* (1957) or *Horror of Dracula* (1958); or one of today's blood-drenched splatter epics such as *Night of the Living Dead* (1968) or *The Texas Chainsaw Massacre* (1974), the one constant, the thing that unites you whether you're still in your teens or over sixty, is this: As a child, you *liked* that creepy feeling you got reaching for the light switch in the basement, that sense that something—*it!*—might be waiting for you when the lights came on. And you're still *hooked* on the adrenaline rush that comes with the anticipation of confronting anything unknown, terrified by what it might be, yet drawn to it—captivated by the need to know what *is* there. The experience of seeing a really scary movie conjures up this same addictive emotion.

Human beings have always felt this way, of course, long before they had the technology to project moving pictures on the screen. But since the advent of the movies at the end of the last century, people have taken to moving pictures as the ideal form for making them feel the emotion of fear.

Moving pictures have the unique ability, through lighting, editing, and other techniques, not only to lead us into that dark basement but then to switch on the lights and *show* us the *it!* that's there waiting for us. They conjure up our deepest, darkest fears and then put a face on them, be it in glorious black and white or full-blooded Technicolor.

From the beginning of the motion-picture medium, directors (indeed some of the cinema's greatest) have shared the view that film was an ideal form for transferring the emotion of fear to an audience—since one of the definitions of the art of directing, in the words of film historian Kevin Brownlow, is, quite literally, the "transference of emotion."

Many directors have also found the medium to be an ideal forum in which to expose their own fears and anxieties or to experiment stylistically with the mechanics of screen fearmaking. And their efforts to feed our insatiable appetite for and enjoyment of the emotion of fear on the screen have often led to some sublime—and not so sublime, but still enjoyable—cinematic achievements.

Regrettably, the bulk of these achievements—including a number discussed in this book—have been lost to us forever due to the combustible nature of early celluloid as well as to neglect and outright destruction by producers who no longer believed such works had any value, commercial or otherwise, once sound came in.* It is, therefore, virtually impossible to assess the entire body of work in the vein of fearfilm, since much of it is no longer available to us for study. Gone are films of potentially incalculable value to our complete understanding of all the genre has had to offer and how it evolved, especially during the cinema's early years, such as the pioneering works of Alice Guy-Blaché (1873-1968), arguably the medium's first female director and a specialist in supernatural and horror/fantasy thrillers, whose career ended before the coming of sound; F. W. Murnau's precursor to *Nosferatu*, a pirated adaptation of Robert Louis Stevenson's iconographic horror tale *Dr. Jekyll and Mr. Hyde*, titled *Der Januskopf* (1920); Wallace Worsley's Lon Chaney vehicle *A Blind Bargain* (1922), one of the actor's few outright horror films, despite his enduring reputation as primarily a horror star; and much, *too much*, more.

Enough remains, however, of both the good stuff and the bad in the arena of screen fear and fright for us to know that since the beginnings of film, the fearmakers have been an extremely prolific bunch who learned (and sometimes stole) from one another, and were never content just to stand still; instead, they continually pushed the genre into new and exciting directions.

That's the real subject of this book: the makers of screen fear—not the emotion of fear itself. *The Fearmakers* discusses twenty practitioners of the art of screen fearmaking, from the silent era to the present day, whose contributions to and influence upon the genre in terms of theme, style, and technical and other innovations remain significant. (Since fear is one of the most primal human emotions, the fearfilm has often been prone to purely exploitative work, of course, and many of the model directors in *this* regard will be dealt with in a forthcoming volume, titled *The Sleaze Merchants: Adventures in Exploitation Filmmaking*.)

While many important directors ranging from Michael Curtiz to Stanley Kubrick have dabbled in fearfilm, and many others such as Sam Raimi and Joe Dante have devoted most of their careers to making movies of terror, horror, and fright, providing some

significant contributions to the genre along the way, I deem the architects of screen fear chosen for discussion in this book to be the genre's twenty *most* important and influential grand masters, honorable practitioners and up-and-comers, each of whom has sought or continues to seek, with varying degrees of success, to take the genre to a place it has never been before, or at least to follow his own distinctive route to the same place.

They include: **Benjamin Christensen,** the Dutch expatriate who delighted in making old-dark-house comedy thrillers but whose most famous work in the genre was banned from America's screens for decades; **James Whale,** whose four seminal fearfilms for Universal in the early 1930s influence the genre still; **Roman Polanski,** whose fearsome studies of paranoia and mental breakdown on the screen have yet to be matched for their realism, psychological insight, and shivery force; **Jacques Tourneur,** the screen's undisputed master of shadowy substance, whose hokey but stylish 1958 thriller *The Fearmakers*, which is about a very different type of scare—the Communist menace— provided this book with an ideal title; **Henri-Georges Clouzot,** "the French Hitchcock"; and many more.

These profiles are arranged chronologically rather than alphabetically in order to give the reader a sense of how the genre has changed and developed over time.

One final note: Some readers will no doubt ask, "Why only twenty?"

My answer to that is this: To keep the book a manageable (and therefore affordable) length, I chose to discuss twenty directors in reasonable depth rather than trying to examine briefly the careers of scores of fearmakers.

Other readers will then ask, "How come you selected so-and-so and not so-and-so?" To that, I can only restate my position that while my selections may be subjective, they were not made arbitrarily. These are the twenty fearmakers above all others whom I believe have made the most impact on the genre—for good or ill—during its more than eighty-year history.

The only name I opted not to include—even though his contribution to and impact on the art of screen fearmaking has been enormous—is that of Alfred Hitchcock. I did so simply because so much has already been written about Hitchcock and his many masterful fearfilms that I felt little could be added here.

I humbly dedicate this book to his memory instead.

*The woeful fate of much of our cinematic heritage is not just confined to silent pictures, although films of the silent era have certainly suffered the most. By some estimates, as much as 50 percent of *all* the films and TV programs ever made in this country are now lost or beyond salvaging, which is why film preservationists are currently mounting such an aggressive drive for (belated) public support, as well as governmental and private funding.

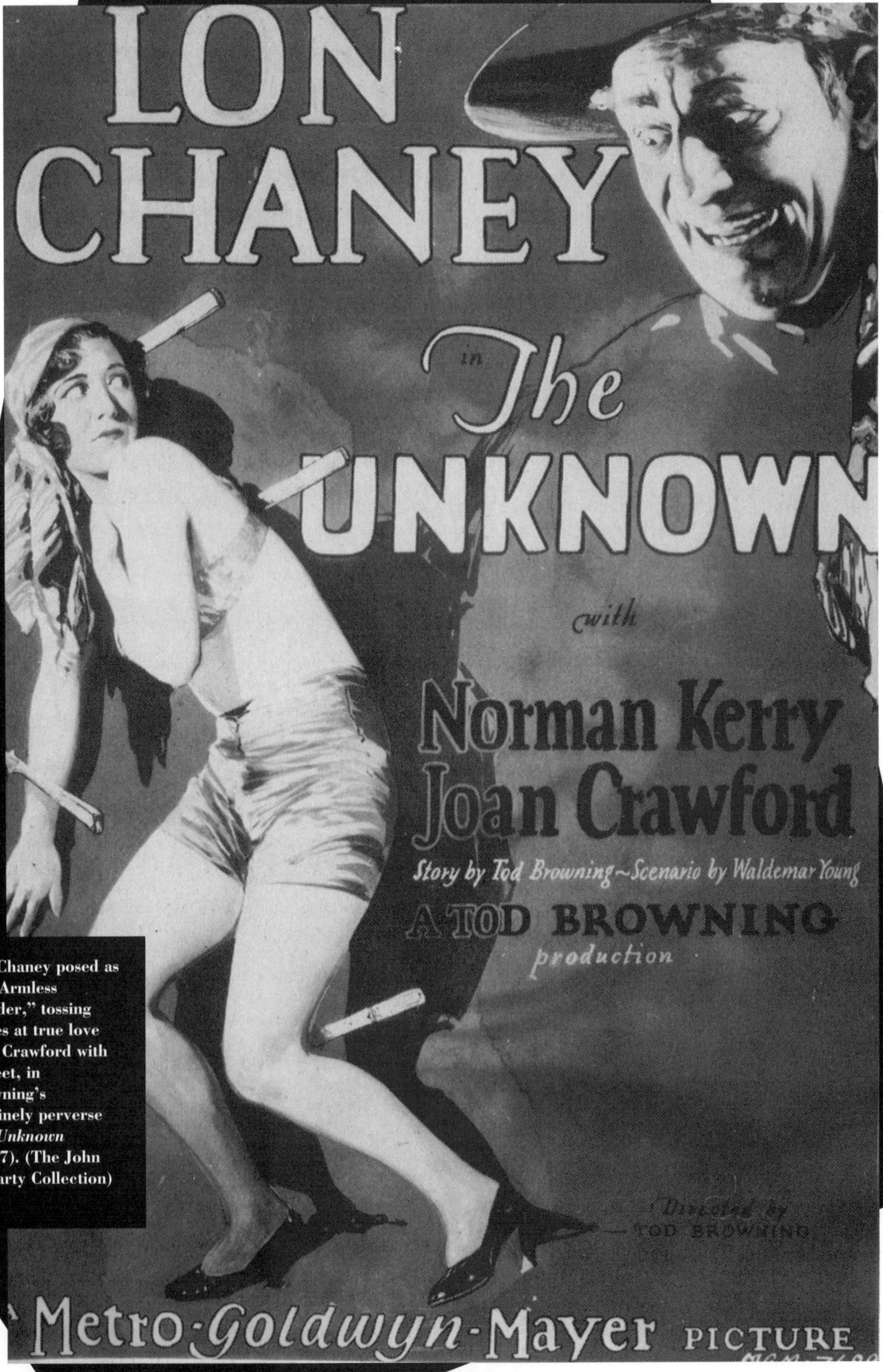

LON CHANEY

in The UNKNOWN

with

Norman Kerry
Joan Crawford

Story by Tod Browning ~ Scenario by Waldemar Young

A TOD BROWNING
production

Directed by
TOD BROWNING

Lon Chaney posed as "the Armless Wonder," tossing knives at true love Joan Crawford with his feet, in Browning's genuinely perverse *The Unknown* (1927). (The John McCarty Collection)

A Metro-Goldwyn-Mayer PICTURE

JOHN MCCARTY

TOD BROWNING

A contortionist and killer hiding out in a circus where he's billed as "the Armless Wonder" falls in love with a girl suffering from a pathological fear of being embraced—and has his arms removed for real to win her over, only to find once the operation is over that she's fallen for the circus strongman (*The Unknown,* 1927).

In a Hungarian circus where the featured sideshow attraction is Salome's beheading of John the Baptist, a love triangle turns deadly when a member of the triangle tries to kill the other with a poisonous Gila monster (*The Show,* 1927).

A trapeze artist and her strongman paramour concoct a scheme for her to marry a sideshow dwarf for his money, then get him out of the way with poison, but the dwarf's fellow human oddities catch on and vengefully cut the full-sized lovers down to size (*Freaks,* 1932).

A crippled music-hall magician turned jungle trader revenges himself on the man who caused his affliction and ran away with his wife by dragging the man's virginal daughter to ruin, then discovers the girl is his own flesh and blood (*West of Zanzibar,* 1928).

The ghoulish plots of these and other Tod Browning films of the silent and early sound period have led to the critical conclusion that here was one

fearmaker who truly let his hair down and revealed his dark side to us on the screen in film after film with a remarkable degree of consistency and relish. Terms like *castration fear, loss of identity, displaced sexuality, obsessive perversity,* and *misogyny* run throughout auteurist studies of Browning's oeuvre like a torrent of psychobabble, conjuring up a picture of the man as the first great twentieth-century American Gothic artist and the cinematic inheritor of the mantle of Edgar Allan Poe.

My own view of Browning is somewhat different. I see him not as a purveyor of dark themes who consistently let loose his private demons on an unsuspecting—yet eager—public with the help of big studio backing through picture after picture but as a pioneer in the craft of exploitation filmmaking, whose artistic credo rang with the call of his step-right-up carny-man career. He was a showman who knew firsthand that a sucker was born every minute and who knew how to separate that sucker from

Carny man turned exploitation film pioneer Tod Browning ringed by some of his human-oddity stars on the set of *Freaks* (1932), the commercial failure of which was a calamity from which his career never quite recovered. (Copyright © 1932 MGM)

his money with the lure of the unknown, the perverse, the forbidden.

Frankly, probing the so-called themes of Browning's work to reveal the man is, I think, about as fruitful as analyzing such a thematically empty, purely exploitative work as the splatter film *Blood Feast* (1963) to get a fix on the psyche of its director, Herschell Gordon Lewis. It's not in the submerged contents of his films where the "real" Tod Browning is to be found but in their sensational, amazingly up-front, and often taboo-breaking concepts.

A son of the South like his mentor in the movies, D. W. Griffith, Charles Albert "Tod" Browning was born in Louisville, Kentucky, on July 12, 1880 (or 1882, according to some accounts). Lured by the siren call of adventure, he left home at the age of sixteen to join a traveling carnival as a roustabout and occasional barker. He later turned to performing, first as a clown, then as a contortionist and illusionist with an act called "the Living Hypnotic Corpse," which he performed on various riverboats along the Mississippi. He subsequently entered vaudeville, where he performed the same acts onstage, as well as doing some comedy and song and dance routines.

Thoroughly hooked on a showbiz career and well grounded in the art of the shill from his years as a carny man, he met Griffith through a mutual acquaintance in 1913 and quickly recognized the unlimited crowd-pleasing potential—and potential for steady employment—of the infant medium in which Griffith was fast gaining a reputation. Browning

jumped at the chance to join the Griffith team as an actor, stuntman, and assistant director. When Griffith went west to make bigger pictures in the sun-drenched valleys of a place not yet famous as Hollywood, Browning went with him, and it was there that he directed his own first films, a series of two-reelers with such exploitable titles as *The Living Head* (1915), *The Burned Hand* (1915), and *Everybody's Doing It* (1916). It was also during this period that Browning, a high roller with a fondness for gambling, liquor, and fast cars who now had enough steady income to indulge all three, was involved in a terrible car crash that catapulted his name into the headlines.

Drunk and at the wheel, Browning had plowed his roadster into a carload of street rails one morning (ostensibly on the way home from an all-night party), instantly killing one of his passengers, Griffith actor Elmer Booth, and severely injuring himself and a second passenger, George A. Seigmann, another member of the Griffith unit. It has been widely speculated over the years that in addition to giving him sudden recognition in the moviemaking community (if not exactly the most welcome kind), the accident—and Browning's unstated injuries from it—resulted in the loss of his genitals, a trauma that turned him to alcoholism and an obsessive preoccupation with themes of sexual frustration, castration, and other forms of mutilation. Many theorists point to the odd, unexplained line of dialogue tossed off by Wallace Ford to the girl (Leila Hyams) attracted to him in *Freaks*—often termed Browning's most personal film—

The Fearmakers

that she should have met him before his accident as a reference by Browning to the true nature of his injuries from the car crash.

In fact, there's little evidence either to confirm or to deny the castration theory. It is true that Browning suffered from alcoholism, but it appears he was well on his way to it even before his famous accident, and he fought to overcome the disease throughout his life. It is also true that he died childless (as far as we know), but he remained married to the same woman to the end of his life in 1962, certainly a frustrating situation for her all those years if the theorists are correct.

One thing is certain, though: The accident didn't slow Browning down any. Less than a year after the crash, he was back behind the wheel, acting the part of the speedster who races Mae Marsh to save her husband from the gallows at the conclusion of Griffith's epic *Intolerance* (1916), a sensational and highly exploitable bit of typecasting to which neither Griffith nor Browning were oblivious.

Browning codirected his first feature-length film, the Civil War drama *Jim Bludso,* in 1917. Within the same year, he moved to Metro (not yet Goldwyn-Mayer) Pictures, where he directed a number of films with such alluring titles as *The Jury of Fate* (1917), *The Legion of Death* (1918), *Revenge* (1918), and *The Eyes of Mystery* (1918), a haunted-house melodrama that foreshadowed the macabre direction his career would ultimately take. None of these films are known to have survived, however.

In 1919, Browning contracted with Universal to direct *The Wicked Darling,* an early example of the gangster film, another popular genre with which Browning would become closely associated throughout his career. That film also marked the beginning of Browning's long association with Lon Chaney, an up-and-coming actor about the same age as Browning who played the villain in the film opposite Priscilla Dean's innocent-gone-wrong jewel thief. Browning and Chaney became friends, no doubt drawn by their similar showbiz backgrounds. More to the point, they began a professional relationship that lasted until Chaney's death in 1930 and had a profound impact on the careers of both men.

Still revered as one of the silent film's most gifted

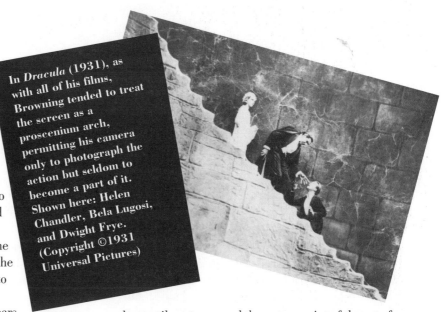

In *Dracula* (1931), as with all of his films, Browning tended to treat the screen as a proscenium arch, permitting his camera only to photograph the action but seldom to become a part of it. Shown here: Helen Chandler, Bela Lugosi, and Dwight Frye. (Copyright ©1931 Universal Pictures)

and versatile actors—and the patron saint of the art of movie makeup—Chaney specialized in roles that required him to disguise his features and contort his appearance to such an extent that he became known as "the Man of a Thousand Faces" and the silent cinema's reigning "Man of Mystery." Chaney historians often discuss the artistic and psychological motivations behind Chaney's penchant for such roles, but they usually fail

Browning reworked elements from his most popular Chaney film, *The Unholy Three* (1925), into *The Devil Doll* (1936), complete with Lionel Barrymore in a Chaneyesque old-woman disguise. (Copyright © 1936 MGM)

to note what a canny business move they were on Chaney's part, for his filmic disguises were also a highly exploitable gimmick that enabled Chaney to carve out a niche for himself that eventually resulted in his becoming MGM's biggest box-office draw, second only to Garbo. And in Tod Browning, Chaney found a writer-director eager to exploit that gimmick in ever-more-sensational ways. Chaney played monsters and bad guys for other directors, of course, but the Browning-Chaney collaboration was a unique one that sustained itself through ten pictures, more than Chaney made for any other single director.

As Browning himself stated in one of the rare interviews he gave about his career, his films with Chaney seldom evolved in the traditional way. Rather than selecting the story first, he would come up with the concept of the type of role he wanted Chaney to play, then find or write a story to fit that role—or roles, for in Browning's films Chaney frequently played dual or multiple parts. This gimmick often resulted in some choice cinematic moments, as in *Outside the Law* (1921), a gangster film in which Chaney plays the villainous Black Mike Sylva and the Chinese Ah Wing, who shoots Black Mike in the film's cleverly edited conclusion. The gangster films *The Unholy Three* (1925) and *The Blackbird* (1926), arguably Browning's finest film, and Browning's Dracula warm-up, *London After Midnight* (1927), are other notable films in which Browning used the gimmick of more than one Chaney to creative and lucrative advantage.

The teaming of Browning and Chaney also resulted in some daring and perverse plotlines, as in *The Unknown* (1927), the synopsis of which heads this chapter and is enough to make the skin crawl, and *Where East Is East* (1929), their final collaboration set in Indochina, where Chaney plays Tiger, hot-blooded trapper of wild animals for the circus. His scenes with his equally hot-blooded daughter (Lupe Valez) as she nibbles excitedly on his scarred arms reek with the suggestion of incest—a taboo topic that lurks throughout the whole film, the plot of which centers on Chaney's efforts to prevent Valez's fiancé (Lloyd Hughes) from being stolen away by a worldly-wise older woman (Estelle Taylor), who happens to be his ex-wife and Valez's mother.

Browning was equally quick to see the value of having his star appear sans makeup and grotesquerie, as in their gangster film *The Big City* (1928), another huge critical and commercial success for them that was hailed by the critics for giving Chaney the chance to demonstrate his talents playing a role without resorting to makeup tricks.

The picture for which Browning is best remembered, though, is the 1931 version of *Dracula*, starring Bela Lugosi, the film that launched the first great cycle of screen horror in the American cinema.

Ironically, *Dracula* is also the one Browning film critics often point to as a missed opportunity for greatness on Browning's part, despite its classic status. This has become especially true in recent years since the release on video of the long-unseen Spanish-language version of *Dracula*, which was shot simultaneously with the Browning version and used the same script and sets but a different crew and actors. The general consensus now is that the Spanish version, directed by George Melford, is the superior of the two films, despite the absence of the inimitable Lugosi in the title role. (Mexican actor Carlos Villarias donned the cape instead.) This opinion is based on the fact that Melford, an otherwise-undistinguished director who, like Browning, began his career in the silent period, brought a bit more stylistic verve to his version of the story—and the view that the resulting film, which retains a number of scenes cut from the Browning film and runs almost half an hour longer, is altogether better paced and more exciting. While it is true that Melford's film boasts a few scenes—shots actually—that are cinematically more inventive than Browning's, an objective comparison of the two films reveals the contest to be pretty much of a draw. Both films have their pluses and their minuses, but the end product in each case is slow-moving, antiquated, and dull—especially when contrasted with James Whale's technically dazzling and not a bit tedious *Frankenstein*, made at the same studio the same year.

In any event, the lack of stylistic flourishes in Browning's direction of *Dracula* was by no means a sudden shifting of gears for him, nor was it a case of failing creative batteries leading to a missed opportunity. While some of his silents with Chaney are indeed more exciting than *Dracula*, and some of his later films—*Freaks*, for instance—more gripping, Browning was never the most cinematic of directors. In the tradition of the stage, where he learned his craft, he tended to treat the screen as a proscenium arch, relying on sets, lighting, and performers for impact, permitting his camera only to photograph the action but seldom to become part of it. Even during the closing days of the silents when the fluid camera techniques of the great German filmmakers Murnau,

Lang, and Dupont resulted in a visual transformation of the American film and Hollywood hacks as well as artists began using the camera in ever-more-stylish ways to involve the audience, a gun figuratively had to be put to Browning's head to get him to do a brief dolly shot—and his technique did not change in the talkie era, even after the camera was freed from the cumbersome shackles imposed by early sound-recording equipment. Nor did he change his approach to storytelling, which was often quite slapdash.

The greatness of Browning's *Dracula* and its unique position in the history of the fearfilm lie in its concept. Browning was not stupid. He knew that *Dracula* was about eroticism and sex—elements that always spelled big box office. He also saw the opportunity to portray these elements in a story that was atypical of the American horror cinema up to that time, for in most such films, the supernatural ingredients were typically used as a bogus mask for some mystery or comedy plot and were explained away at the conclusion. The monsters were never "the real thing." *Dracula* was different, and therefore highly exploitable, and it was a project Browning had fixed on for years. He tried without success to purchase the screen rights to the renowned Hamilton Deane stage adaptation of Bram Stoker's

Edna Tichenor as the Bat Girl and Lon Chaney as the vampire in *London After Midnight* (1927) and a virtually identical shot of Bela Lugosi and Carol Borland in the same roles in *Mark of the Vampire* (1935), Browning's talkie remake. (Copyright © 1935 MGM)

novel even before the play crossed the Atlantic and became a hit on the Broadway stage. When he failed, he wrote his own vampire tale in a similar vein, called *The Hypnotist*, which he filmed at MGM as *London After Midnight*, starring Lon Chaney in two roles, one of them a vampire, and released it just two months after the Deane play's 1927 London premiere, riding in on the play's coattails, as it were. Typical of its genre, the film (now lost) again presented the supernatural elements of the story as bogus come the final fade-out, but in other respects it was clearly a dress rehearsal for the groundbreaking vampire film Browning ultimately did bring to the screen in 1931—albeit sans Chaney, the actor he'd always wanted for the part of Count Dracula, but who had died the year before.

Browning's instincts proved correct. *Dracula* was one of the biggest successes of his career, and his most successful talkie. Capitalizing on that success, he subsequently doubled back and remade his earlier dress rehearsal as *Mark of the Vampire* (1935), featuring Lugosi himself in the vampire role earlier played by Chaney. The film was even more like *Dracula* than *London After Midnight* had been, and he and MGM were immediately slapped with an injunction by Universal because of the similarities. The court ruled against Universal, however, because Browning had cannily retained *Midnight*'s original ending, which revealed the vampire to be a fake and the supernatural elements to be a ruse aimed at unmasking a murderer (Jean Hersholt)—a gimmick that struck audiences and critics in the post-*Dracula* era as a fresh twist.

With the death of Lon Chaney, Browning had lost

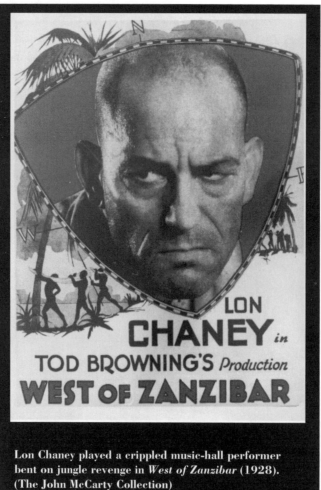

Lon Chaney played a crippled music-hall performer bent on jungle revenge in *West of Zanzibar* (1928). (The John McCarty Collection)

a prime ingredient in his filmmaking formula: an actor who was not only willing but able to contort his body and transform his features in order to disappear into whatever bizarre character Browning conjured up next. Despite the splash he'd made in the role of *Dracula*, Lugosi was neither equipped to step into the chameleon Chaney's shoes nor willing to do so, as he balked at the idea of disguising himself under pounds of makeup to play the part of the Monster in Universal's *Frankenstein*, and the star-making role went to Boris Karloff. Rather than keep looking for another Chaney, Browning opted instead to take his winning formula a sensational step further by casting his next film not with actors donning makeup but with sideshow performers whose twisted shapes and missing limbs were grimly genuine. The result was *Freaks*, a film that critics have since hailed as the most compassionate horror film ever made. But it's clear from watching the film itself that what Browning was really after was shock value. What he did not count on was that sensation-hungry audiences would find the film's authentic grotesquerie so shocking to their sensibilities that they would shun it. The illusion of Chaney pretending to be legless was obviously much more palatable to them than the sight of a bona fide "armless and legless wonder" lighting a cigar with his teeth. The film drew heavy fire from state censor boards and critics, and despite all the notoriety surrounding its "sensational aspects," it was a box-office disaster that MGM quickly pulled from release and locked away in its vaults for years.

The failure of *Freaks* was a calamity from which Browning's career never quite recovered. He'd been ahead of his time with this one, the first great exploitation picture of the talkie era, and the bible on a conceptual level for every fringe and exploitation filmmaker ever since. Browning was never able to go quite as far again. In fact, he began looking backward and rehashing what he'd done before. *Mark of the Vampire* was an outright remake of one of his earlier triumphs, though he attempted to spice it up a bit by injecting the theme of incest into a flashback dealing with the Lugosi character, but the sequence was cut by the studio prior to the film's release. And despite its clever effects work, *The Devil Doll* (1936), a loose adaptation of A. Merritt's horror-cum-gangster novel *Burn Witch Burn*, was little more than a reworking of elements from his most popular Chaney film, *The Unholy Three*, complete with Lionel Barrymore in a Chaneyesque old-woman disguise.

Browning made his last film, *Miracles for Sale*, a routine murder mystery with a magic-show background, in 1939. His instincts hadn't quite left him, however. For several years, he tried to get MGM to back a film version of Horace McCoy's taboo-breaking novel about the Depression, *They Shoot Horses, Don't They?* But it was not to be, and in 1941, he retired in bitterness, refusing to discuss his career publicly for the remainder of his life.

Filmography

1915: *The Lucky Transfer** (director), *The Highbinders** (director), *The Living Death** (director), *The Burned Hand** (director), *The Woman from Warren's** (director), *The Slave Girl** (director), *An Image of the Past** (director), *The Smell of the Poppy** (director), *The Electric Alarm** (director), *Little Marie** (director); 1916: *The Fatal Glass of Beer** (director), *Everybody's Doing It** (director), *Puppets** (director); 1917: *Jim Bludso* (codirector), *A Love Sublime* (codirector), *Hands Up!* (codirector), *The Jury of Fate* (director), *Peggy, the Will O' the Wisp* (director), *The Eyes of Mystery* (director); 1918: *The Legion of Death* (director), *Revenge* (director), *Which Woman?* (director), *The Deciding Kiss* (director), *The Brazen Beauty* (director), *Set Free* (director/writer); 1919: *The Wicked Darling* (director), *The Exquisite Thief* (director), *The Unpainted Woman* (director), *A Petal on the Current* (director), *Bonnie, Bonnie Lassie* (director/cowriter); 1920: *The Virgin of Stamboul* (director/cowriter); 1921: *Outside the Law* (director/cowriter), *No Woman Knows* (director/cowriter); 1922: *The Wise Kid* (director), *Under Two Flags* (director/cowriter), *Man Under Cover* (director); 1923: *Drifting* (director/cowriter), *White Tiger* (director/cowriter), *The Day of Faith* (director); 1924: *The Dangerous Flirt* (director), *Silk Stocking Sal* (director); 1925: *The Unholy Three* (director), *The Mystic* (director/cowriter), *Dollar Down* (director); 1926: *The Blackbird* (director/cowriter), *The Road to Mandalay* (director/cowriter); 1927: *London After Midnight* (director/cowriter), *The Show* (director), *The Unknown* (director/cowriter); 1928: *The Big City* (producer/director/cowriter), *West of Zanzibar* (director); 1929: *Where East Is East* (producer/director/cowriter), *The Thirteenth Chair* (producer/director); 1930: *Outside the Law* (director/cowriter); 1931: *Dracula* (director), *The Iron Man* (director); 1932: *Freaks* (producer/director); 1933: *Fast Workers* (producer/director); 1935: *Mark of the Vampire* (director); 1936: *The Devil Doll* (director/cowriter); 1939: *Miracles for Sale* (director); 1946: *Inside Job* (cowriter).

* short film

The face of the Dracula that never was? Lon Chaney as the bogus vampire in *London After Midnight* (1927), Browning's warm-up for his groundbreaking 1931 Lugosi film. (The John McCarty Collection)

Montagu Love
threatens Thelma
Todd in an
atmospheric scene
from Christensen's
lost horror comedy
The Haunted House
(1928), cowritten
by William Irish,
a.k.a. Cornell
Woolrich. (George
Eastman House)

137-131X

J O H N   M C C A R T Y

BENJAMIN CHRISTENSEN

The all-but-forgotten Danish film director Benjamin Christensen was responsible for one of the most unusual fearfilms of the silent (and any other) era, the legendary *Häxan,* or, as it is more familiarly known, *Witchcraft Through the Ages.*

Christensen never particularly liked the film's more famous English title, even though *Witchcraft Through the Ages* more clearly lays out the film's content and reveals the director's artistic intentions: to chronicle realistically the history of witchcraft in Europe from the Middle Ages to modern times (the twenties) in quasidocumentary fashion.

The prefix quasi is apt, for *Witchcraft Through the Ages,* like the magic-obsessed creatures it imaginatively and often surrealistically evokes, frequently soars into wild flights of fancy. One such moment occurs near the end of the film when the reemergence of witchcraft in the post-Freudian age is linked to a "natural inclination among the female of the species to hysterical behavior." As anyone knows who lived through the 1960s—when renewed interest in occult matters became a sort of national pastime (and at the height of which, 1969, *Witchcraft Through the Ages* was rereleased with sound effects and narration delivered by literary wild man William S. Burroughs)—such behavior is by no means the exclusive province of women.

Born in 1879, Benjamin Christensen studied to be a doctor, then shifted to a theatrical career shortly after the turn of the century.

Captivated by the nickelodeons and earliest movies, he gave up a promising stage career as a singer and actor to write scenarios for the pioneer Danish film director August Blom. However, Christensen's first two films as a director in his own right, *The Mysterious X* (1913) and *Night of Revenge* (1915), revealed the influence of his true artistic mentor, Louis Feuillade, the flamboyant French director of some of the most popular and visually baroque detective and fantasy serials of the pre-World War I period: *Fantômas* (1913-1914), *Les Vampires* (1915-1916), *Judex* (1916), et al.

On the strength of the technical sophistication and narrative strength he demonstrated in his first two films—one a spy thriller, the other a circus and crime drama—Christensen was invited by one of Sweden's two major film companies, Svensk Filmindustri, to make a film for them shortly after the war. The result was the notorious *Witchcraft Through the Ages,* Christensen's most ambitious and visually spectacular film up to that time.

The medieval episodes of

Comedienne Louise Fazenda eavesdrops on some plotters in *The House of Horror* (1929), which was released with music, sound effects, and a talking sequence on Vitaphone disc. Regrettably, they and the film are lost. (George Eastman House)

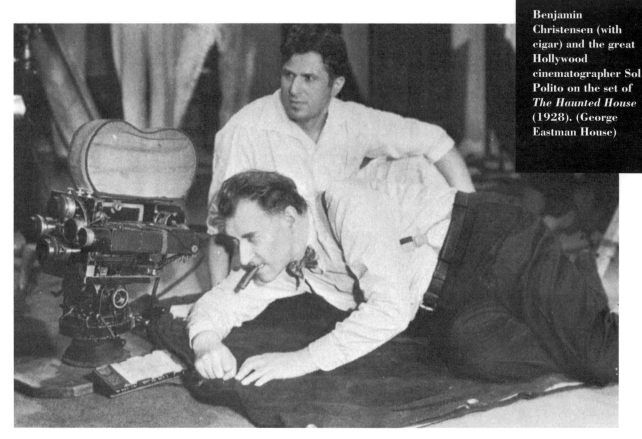

Witchcraft—the film's first half—are the best. In them, Christensen evocatively (and provocatively) illustrates such arcane lore as what ingredients went into the making of the most potent potions (an explicit and particularly revolting sequence); how a witch could be identified by means of a "devil's mark" etched into her person; the sadistic tortures inflicted on witches for engaging in their diabolic craft; and how witches came to use brooms as a way to signal one another that they were "sisters in the craft." All of these fantastic elements culminate in a hallucinatory Walpurgisnacht sequence where the witches fly through the air on their brooms to join their pudgy master, Satan (played by Christensen himself), in an all-nude black mass. The film's modern sequences, beset by stilted acting and a lot of psychobabble, are slow-moving, uninspired, and often unintentionally hilarious by comparison.

Witchcraft's ghoulishness and especially its nudity got it banned from the screens of most theaters outside of its native Sweden for decades. Begun in 1919 but not completed until 1922, the 110- to 120-minute film reached American shores in a severely truncated version in 1929. For its New York City premiere, it was coupled with, of all things, a Laurel and Hardy short comedy called *Liberty.*

Film Daily called the film's "subject matter too grim for most picture houses." Exhibitors must have agreed, for despite its notoriety, *Witchcraft Through the Ages* received limited distribution in the United States and was not a box-office success. It was a critical success, however. The influential *New York Times* termed the picture "fantastically conceived and directed, holding the onlooker in a sort of medieval spell. Most of the characters seem to have stepped from primitive paintings."

The film's notoriety in Europe and the critical accolades it received abroad and, for the most part, in the United States as well caught the attention of Hollywood, and Christensen journeyed to MGM, where he enjoyed a brief but memorable career directing two of the studio's top stars, Norma Shearer (in the 1926 *The Devil's Circus,* which was not a sequel to *Witchcraft,* nor even a horror film, despite its suggestive title) and Lon Chaney (in the 1927 *Mockery,* a tale of unrequited lust and requited love set during the Russian Revolution).

On the heels of these two critical and commercial successes, Christensen was lured to First National (later Warner Brothers-First National) to make a series of three horror/comedy thrillers that today rank among the most tantalizing and sought-after fearfilms of the silent era due to the regrettable fact that two appear not to have survived the ravages of time and nitrate decomposition and the third is all but impossible to see.

With the exception of Lon Chaney's occasional forays into cinematic grotesquerie, most fearfilms predating Universal's successful cycle of Dracula, Frankenstein, and mummy movies were haunted-house comedy thrillers rather than outright monster shows. The format was established by the huge stage and subsequent movie version successes of such archetypal old-dark-house, masked-killer, sliding-panel, will-read-at-midnight chillers as Mary Roberts Rinehart and Avery Hopwood's *The Bat* and John Willard's *The Cat and the Canary*. By the mid-twenties, this type of melodrama had become so popular and pervasive and its clichés so well-worn that it became the subject of satire in such theatrical hits as Crane Wilbur's *The Monster* (filmed by MGM in 1925 with Lon Chaney) and Owen Davis's *The Haunted House: An American Comedy in Three Acts,* the play upon which the first of Christensen's three comedy thrillers for First National was based. The subtitle was dropped, however, and the now-lost film was released, with accompanying sound effects and music on Vitaphone disc, as *The Haunted House* (1928).

Adapted by Richard Bee and Lajos Biro with intertitles provided by an up-and-coming suspense writer named William Irish (a.k.a. Cornell Woolrich), the film dealt with an eccentric millionaire (Edmund Breese) who decides to ferret out which of his four heirs is most deserving of his fortune by putting them to a nightmarish test. He gives them a sealed letter, with instructions that it not be opened until his death. But they ignore his instructions and read the letter, which tells of a fortune in cash hidden somewhere in the millionaire's allegedly haunted mansion. Spurred by curiosity—and greed—the quartet of treasure hunters head for the haunted house to locate the loot (or prevent one another from locating it) but instead encounter all manner of apparitions, lunatics, weird noises, and other trappings of the genre to strain their nerves and test their mettle. In a twist ending lifted from *Seven Keys to Baldpate* (but typical of most such comedy thrillers, it must be said), the weird characters and bizarre goings-on prove to be bogus. The ghouls and goblins turn out to be actors hired by Breese to terrify the presumptive heirs into revealing their true natures. The youthful hero (Larry Kent) proves to be the most stalwart and least greedy of the bunch, so Breese declares him the rightful heir.

Although the film was a popular success, reviews tended to be mixed. Critic Mordaunt Hall called *The Haunted House* a "synthetic

It was erotic scenes like this that got *Witchcraft Through the Ages* (1922) banned from world screens for decades. (The John McCarty Collection)

The Fearmakers

spookshow" that was "as impossible [to swallow] as other stories of its kind, [but possessed] the virtues of being mildly amusing during some of its stretches and judging by the demeanor of the audiences [contained] sufficient suspense to hold the attention." Nevertheless, he, and most of his colleagues as well, admired the filmmaker's obvious affection for the genre and the care and the Feuillade-like manner in which Christensen successfully alternated "spine-chills and giggles." They also took note of the film's abundant "weird" camera angles, sinuous camera moves, atmospheric lighting, and other stylistic flourishes, which they considered "more than slightly reminiscent" of director Paul Leni's work in the old-dark-house classic *The Cat and the Canary* (1927)— even though Christensen had already employed similar techniques in his virtuoso *Witchcraft Through the Ages* and in his two films for MGM, as well.

Christensen returned to the bizarre subject matter of his notorious *Witchcraft Through the Ages* in his next old-dark-house chiller for First National, *Seven Footprints to Satan* (1929).

Released with talking sequences, sound effects, and music on Vitaphone disc, this is the only one of Christensen's three haunted-house comedy thrillers for First National that can still be seen

"Beautifully shot, sharply cut . . . exciting and full of surprises," says silent-film historian Kevin Brownlow of *Seven Footprints to Satan* (1929), the only one of Christensen's horror comedies for First National to have survived. From left to right: Creighton Hale, Angelo Risetto, William V. Mong, and Thelma Todd. (George Eastman House)

Treasure hunter Larry Kent has his mettle tested in *The Haunted House* (1928), the first of a series of over-the-top comedies Christensen made for First National. (George Eastman House)

today. A print is housed in the film archive of New York's Museum of Modern Art. The film's Vitaphone disc is lost, however.

The film was adapted from an extremely popular suspense novel by noted SF and fantasy writer A. Merritt, which first appeared as a five-part serial in the July-November 1927 issues of *Argosy-All Story* magazine. First National quickly snatched up the rights to the cliffhanger, which was published in book form in February 1928 to tie in with the film's release.

A forerunner of *Rosemary's Baby*, Merritt's tale deals with a cult of modern-day devil worshipers whose nefarious activities are overseen by the master of lies, Satan himself. Victims of the cultists' intrigues are lured to Satan's monster-ridden château on Long

Lon Chaney and Barbara Bedford in Christensen's *Mockery* (1927), working title *Terror*, a tale of love and lust set against the Russian Revolution. (The John McCarty Collection)

Island, where they are forced to play a deadly game for their lives. The game involves overcoming a series of nerve- and soul-shattering obstacles thrown in their path as they ascend a precarious staircase—the seven steps to the throne of Satan. Those who successfully reach the top of the staircase are spared. But since Satan is known for stacking the deck in his favor, chances of this are nil.

Bored by the lack of challenge, the egocentric fiend kidnaps a daredevil explorer, Jim Kirkham, and two other people—a gutsy girl named Eve and a stalwart Englishman—and puts all three of them to the test. In Kirkham, however, Satan finally meets his match. Kirkham turns Satan's lies against him and, with Eve and the Englishman's help, successfully outwits the fiend. As the trio make their escape, the château is destroyed by an explosion and Satan and his monstrous minions are consumed within.

Christensen saw in the material an opportunity to create his creepiest, most visually flamboyant Feuillade-like thriller up to that time. And he seized it,

although screen adapters Richard Bee and William Irish altered the ending of Merritt's story by rationalizing the nightmarish adventures Kirkham (Creighton Hale) and Eve (Thelma Todd) get put through as a series of practical jokes. Notes Phil Hardy's *The Encyclopedia of Horror Movies* of this classic early horror film: "*Seven Footprints to Satan* is dazzling in its virtuosity. . . . Christensen's parade of madmen, monsters, witches, dwarfs and gorillas waving guns and manipulating secret panels becomes a startling symphony of light and shadow, sometimes chillingly bizarre, sometimes strikingly beautiful, always invested with a darkly mocking wit." Silent-film historian Kevin Brownlow agrees, calling the film a "beautifully shot, sharply cut haunted-house comedy [that is] very exciting and full of surprises [in which] the supporting cast of monsters [is] disturbingly convincing."

Released a few months after *Seven Footprints to Satan,* in April 1929, *The House of Horror* was the last of Christensen's comedy thrillers for First National.

Richard Bee again wrote the script (an original this time around) and Tom Miranda provided the tongue-in-cheek intertitles. William Irish wrote the dialogue for a talking sequence that was included in the film, along with sound effects and a music score courtesy of Vitaphone disc. Unfortunately, neither the film's original negative and prints nor its accompanying Vitaphone disc appear to have survived. All we have to go on are some surviving stills from the production, which, judging by contemporary reviews,

appears to have been less visually flamboyant than *Seven Footprints* but just as over the top in terms of mixing shudders with laughs.

Former Keystone Kop Chester Conklin (who had also appeared in Christensen's *The Haunted House*) and Louise Fazenda provided the comic relief as the skittish owners of a none-too-thriving antique shop who are drawn by the promise of wealth to the foreboding estate of their eccentric uncle, a miserly millionaire who lives as a recluse and is surrounded by

duplicitous servants and an assortment of other weird characters and hangers-on who occupy their time waiting for him to kick off. Posing as young marrieds, two hotshot reporters on the trail of a story involving a fabulous missing diamond also descend on the house of horror, and they, too, get swept up in the film's serial-like high jinks, involving murder, masked identities, secret rooms with trapdoors, ghostly visitations, and sliding panels—in other words, virtually all the ingredients of the old-dark-house genre rolled up into one big all-stops-out soufflé.

James Ford played one of the reporters and Thelma Todd, a veteran of all three of Christensen's old-dark-house comedy thrillers, played the other.

Christensen's Hollywood career ended unhappily. After completing *The House of Horror*, he went back to MGM to direct a big-budget version of Jules Verne's SF adventure *The Mysterious Island* (1929). He was signed to act in the film, as well. But studio executives disapproved of his painstaking directorial methods, which were causing the already-expensive film to go way over budget, and he was dismissed. Maurice Tourneur replaced Christensen but was soon dismissed for the same reason, and the film, a dreadful hodgepodge of elaborate FX and stodgy performances, was completed by Lucien Hubbard.

Unable to cope with the increasing power of the producer in Hollywood and the technical restrictions imposed on his remarkably fluid camera style by the early talkies, Christensen returned to his native Denmark shortly thereafter. He remained there, returning briefly to stage work and making but a handful of films until his death in 1959 at age eighty.

A revival of Christensen's surviving work—and a renewed effort to locate some of his tantalizing lost films (surely some archive or collector somewhere in the world must have a print locked away)— is definitely in order, for on the basis of *Witchcraft Through the Ages* and *Seven Footprints to Satan* alone, he was a gifted visual stylist and a skilled cinematic craftsman whose influence, not just in terms of subject matter but also with regard to the often surrealistic manner in which it is presented, can clearly be seen in such later films about demonism and witchcraft as Roman Polanski's *Rosemary's Baby* (1968) as well as the same director's 1971 version of *Macbeth*.

Though some of *Witchcraft*'s psychology is outdated hokum, the visual qualities of the film are remarkably contemporary. It is full of mobile and at times ingenious camerawork, rapid cutting, slick animation, and other special effects. It is also exquisitely and eerily photographed. As one critic noted at the time of its initial release, it creates a "truly fantastic mood." And, depending on the quality of the print one sees, it does so to this day.

The medieval episodes of *Witchcraft Through the Ages* (1922) provocatively illustrate such arcane lore as the making of potions and witches' use of brooms. (Moving Image and Sound Archives)

Filmography
1913: *The Mysterious X* (director/writer/actor); 1915: *Night of Revenge* (director/writer); 1922: *Witchcraft Through the Ages* (director/writer/actor); 1923: *Among Jews* (director); *His Mysterious Adventure* (director/writer); 1925: *The Woman Who Did* (director); 1926: *The Devil's Circus* (director/writer); 1927: *Mockery* (director/cowriter); 1928: *The Hawk's Nest* (director/writer), *The Haunted House* (director); 1929: *Seven Footprints to Satan* (director), *The House of Horror* (director); 1939: *Children of Divorce* (director/writer); 1940: *The Child* (director/writer); 1941: *Come Home with Me* (director); 1942: *The Lady with the Colored Gloves* (director).

From *The Bat Whispers* (1930): Grayce Hampton, William Bakewell, and Una Merkel on the stairway; Spencer Charters, Maude Eburne, and Charles Dow Clark watching from the floor. (The Raymond G. Cabana, Jr., Collection)

R A Y M O N D   G .   C A B A N A ,   J R .

ROLAND WEST

T he newspapers named him 'The Bat' because he moved with incredible rapidity—always at night—and he seemed to be able to see in the dark."

So goes a line of dialogue in *The Bat*, the 1920 play by Mary Roberts Rinehart and Avery Hopwood that established the prototype for the old-dark-house form of mystery-comedy thriller. *The Bat* was a Broadway sensation that was later made into a 1926 silent film and a 1930 talkie, both of which were thought to be lost until recently. Their availability now makes it possible to shed some light on the reputation of their eccentric director: Roland West.

West has been variously described as "very closed in," "a very odd man," and "vacant." The fact that he kept to himself as much as he did—even shutting himself off from those he worked with—has rendered him something of a mystery man. It therefore seems fitting that the films he is best remembered for today are those derived from the classic mystery play *The Bat*.

West was born Roland Van Ziemer in Cleveland, Ohio, in 1887. His mother was a stage actress and his aunt a local theater producer. It was the latter who gave West his first taste of the theater by casting him in her 1899 production of *The Volunteers*. By 1904, the young man had become an accomplished stage performer; he had also changed his name to Roland West. At nineteen, he cowrote and starred in a vaudeville sketch titled *The Criminal* (later retitled *The Under World*), which foresaw the direction his career would ultimately take.

Variety described the sketch as "a tale of murder, robbery and police inquisitions [in which] five distinct characters are drawn . . . with a remarkably short time elapsing for [costume] changes. . . . Voice, action, manner and method are completely changed

with each." The versatile West played all five parts. West's biographer Scott MacQueen has termed the sketch "West's career in embryo: its melodramatic turns of plot and preoccupation with the criminal mind occur in every one of his later projects."

Despite his success on the boards, West decided to give up acting and become a film producer. During his years of performing on the Loew's circuit, he befriended Joseph M. Schenck, then Loew's general manager in charge of bookings, who also had dreams of a film career. By the time Schenck became chairman of United Artists in the mid 1920s, West had also relocated to Hollywood and had produced and directed a string of modestly successful, if not remarkable, romantic melodramas for a variety of independent companies, as well as the Lon Chaney vehicle *The Monster*, based on Crane

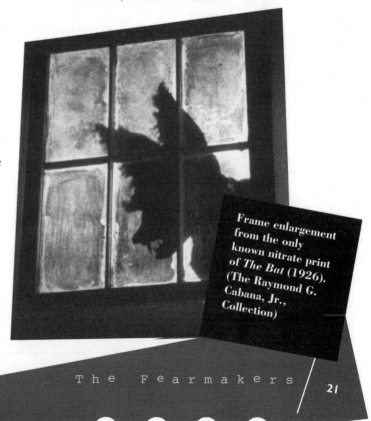

Frame enlargement from the only known nitrate print of *The Bat* (1926). (The Raymond G. Cabana, Jr., Collection)

Wilbur's popular play of the same name, for MGM, so Schenck signed his old friend as a producer and gave him complete autonomy. Given West's obvious fondness for mystery-comedy thrillers, it is not surprising that he chose the most popular of the bunch for his first project under his new contract.

In 1917, Mary Roberts Rinehart decided to convert her 1908 mystery novel, *The Circular Staircase*, into a play. The book, a long, rambling affair, had to be modified heavily to work on the stage. Its plot revolved around a large sum of stolen money concealed in a once vacant house whose new tenants are terrified by a fiend bent on reclaiming the loot. In transferring the story to the stage, Rinehart eschewed the rather unspectacular housekeeper-murderess of her original and substituted a master criminal she dubbed "the Bat." She then compressed the book's protracted time frame into a single night of terror. With the assistance of playwright Avery Hopwood, the play, christened *The Bat*, was finally completed, and in 1920, it made its Broadway debut at the Morosco Theatre. One of the most popular plays of its day, it ran for 867 performances. There were also innumerable road-company presentations. And, in 1926, Rinehart novelized her play, a book that is still in print today.

Because of the success of *The Bat*, an inevitable string of similar plays followed. John Willard wrote, and starred in, *The Cat and the Canary* (1922), a play that inspired D. W. Griffith to make *One Exciting Night* (1922), which borrowed heavily from both plays. The result was a concurrent cycle of mystery-comedy plays and silent films in a similar vein. These so milked the formula established by *The Bat* that, as early as 1925, the release of West's Lon Chaney's mystery-comedy thriller, *The Monster*, the story of a mad scientist (Dr. Ziska) who waylays motorists and uses them for ghoulish experiments in raising the dead at his private sanitarium, prompted the movie critic of the *New York Post* to bemoan: "The only thing against the show is that it is becoming well worn out." But West was not deterred, and he set out to make yet another such thriller—his first film version of *The Bat*.

His silent version of *The Bat* is from beginning to end a blueprint for West's penultimate and most enduring fear film, *The Bat Whispers* (1930). Arthur Edeson's moody camerawork and William Cameron Menzie's striking set designs established new standards for the genre. Summing up the opinions of most reviewers, P. S. Harrison, publisher of a thirties film guide called *Harrison's Reports*, wrote of the silent version, "Few pictures have been released lately that hold the spectator as breathless as does *The Bat*, and not only does it hold him breathless but it thrills

Roland West, eccentric fearmaker, circa 1923. (The Raymond G. Cabana, Jr., Collection)

him and at the same time makes him laugh to his heart's content."

One major difference between West's silent and sound versions of the tale, however, is the appearance of the titular fiend himself. In the silent, he wears a hideous mask that gives him the look of an actual bat. The talkie replaced this visage with more traditional, though still striking, hood-and-cloak garb. Seeing the film as a boy, cartoonist Bob Kane found the villain's batlike costume in the film "quite awesome." Remembering the image years later, he patterned the look of his Batman character on it.

Fate was not to favor West's talkie version, although the circumstances attending the release of both films were remarkably similar. The advent of sound in motion pictures revitalized the mixture of humor and horror established on the stage by *The Bat*, for now the conventional visual elements could be infused with the creepy noises and loud thunderclaps that went with them. A second cycle of haunted-house thrillers was inaugurated with Warner Brothers' *The Terror* (1928), after which came talkie versions of genre favorites such as *Seven Keys to Baldpate*, *The Cat and the Canary* (retitled *The Cat Creeps*), and *The Gorilla*, all of which were remade as talkies within a few years of their silent counterparts.

Audiences quickly reached a saturation point, however, and it was at this point, in November 1930, that West's *The Bat Whispers* was released. *Variety*, although favorably disposed toward West's production

and its many striking innovations, lamented that it "must follow all the other mystery-haunted-house films" and advised its distributor, United Artists, to give it "plenty of heavy exploitation." UA disregarded this sage advice and poured most of its promotional dollars into exploiting its concurrent releases of Howard Hughes's aviation epic, *Hell's Angels,* and Eddie Cantor's all-Technicolor musical, *Whoopee!,* both of which went on to become huge money-earners. *The Bat Whispers* failed to attract enough patrons to earn back its substantial cost.

In addition to shooting the film in the standard 35-mm format, West experimented by making a separate wide-screen 65-mm version, as well. Considering the film's subject matter, which stressed dimly lighted interiors, many critics questioned the value of such panoramic photography. Theater owners agreed and refused to go to the expense of installing the costly

Frame enlargement of the title card from the 65-mm version of *The Bat Whispers* (1930). The aspect ratio is 2:1. A lack of industry standards regarding wide-screen motion pictures caused discontent among exhibitors, which resulted in the Hays Office banning the large-gauge formats shortly after Roland West's film was released. (The Raymond G. Cabana, Jr., Collection)

equipment required to show the 65-mm film. Thus, the wide-screen version saw limited release and was also a commercial failure.

West's technical experiments went beyond wide-screen photography, however. To achieve the film's startling "bat's-eye view" effects, Charles Cline, a United Artists technician, developed a camera dolly capable of zooming the camera eighteen feet in a fraction of a second. A large scaffold was also constructed, from which the camera could be hurtled along tracks or, suspended by a steel cable, swung through space.

In an irony of Hollywood history, Effie Asher, the associate producer of Universal's upcoming production of *Dracula* (1931), contacted West to ask if Chester Morris, then under contract to West and starring in *The Bat Whispers,* might be available to play the part of Count Dracula. West declined the offer, claiming that he was only seeking romantic roles for his new star (an odd reply considering Morris's part in *The Bat Whispers* was decidedly unromantic, indeed the most

Frame enlargements from the only known nitrate print of *The Bat* (1926). (The Raymond G. Cabana, Jr., Collection)

unromantic of his long career). Universal finally gave the part to Bela Lugosi, the Hungarian actor who had played the part on the Broadway stage, and the film was a huge success.

The Bat Whispers presents its cast in the manner of a filmed playbill: The actors' names appear on a crawl in the order of their appearance. This is accompanied by the ominous tolling of a clock. The picture then opens with a shot of the clock tower itself. The camera pulls back, then tilts down to reveal a busy street below. It then plummets down the face of the building and, just as it is about to collide with the traffic, levels off to reveal the entrance of the building, marked POLICE HEADQUARTERS. The scene then dissolves to the interior of a squad car racing through the congested street as a radio bulletin blares an update of the Bat's latest murder threat. The squad car arrives at the town house where the intended victim lives, and the camera swoops up to the top floor, passing through an open window and into the room beyond, to a shot of the victim sitting in a chair. He rises and moves to the window, looking down at his guards below. One of them remarks on the fact the building does not have a fire escape, which will make it difficult for the Bat to gain access. But the Bat doesn't require such conventional forms of entry; he suddenly appears outside the victim's window, hanging upside down like a real bat, reaches in, and garrotes his victims.

This amazing sequence then dissolves to a shot of another clock striking midnight, its dial quickly replaced by the spinning wheels of a train. A panoramic view of the city appears briefly, viewed from within the fast-moving train; the camera then assumes the perspective of the train's engine as it rushes along the track, its lights picking up a sign that reads OAKDALE. A curve in the track jostles the train, and the railway dissolves to a road. Now the viewer is inside a speeding car; its lights catch the shadow of a bat fluttering across the facade of the Oakdale Bank—the scene of the Bat's next crime.

The problem with this bravura opening sequence is that it establishes a pace and virtuosity of style that was all but impossible to maintain in an early talkie, when dialogue was still being

The lightweight Cline dolly built for *The Bat Whispers* (1930). Left to right: Chester Morris, Ray June, Robert Planck, and Charles Cline. (The Raymond G. Cabana, Jr., Collection)

emphasized over camera movement. Because the picture is based on a play, dialogue abounds in *The Bat Whispers*, and in some cases, it is very drawn out. This tends to place the daring camerawork in the opening scenes in bolder relief, rendering the film an eccentric piece of work.

The story proper is restricted to the "haunted" mansion, which spinster Cornelia Van Gorder (Grayce Hampton), accompanied by her niece (Una Merkel) and maid (Maude Eburne), has leased for the summer. Weird things start to happen when various characters attempt to find some stolen bank funds secreted on the property. The Bat, too, is after the loot, and his perambulations intensify the night of terror for the house's beleaguered inhabitants. The film climaxes when all the characters converge in the attic, the money is found, and the identity of the Bat is revealed in a surprise twist. He turns out to be Detective Anderson, the lawman ostensibly in charge of the case.

For the stage play, producers Wagenhals and Kemper selected Harrison Hunter for the part of Detective Anderson but purposely withheld from him (and the rest of the cast, as well) that his character was actually the Bat in disguise. As revealed in the climax, the Bat had waylaid the real Detective Anderson, who thereafter ranged the house and grounds in a state of amnesia. Believing himself to be the hero of the piece, Hunter fashioned his performance accordingly. The final scene wasn't given to the cast until just before dress rehearsal. Hunter was not only shocked but also outraged, and he railed against what he considered to be a "low joke."

Nevertheless, he went on with the show,

and the ruse proved to be quite effective. His performance as the ersatz detective proved to be so convincing that the double-twist ending shocked audiences as much as it had initially shocked him.

In *The Bat Whispers*, Anderson/the Bat was played with a businesslike attitude leavened by a wicked sense of humor by a very young Chester Morris, whose temples were grayed to make him appear older. As the narrative progresses and Morris's bogus Anderson is repeatedly frustrated in his attempts to locate the hidden money, his behavior and appearance degenerate. When he is finally unmasked as the Bat, his visage, hellishly intensified by flickering firelight as he laughs maniacally, boasting of his evil brilliance, becomes terrifying indeed. This image closely approximates Rinehart's description of the fiend in the novelization of her play as being "as grim and menacing a figure as a man just arisen from the dead."

The device of the guilty detective did not originate with *The Bat*. Gaston Leroux, best remembered today as the author of *The Phantom of the Opera*, employed it as early as 1907 in his novel *The Mystery of the Yellow Room*, which Agatha Christie later credited as sparking her interest in writing mysteries. She virtually admitted that Leroux's *Yellow Room* served as the model for her own novels *Murder on the Links* (1923) and *The Secret of Chimneys* (1925). But she failed to credit the influence of either *Yellow Room* or Rinehart's *The Bat* on her famous 1952 play, *The Mousetrap*, which also featured a phony policeman who is unmasked as the murderer.

"Like a bat, he chose the night for his work," wrote Rinehart of her criminal mastermind. The same was true of Roland West. To avoid the prying eyes of studio executives, he shot *The Bat Whispers* from dusk to dawn, providing dinner for his cast and crew at midnight, the witching hour. Appropriately enough, the film takes place at night; it even concludes with the Bat vowing to return "At night!"

West was to make only one more picture after *The Bat Whispers*—a gangster melodrama called *Corsair,* which United Artists released in 1931. The film served mainly as a vehicle to reintroduce Chester Morris to cinema audiences after the failure of *The Bat Whispers*. (In between the two films, Morris had taken an extended vacation to recuperate from a severe case of "klieg eyes"—scorched retinas—which he'd suffered when West had him step before one of the studio's powerful arc lamps to achieve a menacing shadow effect in *The Bat Whispers*.) *Corsair* featured impressive camerawork by Ray June and Robert H. Planck (the team responsible for *The Bat Whispers*), but some of the film's editing and dubbing is so crude that *Corsair* looks like a much earlier release.

Like *The Bat Whispers*, which had been obscured by a profusion of similar releases, *Corsair* made little impression at the box office due to the torrent of other gangster pictures then flooding theaters; West abandoned filmmaking altogether. Instead, he channeled his energies into transforming a three-tiered Mediterranean-style house he'd bought in Pacific Palisades into a restaurant. He died in obscurity in 1952. Today he is remembered less for his films than for his involvement with ill-fated actress Thelma Todd. A top comedienne of the silent and early talkie period, Todd died under still-mysterious circumstances when her body was found stuffed behind the wheel of her car, the engine still running, in the locked garage of her own house of horror in California's Pacific Palisades. Her death was ruled a suicide, caused by carbon monoxide poisoning. But the number of bruises on her body (did she beat herself up first before turning on the engine?) prompted many people to believe she had been murdered. In a 1989 book about the case, *Hot Toddy*, author Andy Edwards claimed that Todd was the victim of a mob hit ordered by Mafia chieftain Lucky Luciano, with whom the young actress was allegedly having a hot-and-cold romantic and professional relationship at the time. Others have speculated that she was done in by her jealous longtime companion, Roland West. To this day, no one really knows "who done it," although the Los Angeles police officially closed the books on the case following West's death in the early 1950s, which gives some idea of where their suspicions apparently rested.

West's body of work remains woefully incomplete. Few of his films are extant, but fortunately the two productions on which his reputation largely rests—*The Bat* and *The Bat Whispers*—are preserved by the UCLA Archive.

The wide-screen version of *The Bat Whispers* received its first public screenings in almost fifty years at UCLA and the Museum of Modern Art in New York in the spring and summer of 1988, respectively. The show print retained the film's original 2:1 aspect ratio and boasted a full-range rerecorded sound track utilizing DBX noise reduction. In the New York showing, which I attended, the pervasive thunderclaps that continually erupted on the sound track seemed synchronized with the vibrations caused by the passing subway cars nearby. It made for quite an effect—one worthy of Roland West himself.

Filmography

1916: *A Woman's Honor,* a.k.a. *Lost Souls;* (producer/director); 1918: *De Luxe Annie* (director/cowriter); 1921: *The Silver Lining* (producer/director/cowriter), *Nobody* (producer/director/cowriter); 1923: *The Unknown Purple* (director/cowriter); 1925: *The Monster* (producer/director); 1926: *The Bat* (producer/director/writer); 1928: *The Dove* (producer/director/cowriter); 1929: *Alibi* (producer/director/cowriter); 1930: *The Bat Whispers* (producer/director/writer); 1931: *Corsair* (producer/director/cowriter).

The Bat (Chester Morris), unmasked and insane, threatens his captors and the audience in this nightmarish close-up of the finale of the wide-screen version of *The Bat Whispers* (1930). (The Raymond G. Cabana, Jr., Collection)

Above: Typical of a Whale protagonist, Griffin (Claude Rains, right) is simply different from those around him, as the positioning of the characters within the frame of this shot from *The Invisible Man* (1933) suggests. (Copyright © 1933 Universal Pictures)

Right: Una O'Connor and Claude Rains in *The Invisible Man* (1933), the first Whale film to combine creator and creation into a single figure. (Copyright © 1933 Universal Pictures)

K E N   H A N K E

JAMES WHALE

Who exactly was James Whale? Most fearfilm fans will be able to tell you Whale directed the genre classics *Frankenstein* (1931), *The Old Dark House* (1932), *The Invisible Man* (1933), and *The Bride of Frankenstein* (1935). The more knowledgeable fan might be able to stray beyond the genre with which Whale is most identified and add the memorable *Journey's End* (1930), *One More River* (1934), *Remember Last Night?* (1935), and *Show Boat* (1936) to Whale's list of credits. They will speak of his unique mix of theatricalism and cinematic inventiveness, his oversized close-ups, quirky sense of humor, odd camera angles, elaborate tracking shots, and shaved sets. But these are just surface elements. They tell us nothing of James Whale himself.

Whale was seldom trustworthy in his published remarks about himself. Born in England in 1889, the working-class son of a religious fanatic mother, he presented a life story to the world at large that he felt ought to have been true. In effect, he re-created himself as the product of the English upper crust he admired so much. Whale the artist, on the other hand, was invariably honest.

A onetime graphic artist, newspaper cartoonist, and theater director, James Whale is firmly typed in our cinematic consciousness as a horror-movie specialist. But in fact, he moved to the horror genre mainly to escape being typed as a creator of war films—a distinct threat after his back-to-back work on *Hell's Angels* (1930) and *Journey's End* and then his first assignment at Universal, another war film, titled *Waterloo Bridge* (1931). Universal was so impressed by its new directorial catch (soon to be dubbed "the ace of Universal") that Whale was offered the pick of any material the studio owned. He opted for *Frankenstein* almost out of desperation. The rest is tangled history.

Universal, having struck gold with Tod Browning's *Dracula* (1931), was eager to follow up with another Bela Lugosi horror film. It first offered *Frankenstein* to director Robert Florey, who envisioned the project as his Hollywood breakthrough. Whether or not Whale realized he was stepping on Florey's toes by asking for this particular project is unknown. But his decision to do so altered not only his own fate but those of Florey, Bela Lugosi, and a small-time character actor named Boris Karloff. What a Florey-Lugosi *Frankenstein* might have been like is anybody's guess, though admirers of Florey argue loudly, long, and unpersuasively that Whale merely reaped the fruits of Florey's preproduction labors— and made an inferior film in the bargain. On the other hand, Whale's decision to replace Lugosi clearly delighted Lugosi himself, who hated the inarticulate role of Frankenstein's monster—just as it equally delighted Karloff to inherit the part. None of this matters except as historical perspective. What matters is the film Whale made.

The key to Whale's work on a thematic level lies, in my opinion, in the director's well-known homosexuality. Shortly before his debut in Hollywood, Whale had been rejected by the one great lady love of his life, Doris Zinkeisen, although the two remained friends; in fact, she designed the costumes for *Show Boat*. According to many of his associates, Whale had a tendency to blame this rejection on his inability to lead a "normal" life. Whale turned this rejection into an elaborate fantasy ideal about "redemption through the love of the right woman," a romantic delusion he explored and ultimately rid himself of in his four classic horror films for Universal.

In the first of the series, Henry Frankenstein (Colin Clive) is clearly playing at being God in his experiments. But there is more going on here than this relatively simple conceit. In view of the fact that strict

The Fearmakers

Christian dogma insists that the homosexual is an "abomination" in the eyes of God, there is good reason to suppose that Frankenstein, Whale's ersatz God, is a kind of satire of the biblical God. Frankenstein creates his "abomination" and almost immediately locks it away in a dungeon (for all intents and purposes, a closet). The Monster is stripped of its humanity and soon referred to no longer as "he," but "it." Frankenstein's personal redemption occurs only when he accepts his responsibility for the Monster's existence and restores the Monster's humanity by again calling the creature "he." If we accept the concept (which the devout, then as now, assure us is the case) that God had a hand in creating the homosexual Whale, then the biblical God is as responsible for him as Frankenstein is for his creation.

This is Whale's point in the film, and he is outraged by the situation; his fury finds its voice in the encounter between creation and creator in the windmill at the film's fiery climax. It is here that the Monster comes face-to-face with his god, and, in a bone-chilling moment of disgusted realization, he utterly rejects Frankenstein by casting him from the top of the mill, even though by doing so he also throws away his only protection against destruction. This is

quite the starkest moment in any Whale film, and its powerful depiction of a deliberate rejection of God remains unmatched in any other film.

In the film's heroine (Mae Clarke), there is, perhaps, a glimmer of Whale's perception of the truth about his own relationship with Doris Zinkeisen. Taking the homosexuality angle a step further, we can view the Monster not only as Frankenstein's creation but as the living embodiment of his sexuality (and, by logical extension, Whale's). It is this aspect of himself that he attempts to closet away, to deny. The results are not only futile but disastrous—and nearly fatal for Frankenstein's fiancée.

Whale's next horror opus was *The Old Dark House.* It was a project that originated with the director, who talked Universal into buying J. B. Priestley's novel *Benighted* as an ideal vehicle for the next Whale-Karloff outing. Whale then proceeded to turn Priestley's thoughtful and difficult tale into a film that deftly managed to be true both to himself and to the original novel. The film tells the story of several travelers, one of whom is a burned-out World War I veteran, who seek shelter at a secluded house peopled by a family of eccentrics and psychos and face a night of terror to survive. It effectively condenses and suggests the book's deeper implications on the topic of post-World War I malaise while making a few telling departures, the most oft-cited of which is the change to a happy ending. Priestley had written the novel just after his twenty-five-year-old wife's death from cancer, and the attendant sense of gloom for its own sake in the book's "tragic" ending seems, if not grafted on, at least

The Monster out of the closet. Director James Whale (right, with cigar) and his symbolic alter ego (Boris Karloff) on the set of *Frankenstein* (1931). (Copyright © 1931 Universal Pictures)

Clockwise from upper right: The Monster (Boris Karloff) unwittingly murders a little girl by tossing her in a lake to see if she will float like a flower, a scene cut from the film prior to its release but finally restored more than fifty years later—from *Frankenstein* (1931). (Copyright © 1931 Universal Pictures) An abomination in the eyes of God. Boris Karloff as the Monster, locked away in a dungeon, in James Whale's *Frankenstein* (1931). (Copyright © 1931 Universal Pictures) The Monster (Boris Karloff) comes face-to-face with his god and creator (Colin Clive) in the windmill and rejects him, at the film's fiery climax—from *Frankenstein* (1931). (Copyright © 1931 Universal Pictures)

slightly beside the point. The significance of Whale's change to a happy ending (Priestley never raised any objections to the change) becomes clear when the film's war hero protagonist, Penderel (Melvyn Douglas), accepts a sense of responsibility for the well-being of the inhabitants of the old dark house and is rewarded, by Whale, with life rather than death.

Significant as this change is, the most fascinating alteration from novel to film lies in the very different presentation of Saul (Brember Wills), the pyromaniac brother of the bizarre inhabitants of the old dark house, who, much like the Monster in *Frankenstein*, has also been locked away out of sight.

In the novel, Saul is a great, brutish homicidal beast who merely breaks loose, runs amok, and expires, along with the hero, in a pitched battle. In the film, Saul is an elderly, repressed little man. In the book, the character never speaks. In the film, he chatters away incessantly, often quoting the Bible at great length. Saul is the worst and most dangerous secret of the titular old dark house, and as such he embodies Whale's view of his own homosexuality. Significantly, the hero (Whale's on-screen alter ego) must face up to Saul. It is also significant that the

Elsa Lanchester and Colin Clive in *The Bride of Frankenstein* (1935). (Copyright © 1935 Universal Pictures)

character in the film with whom the hero identifies most strongly—but dislikes intensely—is Saul's effeminate, self-romanticizing, and cynical sibling Horace (Ernest Thesiger), a character possessing many of Whale's own personal traits.

Unfortunately, *The Old Dark House*'s status for many years as a lost film and the subsequent legal entanglements after a print of it was discovered have kept the film from being widely seen and becoming as well known as Whale's other horror films. It has never been sold to television or legally released on video. This is too bad, because not only is it a very personal work and key Whale film, it is also Whale's most genuinely frightening. In it, Whale seems to have consciously aimed for pure shock effect time and again. And he scores each time.

Better known by far is *The Invisible Man.* While some purists may carp that it is more science fiction than horror (a debatable point), it is *the* film that lays the thematic groundwork for Whale's masterpiece, *The Bride of Frankenstein.* More visually striking than its predecessors, *The Invisible Man* is also a much more modern work. It is the first Whale horror film to present its horrors as something that can exist in everyday life. And it is the first (and only) Whale film that combines creator and creation into a single figure; by doing so, it suggests a movement away from the concept of "closeting" the alter ego seen in the earlier films.

True to H. G. Wells's novel, *The Invisible Man* is also the most clearly class-conscious of Whale's horror films. Its antihero, Jack Griffin (Claude Rains), becomes an invisible man in an effort to better his station in life, to make himself worthy of the daughter of his employer by doing something "no other man in the world ever dreamed of doing." His obsessive behavior on this point is pronounced and he constantly refers to his impoverished status: "I was just a poor, struggling chemist working in your father's laboratory"; "I was so pitifully poor"; and so on. Griffin's discovery leads to madness and ever-increasing greed for money and power, none-too-pretty aspects of his character. And yet Whale's sympathies lie completely with him. Typical of a Whale protagonist, Griffin is simply different from those around him. The true target of Whale's satirical wrath is Griffin's stodgy middle-class coworker, Dr. Kemp (William Harrigan). Kemp is consistently presented not only as an unimaginative dullard but as a boringly conformist materialist with no regard for anything but his own comfortable position. Kemp is worse than a villain in Whale's view. His sense of responsibility extends only so far as it affects him personally, making him both a physical and moral coward. His death at Griffin's hands actually seems deserved, and no one could argue with Griffin's summation of Kemp's character just prior to the deed: "I always said you were a dirty little coward, Kemp. You're a dirty, sneaking little rat as well!"

On a purely creative level, Whale's most striking accomplishment, apart from the film's technical virtuosity, is the deftness with which he and screenwriter R. C. Sherriff make murder (mass murder, no less) not only entertaining, but palatable. The film deliberately hardens the viewer to the invisible man's acts of violence, the first of which are a series of pranks designed to scare the locals. Even the film's first murder (and only deliberately horrific moment), where Griffin kills "a stupid policeman" by savagely bashing his head in with a stool, is quickly dispelled by distancing it from the later murders with more prankish high jinks, such as the theft of a policeman's trousers and a comic bank robbery. By the time we get to Griffin's major acts of violence, they seem less horrific and more a logical extension of events.

The once-heroic villagers now transformed into a bloodthirsty mob bent on tormenting the ill-fated Monster (Boris Karloff)—from Whale's masterpiece, *The Bride of Frankenstein* (1935). (Copyright © 1935 Universal Pictures)

The moralistic ending, where Griffin dies muttering, "I meddled in things that man must leave alone," seems to address directly Whale's consistent theme of avoiding responsibility by subverting nature—specifically one's own nature. However, the real point is that it shatters Whale's previous concept of redemption through the love of a good woman. Not only does this love solve nothing, Whale now proposes, but the pursuit of it is at the bottom of Griffin's troubles in the first place.

Whale had long resisted making a sequel to *Frankenstein*. In fact, Universal was planning to go ahead with the project (then known as *The Return of Frankenstein*) without him. Kurt Neumann had been signed to direct. But the studio recognized that Whale was a critical ingredient in the first film's success, so they enticed him by offering him complete artistic control. Whale found this offer irresistible, and the result was his most technically accomplished and satisfying film—and the jewel in Universal's series of *Frankenstein* horror films, despite the fact that Whale's follow-up almost isn't a horror film at all. The trappings of *The Bride of Frankenstein* are pure Whale gothic. But while preserving the veneer of the horror/fear film, the events the film depicts are scarcely ever horrific. *The Bride* contains no more than two stock horror sequences: the opening attack on a villager and his wife by the supposedly dead Monster and the Monster's accidental menacing of a shepherdess. Whale had clearly grown bored with the mechanics of the standard horror film (the very mechanics he had helped define) and was casually subverting the genre to his own ends.

This time around, Henry Frankenstein (Colin Clive) is a god of somewhat lesser status, while his creation, or "son" (Boris Karloff), has developed into an almost Christ-like figure. At one point, the Monster is even crucified. The difference in Whale's approach is apparent as soon as the campy, in-joke prologue, wherein Mary Shelley (Elsa Lanchester), Percy Shelley (Douglas Walton), and Lord Byron (Gavin Gordon) recap the events of the first film as if they were part of Mary's novel, is over. The story proper begins where the first film left off—at the burning mill, the once-heroic villagers surrounding it now transformed into a bloodthirsty mob bent on tormenting the ill-fated Monster. Suddenly, it is no longer religion that is being questioned by Whale, but the abuse of religion by man, and this theme runs throughout the film.

At the same time, *The Bride of Frankenstein* also presents a positive image of the potential for good in religion as seen in the relationship between the Monster and the blind hermit (O. P. Heggie) who befriends him. Both characters are outcasts, reduced by society to the status of "nature's misfits." "It's very lonely here," the hermit tells the injured Monster, "and it's been a long time since any human being came into this hut." The prayer scene that climaxes their first encounter is one of the most satisfying—and least embarrassing—expressions of religious faith in all cinema, and an oddly wide-eyed one to have come from a filmmaker described by one of his biographers as not being a particularly religious man.

The villain of the piece is Dr. Pretorius (Ernest Thesiger). Flamboyant, theatrical, and even more of a showman than Henry Frankenstein was in the first film in the series (where Henry's creation of the Monster was clearly viewed as a theatrical event), Pretorius is the personification of Whale's self-deluding side—the side that bought into the redemptive powers of the "ideal woman" fantasy. This

fantasy, like Pretorius himself, does not survive the film. It is Pretorius who not only forces Henry to create a mate (Elsa Lanchester) for the Monster but puts the idea into the Monster's head in the first place. When the deed is done and the Monster must face up to the fact that this woman who was, quite literally, made for him also rejects him, this fantasy is exploded once and for all and Pretorius, the mate, and the Monster all perish. For Whale, this moment is the culmination of a career based on delving into his own psyche.

Whale's career continued beyond *The Bride of Frankenstein*. But his most vibrant, personal, and successful work was behind him. He found it increasingly difficult to get work and eventually his physical and mental health began to deteriorate. In 1957, his body was found floating in the swimming pool of his Pacific Palisades home. A note hinting at suicide was found on the desk in his study, but the death was officially ruled an accident.

How to account for Whale's precipitous fall from grace in an industry that once considered him "the ace of Universal?" There were probably many reasons. But the *most* probable explanation is simply that Whale had said all he had to say. Even one of his most charming later films, the biographical romp *The Great Garrick* (1937), seems merely to be an exercise in style and sophistication with no particular drive or target.

In the end, it may be that James Whale was ultimately a somewhat selfish artist. He created himself, took himself apart, examined what he found, and then was finished.

From left to right: Gloria Stuart, Lilian Bond, Charles Laughton, Raymond Massey, Melvyn Douglas, Boris Karloff, and Eva Moore in Whale's *The Old Dark House* (1932), for many years a lost film. (The John McCarty collection)

Facing page: Boris Karloff as the brutish Morgan, one of the bizarre inhabitants of Whale's *The Old Dark House* (1932). (The John McCarty Collection)

Filmography

1930: *Hell's Angels* (codirector, uncredited), *Journey's End* (director); 1931: *Waterloo Bridge* (director), *Frankenstein* (director); 1932: *The Impatient Maiden* (director), *The Old Dark House* (director); 1933: *The Kiss Before the Mirror* (director), *The Invisible Man* (director); 1934: *By Candlelight* (director), *One More River;* 1935: *The Bride of Frankenstein* (director), *Remember Last Night?* (director); 1936: *Show Boat* (director); 1937: *The Road Back* (producer/codirector), *The Great Garrick* (director); 1938: *Port of Seven Seas* (director), *Sinners in Paradise* (director), *Wives Under Suspicion** (director); 1939: *The Man in the Iron Mask* (director); 1940: *Green Hell* (director); 1941: *They Dare Not Love* (codirector); 1949: *Hello Out There* (director).

*A remake of Whale's earlier *The Kiss Before the Mirror.*

Tourneur suggested the idea of a voodoo reworking of *Jane Eyre* when the studio assigned Lewton the title *I Walked with a Zombie* (1943) for the team's next film. Tourneur's last film for Lewton was *The Leopard Man* (1943), a conventional murder mystery for two thirds of its length. But the brilliant first third is representative of Tourneur's fearmaking gifts at their most unnerving. (Copyright © 1943 RKO Radio Pictures)

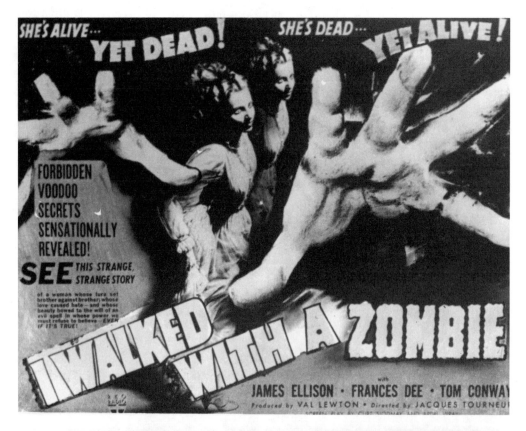

JACQUES TOURNEUR

As a writer whose main area of expertise is film history, I'm frequently asked at gatherings, both public and private, what my all-time favorite film is. My response is usually somewhat equivocal, since, like most people, whether they write about films or not, I cherish many different films and my all-time favorite among them can change on a daily basis depending upon my mood or on which one of them I've seen again most recently. This is not the case, however, when the question is narrowed to my all-time favorite movie, and director, in the genre of fearfilm. It is *Curse of the Demon* (1958), directed by Jacques Tourneur.

Having written so much about so-called splatter movies, an offshoot of the horror/fear film genre for which I'm often criticized (erroneously, I believe) of being a proponent or apologist, this response usually comes as a bit of a surprise, for Tourneur's directorial approach to producing shudders and gasps is about as far removed from the frontal assault of splatter as it is possible to get.

So why is it my all-time favorite? In part, it is because Charles Bennett's ingenious script (with input from producer Hal F. Chester), which is about a debunking parapsychologist and a genial demonologist, his nemesis, who proves to the former once and for all that "evil, supernatural creatures do exist," places more emphasis on character than is customarily found in such fare. And Tourneur's realization of that script actually makes us question our concept of the order of the universe—not only in its unusual juxtaposition of hero and villain but in its straight-faced belief in the possibility of the supernatural. In fact, Tourneur was one of the few fearmakers actually to go on record as believing in the supernatural. He shored up the belief while making

Over Tourneur's objections, producer Hal E. Chester inserted several mismatched long shots of a cheesy-looking monster along with some close-ups of a very different and quite fearsome-looking beast (designed by Ken Adam) into the director's near masterpiece in the powerful art of suggestion, *Curse of the Demon* (1958). (Copyright © 1958 Columbia Pictures)

A retouched publicity still of Simone Simon in *Cat People* (1942), rendering overt what Tourneur's technique had left mostly oblique. (Copyright © 1942 RKO Radio Pictures)

that in this film particularly, and in many of his other fearfilms as well, his skill in this regard remains unsurpassed. Putting it simply, no one has ever succeeded so effectively in making the hairs stand up on the back of the viewer's neck by showing nothing but a long, dark corridor (backgrounded on the sound track by nothing more than an odd pagan chant) as Jacques Tourneur does in *Demon.* I daresay that if Tourneur had lived, had been given the challenge of doing a modern fearfilm in the splatter mode, and had improbably taken on that challenge, he might conceivably have pulled off the most gut-wrenching, stomach-churning, scariest such film ever made—and would have succeeded in doing so, ironically, by not showing us much of anything on the screen at all.

Demon, when for research purposes he interviewed several of England's most famous witches about the spirit world and found, through them, that he possessed some uncanny (albeit unstated) powers himself.

This leads me to my main reason for admiring *Curse of the Demon* above all other films in its vein. Jacques Tourneur's work in the fearfilm genre remains distinctive, and *Demon,* which appeared toward the end of his career, stands out as the apotheosis of that work because it is the film in which all his themes and ideas about the supernatural and the psychology of fear, and his approach to expressing them on the screen, crystallized into an almost perfect whole. I say "almost perfect" because the film was taken over by its producer after Tourneur turned in his final cut, and some of the producer's injudicious tamperings ran counter to what Tourneur had strived to achieve: fearfilm's masterpiece in the powerful art of suggestion.

In short, my admiration of *Demon* is due not just to the fact that Tourneur manages to send chills up my spine with the use of subtlety and sleight of hand but

While most film historians, critics, and fans share my enthusiasm for *Demon* as one of the great modern horror films, they often refer to it as a stylistic throwback to the esteemed series of horror films produced by Val Lewton in the 1940s and admire it chiefly for what they consider its Lewtonesque qualities. What this assessment tends to ignore, however, is the fact that the subtle atmospherics of *Demon* are not only characteristic of the films Tourneur made for Lewton but of many of the short subjects and features he made before joining the Lewton unit and of virtually all the films he made afterward, the bulk of which don't even fall into the category of fearfilm. *Demon* is not a stylistic anomaly like director Robert Wise's *The Haunting* (1963), the only genre film Wise made after leaving the Lewton unit—and he made several—that remotely resembles the work he did for Lewton, and was clearly intended as an homage to his Lewton years. The suggestion that *Demon* reveals the dominating influence of Val Lewton on Tourneur is patently inaccurate. This assessment is wrong on a thematic level as well, for it ignores a very important point about *Demon*—namely the film is boldly about the supernatural. The only

The Fearmakers

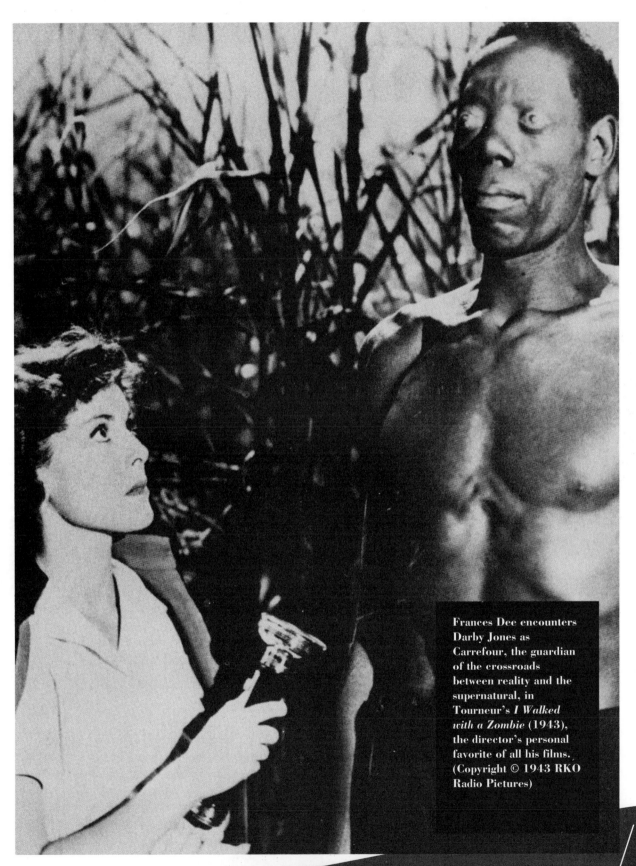

Frances Dee encounters Darby Jones as Carrefour, the guardian of the crossroads between reality and the supernatural, in Tourneur's *I Walked with a Zombie* (1943), the director's personal favorite of all his films. (Copyright © 1943 RKO Radio Pictures)

Lewton-produced films that fall wholly into the same thematic category are *Cat People* (1942) and *I Walked with a Zombie* (1943), both directed by Jacques Tourneur.

These assessments are not really criticisms of Tourneur, however, for even among people who feel he owed everything to Lewton, he is still much admired as a filmmaker. What such assessments do illustrate, though, is that in the fearfilm hall of fame, the name Tourneur remains considerably overshadowed by that of Val Lewton. Ironically, overshadowing (no pun intended) seems to have plagued Tourneur's film career as a whole.

At the outset of his career in Hollywood, Tourneur was overshadowed by the name and reputation of his movie director father, Maurice Tourneur, who, with young Jacques in tow, emigrated from France to the United States during the second decade of this century and went on to become one of the silent cinema's most important pioneers—and, according to some critics, its greatest artist. It was

from studying his father's delicate use of light and shadow on the screen, Tourneur maintained, that he developed the sensibility for subtlety and atmospherics that marked his earliest work as a director and the films he went on to make for Lewton. Tourneur also said he developed a fascination for the subject of psychoanalysis and the works of Freud, Jung, and Havelock Ellis from his father and that this, too, influenced his work as a filmmaker, not only in his direction of actors but in his attention to character and motivation.

In some circles, this belief in the overshadowing of Tourneur *fils* by the reputation of Tourneur *père* still continues. But in terms of achieving a major Hollywood career, Jacques Tourneur was even more overshadowed by the success of his directorial colleagues in the Lewton unit, Mark Robson and Robert Wise, who both went on to become powerful producer-directors with enough clout in the industry to launch their own big-budget projects. Tourneur, on the other hand, wound up his days as a hired hand, directing films on a shoestring for American-International Pictures and working for series television, a medium he despised for what he called its "impersonality." The only one of his TV shows he ever had kind words for was an episode he directed for Rod Serling's *The Twilight Zone*. Entitled "Night Call," it is a minimasterpiece of mood and shadowy terror that is pure Jacques Tourneur.

Tourneur might have enjoyed the same success in the industry as Robson and Wise had he been a bit more choosy in selecting his material. But I doubt that the cinema and fearfilm would have been the richer for it, since, with all respect to Messrs. Robson and Wise, Tourneur's body of work, despite its lack of big budgets, blockbuster hits, and Oscar nominations, remains considerably more distinctive and consistent on both a stylistic and a thematic level, notwithstanding the director's avowed practice of accepting whatever script was offered to him regardless of its content.

Tourneur began his career in film working as a story-idea man, then as an assistant director and editor for his father in Hollywood and Europe, where Tourneur *père*, disgruntled by the increasingly meddlesome role of the producer in American films, returned permanently in the late 1920s. Although he had become an American citizen, the young Tourneur remained in Europe for the next several years. It was there that he directed his first four features, a series of Gallic love stories and comedies, which I have been unable to track down and that may, in fact, be lost.

Determined to break out of his famous father's shadow and carve out a Hollywood career of his own, Tourneur returned to the United States in 1934 and went to work as a second-unit director for MGM. There he also directed many short subjects for the studio's *Pete Smith Specialties, John Nesbitt's Passing Parade,* and *Crime Does Not Pay* series, frequently

using the more American-sounding name Jack for his screen credit. The short subjects proved to be an excellent training ground for Tourneur to hone his trademark skills—and many of them display the visual qualities later dubbed "Lewtonesque." Faced with the combined challenge of low budgets and extremely tight shooting schedules, Tourneur ingeniously used lighting in many of his short films, not only for atmospheric purposes but to mask his lack of elaborate sets and other production values by inexpensively suggesting them and creating other effects with well-placed shadows and silhouettes—techniques he would employ in his Lewton films for similar reasons. Some of his short films also reveal a pre-Lewton interest in dealing with outré themes with subtlety and suggestion; for example, *The Ship That Died* (1938)—the story of the Marie Celeste ghost ship—and *The Incredible Stranger* (1942), the tale of a small-town psycho who lives with waxen images of his dead wife and children.

Another of his short subjects for the *Crime Does Not Pay* series was subsequently expanded by the studio under Tourneur's direction into his first full-length American feature, *They All Come Out* (1939), a full-blown early example of film noir costarring Tom Neal of *Detour* (1945) fame. On the strength of it, MGM assigned Tourneur to direct the first two entries in what would prove to be a short-lived series of noirish mystery thrillers starring Walter Pidgeon—*Nick Carter—Master Detective* (1939) and *Phantom Raiders* (1940). Another feature, *Doctors Don't Tell,* followed in 1941.

In the interim, Tourneur also continued directing short subjects for the studio, as well as directing second-unit work on some of the studio's major productions such as David O. Selznick's *A Tale of Two Cities* (1935). This is the project that introduced him to Val Lewton, an employee of Selznick's then assigned to produce the second-unit sequences. According to Tourneur, he and Lewton became fast friends immediately because of their mutual interests not only in moviemaking but in sailing and art. And so, years later, when Lewton was put under contract by RKO to produce a series of low-budget horror films with outrageous studio-assigned titles, he considered no one else but his friend Tourneur to direct the first one, *Cat People* (1942), and the studio agreed.

The now-famous style of *Cat People* with its innovative emphasis on atmosphere and the

The Fearmakers

41

suggestion of menace was an abrupt departure from the traditions of such influential horror successes as *The Phantom of the Opera* (1925), *Dracula* (1931), and *Frankenstein* (1931). Even today, it is still referred to by film historians as the first monster movie to deny audiences even a glimpse of the monster—the vicious black panther the film's lead character (Simone Simon) becomes whenever her emotions are strongly aroused. In fact, Tourneur does show the monster in a scene where the film's hero and heroine (Kent Smith and Jane Randolph) find themselves confronted by the beast in their darkened office. An insert shot of the panther lurking beneath a drawing table was insisted upon by the front office, but Tourneur and his photographer, Nicholas Musuraca, responded by staging the shot obliquely and without emphasis. What the film does not show, as Lon Chaney, Jr.'s *The Wolf Man* had done the previous year, is the character's actual transformation into the beast, a decision on the part of Lewton and his team that was born out of a combination of artistic judgment and simple expediency. Lewton was convinced that his film (indeed most

horror films) would prove much more effective in the shudders department if the story was presented realistically and straight, emphasizing the psychological elements of fear rather than more blatant horrors, which he felt were best left to the audience's imagination. But on a minuscule budget of slightly more than $100,000 and a tight shooting schedule, he wasn't able to afford elaborate special effects, either. Tourneur shared Lewton's artistic goals of not showing too much and was grounded in the techniques necessary to achieve them on the screen. According to the film's credited scriptwriter, De Witt Bodeen (Lewton, Tourneur, and even the film's editor, Mark Robson, contributed to the story, as well), it was Tourneur who was entirely responsible for the style of *Cat People*. In addition to sketching out the film's basic plot, Lewton also contributed the ideas for the film's famous "busses" (as Lewton dubbed them)—shock sequences aimed at lifting viewers off their chairs with the sudden appearance of an unexpected, and usually everyday, object accompanied by a loud burst of sound, the one technique wholly inspired by Lewton that Tourneur continued to use throughout his horror and nonhorror film career.

"Val was the dreamer and I was the realist, which is why we worked so well together," Tourneur often said of his relationship with Lewton. Interestingly, this

dichotomy in their personalities (and, implicitly, in their approaches to life) is reflected in the characters and central themes of most Tourneur films, wherein it is usually the cause of conflict, not harmony. Simon's conviction that she is condemned by a supernatural curse to turn into a deadly cat creature whenever she is roused to anger, love, or jealousy runs counter to her skeptical, feet-on-the-ground, and even stodgy husband's absolute belief in an orderly universe where such things cannot possibly be. She is the dreamer and he the realist, and it is the inability of his character to understand, accept, or deal with her opposing philosophy that triggers the dire events that befall him and other characters in the film, including Simon herself. This same thematic situation presented itself in Tourneur's next two films for Lewton, the brilliant supernatural tone poem *I Walked with a Zombie* and *The Leopard Man* (both 1943)—a conventional murder mystery—and runs fairly consistently throughout the director's filmography. Most of his protagonists—particularly his male protagonists—share Smith's realistic, pragmatic nature, if not his stodginess, and it usually spells difficulty, if not outright disaster, for them (Robert Mitchum in Tourneur's film-noir classic *Out of the Past*, 1947) unless or until they come to terms with the less orderly nature of their opposites, their adversaries, in themselves and in life in general—or, as is the case with the ultraskeptical, ultrapragmatic, and profoundly destructive debunker (Dana Andrews) in Tourneur's masterpiece *Curse of the Demon*, until they not only come to terms with and accept what they cannot understand but finally embrace it to survive.

Filmography

1930: *Accusée, Levez-vous* (editor); 1931: *Maison de Danses* (editor), *Tout Ça Ne Vaut Pas L'Amour* (director), *Partir* (editor); 1932: *Au Nom de la Roi* (editor), *Les gaîetés de l'Escadron* (editor); 1933: *Pour Être aimé* (director), *Toto* (director), *Les Deux Orphelines* (editor); 1934: *Les Filles de la Concierge* (director), *Le Voleur* (editor); 1935: *A Tale of Two Cities* (second-unit director); 1936: *Harnessed Rhythm** (director), *The Jonker Diamond** (director), *Killer Dog** (director), *Master Will Shakespeare** (director); 1937: *The Boss Didn't Say Good Morning** (director), *The Grand Bounce** (director), *The King Without A Crown** (director), *The Man in the Barn** (director), *Romance of Radium** (director), *The Rainbow Pass** (director); 1938: *The Face Behind the Mask** (director), *The Ship That Died** (director), *Strange Glory** (director), *Think It Over** (director); 1939: *Yankee Doodle Goes to Town** (director), *They All Come Out* (director), *Nick Carter—Master Detective* (director); 1940: *Phantom Raiders* (director); 1941: *Doctors Don't Tell* (director); 1942: *The Magic Alphabet** (director), *The Incredible Stranger** (director), *Cat People* (director/cowriter, uncredited); 1943: *I Walked with a Zombie* (director/cowriter, uncredited), *The Leopard Man* (director); 1944: *Days of Glory* (director), *Experiment Perilous* (director); 1946: *Canyon Passage* (director); 1947: *Out of the Past* (director); 1948: *Berlin Express* (director); 1949: *Easy Living* (director); 1950: *Stars in My Crown* (director), *The Flame and the Arrow* (director); 1951: *Circle of Danger* (director), *Anne of the Indies* (director); 1952: *Way of a Gaucho* (director); 1953: *Appointment in Honduras* (director); 1955: *Stranger on Horseback* (director), *Wichita* (director); 1956: *Great Day in the Morning* (director), *Nightfall* (director); 1958: *Curse of the Demon*, a.k.a. *Night of the Demon* (director), *The Fearmakers* (director), *Fury River* (codirector); 1959: *Frontier Rangers* (codirector); *Mission of Danger* (codirector), *Timbuktu* (director), *The Giant of Marathon* (director); 1963: *The Comedy of Terrors* (director); 1965: *War Gods of the Deep* (director).

* short film

JOHN MCCARTY

HENRI-GEORGES CLOUZOT

In view of the seminal influence his films—one film in particular—have had on the cinema of fear, it is regrettable, but not surprising, that the name Henri-Georges Clouzot isn't better known these days. With the exception of three of his films, Clouzot's features seldom receive much exposure now, even on video. As a result, the name and reputation of this distinguished director of thrillers and shockers, whom the press dubbed "the French Hitchcock" and who died in 1977, has fallen into relative obscurity. This is a situation that sorely needs correcting, for there is, perhaps, no more unsung director in the arena of fearfilm whose body of nerve-racking, often shuddery work is more deserving of revival for the enjoyment and appreciation of today's fans than Henri-Georges Clouzot. Videocassette and laser-disc distributors, please take note.

Born in Niort, France, in 1907, Henri-Georges Clouzot bounced around at jobs in the Navy, law, and newspaper work before settling on a career in show business. He started out as a film editor, then shifted to scriptwriting, and directed his first film, a suspenseful short subject called *La Terreur des Batignolles*, in 1931. Following a sojourn in Germany, where he worked as an assistant director and prepared the French-language versions of several German films directed by Anatole Litvak and E. A. Dupont, he became ill and his show business career was interrupted by a lengthy convalescence in a private sanitorium. Plagued by poor eyesight in addition to a weak constitution, he never did quite recover from his susceptibility to any illness that came along, and he remained sickly all his life. According to those who knew him, he was embittered about the poor health fate had dealt him, and this bitterness, some critics maintain,

"Evil is a necessary thing." Pierre Fresnay as the victimized doctor in Clouzot's *Le Corbeau* (1943). (Moving Image and Sound Archives)

formed the basis of the pessimism and dark view of life that he expressed off and on (mostly on) in his films.

During the German occupation of France, Clouzot made the controversial decision to write screenplays for the Continental Film Company, a pro-Vichy outfit not

Micheline Francey and Pierre Fresnay give premature thanks that the poison-pen letters accusing them of adultery—and worse—have ceased—from *Le Corbeau* (1943). (The John McCarty Collection)
Ginette Leclerc and Pierre Fresnay in *Le Corbeau* (1943), Clouzot's controversial suspense film about an outbreak of poison-pen letters in a small French town. (The John McCarty Collection)

so secretly bankrolled by German moneymen. Out of guilt or conviction, other French filmmakers and actors involved with this German front organization soon sought employment elsewhere, but Clouzot, believing the company's money didn't smell even if its politics did, stayed on and was soon given the opportunity to direct his first feature-length thriller, *L'Assassin Habite au 21* (1942), which he adapted from a popular whodunit by S. A. Steedman in the mold of Georges Simenon's Inspector Maigret detective stories. In his massive *The Story of Cinema*, historian David Shipman writes of the film: "Few directors made a more brilliant start—literally, since after an opening sequence in which a series of grisly murders is discussed in a bar the camera follows

The Fearmakers

one of its patrons along the street and it is gradually clear to the audience that he is being followed by the killer." From this brief description, one sees the evidence of a Hitchcockian influence on Clouzot, for the sequence strikingly recalls a number of stylistic and atmospheric ingredients in Hitchcock's own first thriller, *The Lodger* (1926). Even the English title of the Clouzot film, *The Murderer Lives at Number 21,* shares a certain affinity with the Hitchcock film. In a few years, however, the situation would reverse itself and the master of suspense would reveal the influence of Clouzot in such films as *Vertigo* (1958) and especially *Psycho* (1960).

The iconoclastic Clouzot continued his controversial association with Continental to make his next film, *Le Corbeau* (1943), a suspense thriller about a madman who turns a provincial French town upside down, wrecking the lives of a number of its citizens, by writing a string of vile and accusatory poison-pen letters that he anonymously signs "Le Corbeau" (translated in the film's subtitles as "The Crow," although many American prints and sources insist on translating it as "The Raven"). The film very nearly wrecked Clouzot's career as well, for once the Nazi occupation was over, the newly installed government condemned Clouzot and his cowriter, Louis Chavance, for having defamed the character of the French people in their film. *Le Corbeau* was banned from further showings and officials threatened to have Clouzot and Chavance tried as collaborators and executed. Instead, the two men were forbidden from working in the postwar French film industry. By 1947, however, the political climate had cooled considerably. Clouzot was finally able to get backing for another film, the detective thriller *Quai des Orfèvres,* and he was back in business.

In defense of themselves and their film, Clouzot and Chavance insisted that whereas *Le Corbeau* had indeed been financed by a German front organization and was used by the German occupiers as anti-French propaganda, the story itself had not been written with that purpose in mind. They maintained that their cautionary tale was based on an actual incident that had occurred in France in the early thirties, and that, although specifically set in a French town (Saint-Robin), it was meant to apply universally. An opening title card setting the locale of the film as "a small town . . . anywhere" supports the filmmakers' claim.

Although filmed during the German occupation, the actual period of *Le Corbeau* is rather ambiguous. There's neither a German soldier in sight nor a reference to the war or the occupation throughout. The story could be taking place before the war or conceivably just afterward. In any case, it's easy to see why the film incurred such wrath after the liberation, for its bitter portrayal of lives torn apart by lies, innuendo, and denunciation probably struck quite a sensitive nerve.

For all this, however, *Le Corbeau* is remarkably upbeat for a Clouzot film. In the end, the villainous Crow is vanquished, some of the victims of his perfidy are avenged, and the hero and heroine (Pierre Fresnay and Ginette Leclerc) are at last able to shed the heavy burdens of their respective pasts and begin a new life together. The outcome of the traumatic ordeal is positive, prompting Fresnay to reflect that perhaps "Evil is a necessary thing."

Prefiguring the sardonic conclusions of some of his future fearfilms, Clouzot serves up a disturbing final image, however, by having Fresnay come upon the body of the dead Crow slumped over a desk, his throat cut from ear to ear by the mother of one of his victims. As Fresnay opens a window to let in some air, he sees the avenging woman departing down the street. Dressed in black and wearing a black shawl, she looks very much like a crow herself.

A number of the film's suspense and fear-filled set pieces suggest the Hitchcock influence, as well.

The Wages of Fear (1953), starring Yves Montand, cemented Clouzot's reputation around the world as a maestro of heart-pounding suspense. (The John McCarty Collection)

For example, there's the elaborate tracking shot that opens the film, establishing all the major locations, and the disquieting final shot of Fresnay emerging from a cottage to wash blood from his hands. (One of the town doctors, Fresnay has just saved a woman's life by giving her an abortion—a forbidden practice in this Catholic country—which the Crow reveals in the first poison-pen letter in an attempt to destroy him.)

Other memorable sequences indicate Clouzot was not only learning from Hitchcock but developing a master's touch of his own: the arrest of the nurse Marie, initially suspected of being the Crow, as she breathlessly locks the door of her apartment after being pursued through the distorted-angled streets of the town by a howling mob (which we hear but do not see), spots a shattered mirror, and turns around to see that her sanctuary has already been invaded and its contents thoroughly trashed; the funeral of the boy whom the villainous Crow's missives drove to suicide, during which another poison-pen letter falls to the street from the back of the hearse and the procession of mourners step fearfully around it; and the scene in the church following Marie's arrest as the parishioners give premature thanks for their town's salvation, where the first of another series of letters flutters down to them from the dark rafters above, its spiraling descent captured by Clouzot's camera in a brilliantly choreographed crane shot.

In the manner of Hitchcock, the director also makes bold use of extreme close-ups to suggest guilt and anxiety during an especially tense scene where the principal suspects in the case are rounded up and given a grueling handwriting test to expose the culprit—a test that is perversely conducted, though we don't know it at the time, by the malevolent Crow himself.

After Clouzot captured the director's prize for his next thriller, *Quai des Orfèvres,* at the 1947 Venice Film Festival and his reputation was restored, the ban on *Le Corbeau* was lifted and the film, now considered a suspense classic, became widely shown, capturing the attention of Hollywood. Twentieth Century-Fox bought the rights and assigned director Otto Preminger to do an English-language remake. Titled *The Thirteenth Letter* (1951), the remake starred Michael Rennie in the Fresnay role and Charles Boyer as the villainous letter writer. This film remains an effective chiller in its own right—perhaps because Howard Koch's screenplay and Preminger's direction followed the Clouzot original virtually scene for scene. The locale of the remake was transposed to a small town in Canada, however.

If the controversial *Le Corbeau* established Clouzot's reputation in Europe as a maestro of menace capable of gripping audiences with heart-pounding scenes of suspense and fear, his first big international success, *The Wages of Fear* (1953), cemented it around the world. A fear film of the first order—and a quintessential thriller to boot—the prize-winning *Wages of Fear* stimulated a degree of controversy, as well. Reviewers saw its story of four down-and-outers who risk their lives transporting truckloads of nitroglycerin over hostile South American roads to dowse a U.S. oil company's fire as a stinging attack on American capitalism and Yankee corporate imperialism in the Third World. Condemned as an anti-French fascist for *Le Corbeau,* Clouzot now found himself being vilified as a Communist. In the manner of John Huston's *The Treasure of the Sierra Madre* (1948), a film it superficially resembles, *The Wages of Fear* does cast a critical eye on capitalist greed and the exploitation of the downtrodden masses. But its primary theme, a reflection perhaps of Clouzot's attitude toward his ongoing struggle against ill health, is the fate of the individual who finds himself with all the odds stacked against him. And the conclusion Clouzot reaches couldn't be more bleak. All but one of the four men perish en route—and the one who gets through is killed shortly afterward in a freak accident when he lets down his guard.

The Wages of Fear is by no means a cheerful film. But it is a relentlessly gripping and suspenseful one that, befitting its title, creates a palpable sense of nightmarish dread and white-knuckle fear on a par with the best of Hitchcock from the moment the nitro-filled trucks start rolling all the way through to the bitterly ironic finish. It was the worldwide critical and financial success of *The Wages of Fear,* one of the most nail-biting films of the era, that led to Clouzot's being dubbed "the French Hitchcock." Ironically, Hitchcock had sought to make the film himself, but he lost a bid for the rights to the book upon which the film is based, Georges Arnaud's *Le Salaire de la Peur,* when Arnaud, apparently for purely nationalistic reasons, decided he wanted the film made by a French director instead. Auspiciously, Clouzot was ready and waiting in the wings. Years later, though, Arnaud's thriller was bought up by an American director, William Friedkin, who remade it as *Sorcerer* (1977), starring Roy Scheider. Due to French copyright law, however, Friedkin was prevented from doing an exact remake and therefore his film is quite different from *The Wages of Fear*—and from the novel from which Clouzot's film was faithfully adapted.

Hitchcock's and Clouzot's paths crossed again, even more memorably, over the rights to the novel *Celle Qui N'etait Pas,* a Grand Guignol thriller by the popular French writing team Pierre Boileau and Thomas Narcejac. Inspired by the hard-boiled thrillers of the American writer James M. Cain, Boileau and Narcejac's devious tales usually centered around a murder scheme hatched by a pair of adulterous lovers to get an unwanted wife or husband out of the way for reasons of passion and profit. The authors turned the tables on the Cain formula, however, by exploring the murder scheme from the point of view of the victim or a set-up patsy— a twist they typically revealed

Above: Clouzot dropped several clues to the often-imitated surprise twist of *Les Diaboliques* (1955) in shots like this one where Vera Clouzot, the real victim of the murder plot, is framed in a tight squeeze between her conniving persecutors Paul Meurisse (right) and Simone Signoret (back to camera). (The John McCarty Collection) Facing page: Simone Signoret prepares the drugged Paul Meurisse for drowning as accomplice Vera Clouzot looks on in *Les Diaboliques* (1955), one of the most influential fearfilms of the 1950s. (The John McCarty Collection)

to the reader only on the very last page. *Celle Qui N'etait Pas* (which roughly translates as *The Woman Who Was No More*) is characteristic of the authors' approach. Set in a French boarding school, the novel details the vengeful murder of the school's villainous headmaster by his put-upon wife and abused mistress, then pulls the rug out from under us at the conclusion by revealing that the wife herself is the intended victim of an even more ingenious

murder plot, hatched by the headmaster and his mistress to drive the woman into suffering a fatal heart attack so they can get her out of the way and claim her estate.

Boileau and Narcejac felt the novel, which contains many grisly elements and some supreme moments of carefully calculated suspense, to be ideal Hitchcock material and encouraged their representatives to negotiate a deal for the screen rights. According to some sources, Hitchcock actually made a bid on the book, but the rights went to Clouzot instead because Hitchcock's offer was too low. There may be some truth in this, since Hitchcock was well known for grabbing the rights to the stories and novels he adapted at the most rock-bottom price possible—as was the case with Robert Bloch's *Psycho*, which he bought for a paltry nine thousand five hundred dollars. Other sources claim that Hitchcock declined even to make an offer on the book because he felt the material wasn't really his cup of blood. In view of the influence Clouzot's film version, retitled *Les*

Diaboliques, would have on Hitchcock, however, this claim seems rather improbable—especially since Hitchcock quickly snapped up the rights to Boileau and Narcejac's next thriller, *D'entre les Morts*, which contains many similar elements, and used it as the basis for what is arguably his greatest film, *Vertigo* (1958).

Released in the United States in 1955 as *Diabolique* (a.k.a. *The Fiends* and *The Devils*), Clouzot's film was a huge critical and commercial success—even more of a success than his *Wages of Fear*. Because of its memorable ad campaign, which urged audiences not to reveal the ending and encouraged exhibitors not to let people in after the film began, eager audiences from coast to coast lined up in droves to see the film, an unheard-of experience for any foreign-language release in the United States up to that time. Hitchcock adopted the same advertising gimmick for the release of *Psycho*, with even greater box-office results.

Beyond the similarities of their advertising campaigns and twist endings, these two watershed

Brigitte Bardot in one of her best films and one of Clouzot's last, *La Verité* (1960), a.k.a. *The Truth*. (Moving Image and Sound Archives)

fearfilms are remarkably similar in other ways, too, a fact that indicates Hitchcock had taken more than a passing interest in the Boileau/Narcejac novel—and in Clouzot—for some time. Both films are murder mysteries with horrific overtones and share a common atmosphere of expressionistic and Grand Guignol gloom imposed on a modern, everyday locale. The evil departed appears to have returned from the grave in both films. A murder taking place in a bathroom is the shocking highlight of each film, complete with identical close-ups of water swirling down the bathtub drain after the murder has occurred. *Diabolique,* however, contains two murders set in a bathroom—one faked, the other real. The shot of the deceived wife, played by Vera Clouzot (the director's spouse), slumping lifelessly to the bathroom floor after suffering her fatal heart attack is quite similar to the image of Janet's Leigh's final repose after being slain in *Psycho*. Indicative of the fact that Hitchcock had seen and been impressed by Clouzot's work well before *Diabolique,* however, is the scene in *Psycho* where

Vera Miles enters the fruit cellar, encounters Mrs. Bates's corpse, and knocks an overhead light with her hand as she screams, causing the room to come alive with eerily moving shadows from the swinging light. *Le Corbeau* contains a similarly eerie scene involving a swaying overhead light—a visual effect Clouzot maintained he'd had in his mind for some time before deciding where and when to put it to good use. Hitchcock borrowed it and put it to good use, as well.

Diabolique's dark psychological overtones, macabre humor, and diabolical plot twists hinting of the supernatural rippled throughout a diverse range of fearfilms in addition to Hitchcock's in the years ahead. Director William Castle patterned many of his successful string of fifties shockers (*Macabre, House on Haunted Hill, The Tingler*) in whole or in part on the Clouzot film. While ostensibly based on the works of Edgar Allan Poe, Roger Corman's gothic horrors *The Pit and the Pendulum* (1961) and *The Premature Burial* (1962) made use of the Clouzot film's twist-ending murder plot, as well. In the wake of *Psycho*'s worldwide impact and box-office success, Hammer Films expanded beyond its period horror formula with a series of psychological shockers (*Scream of Fear, Maniac, Paranoiac, Nightmare, Hysteria, Crescendo, Fear in the Night*) that the studio dubbed "mini-Hitchcocks." They might better have been called "mini-Clouzots," however, for the shadow of *Diabolique* fell even more heavily on them. Even such recent psychological thrillers as Phil Joanou's *Final Analysis* (1992), a film intended as a nod to Hitchcock's *Vertigo*, and Harold Becker's *Malice* (1993) remain implicitly a nod to Clouzot's *Diabolique*, and to Boileau and Narcejac, as well.

Eventually, *Diabolique* was twice remade, first as an above average TV movie, *Reflections of Murder* (1974). Although transposed to the United States, the telefilm, scripted by Carol Sobieski and directed by John Badham, otherwise followed the plot and structure of the Clouzot film quite faithfully. Sam Waterston and Tuesday Weld re-created the roles of the duplicitous lovers memorably played by Paul Meurisse and Simone Signoret in the original, and Joan Hackett took Vera Clouzot's part as the mercilessly destroyed wife. A second and vastly inferior made-for-TV remake set in a New Orleans sanitorium followed in 1993. Titled *House of Secrets*, the film starred Melissa Gilbert, Bruce Boxleitner, and Kate Vernon.

Ironically, although Clouzot continued to turn out psychological shockers, many of them quite good, his films failed to secure widespread distribution; as a result, he never again experienced a huge critical and commercial success. Eventually, his style of carefully crafted filmmaking went out of favor in France entirely with the birth of the New Wave and his output grew fewer and far between. In 1977, his chronic ill health finally caught up with him and he died of heart failure at age seventy-one, having survived much longer than he pessimistically believed possible. (His first wife, Vera, a gifted actress and the definitive Clouzot screen victim, died much earlier, in 1960, at the young age of thirty-nine.)

Filmography

1931: *La Terreur des Batignolles* (director/writer): 1942: *Les Inconnus dans la Maison* (writer), *L'Assassin Habite au 21*—U.S. title: *The Murderer Lives at Number 21* (director/cowriter); 1943: *Le Corbeau*—U.S. title: *The Raven* (director/cowriter); 1947: *Quai des Orfèvres*—U.S. title: *Jenny Lamour* (director/cowriter); 1949: *Manon* (director/cowriter), *Retour a la Vie* (codirector/cowriter); 1950: *Miquette et Sa Mere*—U.S. title: *Miquette and Her Mother* (director/cowriter); 1953: *Le Salaire de la Peur*—U.S. title: *The Wages of Fear* (director/cowriter); 1955: *Les Diaboliques*—U.S. title: *Diabolique* (director/cowriter); 1956: *La Mystère Picasso*—U.S. title: *The Mystery of Picasso* (director); 1957: *Les Espions*—U.S. title: *The Spies* (director/cowriter); 1960: *La Vérité*—U.S. title: *The Truth* (director/cowriter); 1968: *La Prisonnière*—U.S. title: *The Female Prisoner* and *Women in Chains* (director/cowriter); 1969: *Messa de Requiem* (director).

HE STRIPPED SOULS AS BARE AS BODIES!

AMERICAN INTERNATIONAL presents

RAY MILLAND
STARRING AS

"X"

THE MAN WITH
THE X-RAY EYES

IN PATHÉCOLOR
AND SPECTARAMA

WINNER OF THE
INTERNATIONAL SCIENCE-FICTION
FILM FESTIVAL

Roger Corman's 1963
film *X—The Man with
X-Ray Eyes* rose above
the level of his previous
teen-oriented movies to
deliver a powerful
fearfilm to an
unsuspecting teen
audience.

ROGER CORMAN

In the mid-1950s, two enterprising gentlemen named James H. Nicholson and Samuel Z. Arkoff founded American-International Pictures, a shoestring production company aimed at exploiting the growing market for teen-oriented movies. In doing so, they helped to define an entire area of the movie industry, one which still thrives.

AIP was the first to see—and to capitalize on—the baby-boom teenagers whose pockets were heavy with unspent allowances, whose hormones had begun to rage, and whose first-generation suburban ennui begged for diversion. To such ripe audiences, AIP offered laughs, scares, and action, all done cheaply enough to ensure a profit, and with enough skill to ensure an audience. And the task of delivering on this challenge fell to Roger Corman, AIP's first and most prolific director, who went on to become the patron saint of low-budget filmmaking in the United States.

Born in 1926, Corman expected to follow in his father's shoes and become an engineer, but after graduating from Stanford University with a degree in industrial engineering, and after serving in the Navy, he responded to the call of Hollywood and found a job as a messenger for Twentieth Century-Fox studios that paid $32.50 per week. He went on his own to produce his first film on a shoestring budget, the grade Z sci-fi opus *The Monster from the Ocean Floor,* in 1954. That same year, he came to the attention of American-International Pictures, then known as American Releasing Corporation, for whom he produced the race-car thriller *The Fast and the Furious.* In a typical Corman cost-cutting move, he performed some of the dangerous stunt driving in the film himself. He made his directorial debut in 1955 with *Swamp Women.*

Corman's first directorial efforts for AIP were *Five Guns West* and *Apache Woman* (both 1955). It wasn't long, however, before Nicholson and Arkoff noticed the lucrative potential of fearfilms with the teen market, and Corman acted as executive producer for the studio's first effort in this vein, the 1955 *The Beast with a Million Eyes.*

After this, Corman began turning out fearfilms for AIP, as well as for its rival for the low-budget pie, Allied Artists, at a furious rate. Shooting schedules were prohibitively short, budgets were cinched tight, and frequently two films were shot back-to-back to save money on set construction. From such circumstances emerged such Corman efforts as *Attack of the Crab Monsters* (1957) and *The Wasp Woman* (1959), films that—quickie production notwithstanding—were competently made, enjoyable fare, just right for preteen chills and older siblings' make-out sessions.

Benefiting from more experience, Corman's films, though just as quickly and inexpensively made, began to flesh out into more subtle, thought-provoking explorations of character and plot. With his 1963 film *X—The Man with X-Ray Eyes,* Corman unleashed upon an unsuspecting teen public a film of quite disturbing power.

The film starred Ray Milland as a scientist who concocts a potion giving him the power to see through opaque surfaces. Its scenes of Milland's more cosmic visions have a surreal quality quite apart from the more familiar rubber-suited space monsters of the director's earlier fare. As Milland's self-administered potion grows more powerful, he begins to see beyond the conventional world, encountering alien things lurking beneath the surface of everyday reality. By the film's conclusion, Milland, whose eyes have turned completely black, has been driven to madness by his enhanced vision. Tortured beyond endurance, he tears out his

offending orbs. Clearly, this was not the same amiably clumsy type of plot exemplified by Corman's earlier efforts.

Even before this, however, Corman had begun to make serious ripples in the Hollywood pond. In 1960, he released the first of his so-called cycle of Edgar Allan Poe films, *House of Usher*, an atmospheric, eerie work distinguished by first-rate art direction, costuming, polished (if at times self-parodying) performances, and an overall look that belied its meager (by Hollywood standards of the time) budget. Corman's director of photography, Floyd Crosby, achieved a persistent sense of gloom in the film, of dankness and corruption well in keeping with the Poe source.

The Poe cycle continued for eight or nine more films, depending on how finely one wishes to split hairs: *The Haunted Palace* (1963), while named after Poe's poem, was actually an adaptation of a story by H. P. Lovecraft. Purist quibbles aside, the series gave Corman a well-earned critical respect not accorded to his earlier works and established him as a director of significant note.

Corman's Poe adaptations work well as pop-psychology character studies because they echo Poe's recurring theme of psychological breakdown. Madness burns away at the protagonists of these films, finally exploding outward in deranged, destructive climaxes. In fact, the image of the mentally unstable hero is a staple of Corman's work, present in films ranging from his early gangster movie, *Machine Gun Kelly* (1958), to his most recent directorial effort, *Frankenstein Unbound* (1990).

Not burdened by pretense or a ponderous sense of mission, Corman played his own Poe series for

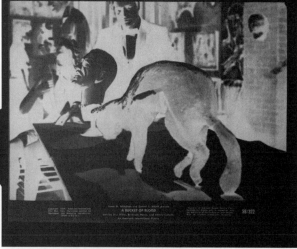

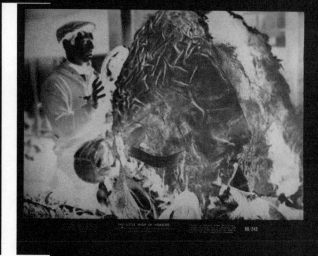

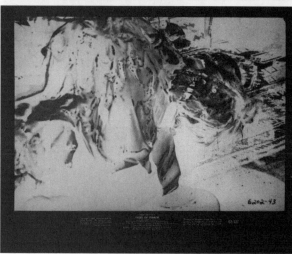

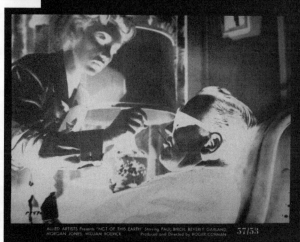

laughs in the 1963 *The Raven*, which featured a perplexed young Jack Nicholson (no relation to James H.) ambling about as the romantic interest, while fearfilm veterans Boris Karloff, Peter Lorre, and Vincent Price ham it up as rival sorcerers. A Poe film in name only, the campy lark nonetheless possesses the same quality of set design and execution that mark the series' more serious entries.

The humorous film was by no means an anomaly in Corman's career, for humor has always had its place in Corman's work. His lonely, tormented heroes have never been the excessively gloomy types familiar to viewers of upscale foreign films. As American as the movies themselves, his characters usually find themselves lost within a spiraling anarchy, in which they follow a series of bad impulses that lead to their own destruction. Seymour Krelboined, the charming simpleton hero of Corman's *The Little Shop of Horrors* (1960), slowly wraps himself in the mantle of his own madness as he feeds the voraciously carnivorous plant Audrey, Jr.

Clockwise from top left: Lost within a spiraling anarchy: Dick Miller and Jonathan Haze as the simpleton heroes of *A Bucket of Blood* (1959) and *The Little Shop of Horrors* (1960), two of Corman's earliest—and best—horror comedies. (Copyrights ©1959, 1960 American-International Pictures and The Filmgroup, Inc.) Nurse Beverly Garland treats vampire from outer space Paul Birch in Corman's *Not of This Earth* (1957). (The John McCarty Collection) The rotting corpse of M. Valdemar in the final episode of Corman's Poe anthology film *Tales of Terror* (1962).

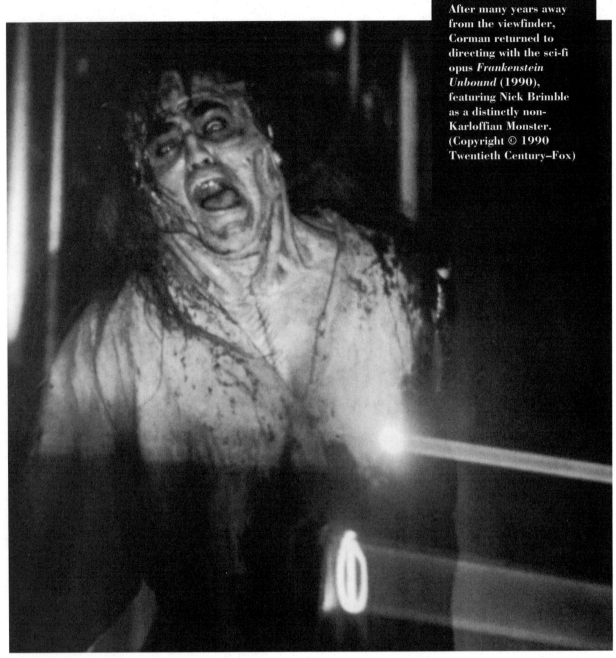

The stable of talent Corman assembled for his films have in common a sense of irony that makes even the films' darkest subject matter appealing. For example, Vincent Price's purring decadence in the Poe films successfully parodies the Anglophile myth of classiness and sophistication that had dogged Corman's poker-faced contemporaries at England's Hammer Films. Jonathan Haze's nebbish Seymour in *Little Shop* is a more relaxed and infinitely more amusing take on the spastic convulsions of Jerry Lewis. In the same film, Jackie Joseph takes Marilyn Monroe's dumb-blonde to an imbecilic extreme, and Dick Miller's dead-pan Everyman is a study in low-key hilarity. As Corman's budgets grew, so did his casting latitude, and he went on to draw performances of deft wit and grand malice out of even more well-known stars such as Shelley Winters, Angie Dickinson, Peter Fonda, and others too numerous to name.

Fraught with Cold War xenophobia, the 1950s gave rise to films dealing with atomic mutation, as well as with more indirect worries about invasion and infiltration. It wasn't long, however, before new threats loomed over the paranoid suburbs of America—the young, with their sudden interests in drugs and politics, ceased to worry about the abstract terrors of atomic mutants and invaders from outer space and began to find more immediate ways of gratifying their hunger for sensation. Corman satisfied these needs with menacing portraits of bikers (*The Wild Angels*, 1966), dope fiends (*The Trip*, 1967), and criminals (an ongoing series beginning with the 1958 *The Cry Baby Killer*, ranging through the 1967 *The St. Valentine's Day Massacre*, and concluding—for the time being, anyway—with the 1975 *Capone*, which, like *The Cry Baby Killer*, Corman produced but did not direct).

Perhaps it's appropriate that at the chronological end of the 1960s, Corman released *Gas-s-s-s* (1970), which, despite having been ruined (by his account) through a studio recut, served as a capper for the hippie era. Built upon the conceit that

everyone over twenty-five is killed by a nerve-gas spill, *Gas-s-s-s* is a film whose corniness and cynicism provides a summation of the times that spawned it. It offers a portrait of a movement in dissolution, concluding with the remergence—as reanimated corpses—of such luminaries of the era as Che Guevara, Martin Luther King, Jr., and John F. Kennedy. In ending the film with the remergence of the undead political martyrs of the time, Corman effectively bookended the decade, closing off the era while calling for a new start.

Vincent Price prepares John Kerr for a close shave in *The Pit and the Pendulum* (1961), Corman's even more successful second entry in the Poe series. (Copyright © 1961 American-International Pictures) Ray Milland stepped into Vincent Price's shoes for *The Premature Burial* (1962), opposite John Dierkes. (The John McCarty Collection)

Vincent Price and Mark Damon in *House of Usher* (1960), Corman's elegant first entry in his so-called cycle of Edgar Allan Poe films. (Copyright © 1960 American-International Pictures)

The 1970s saw Corman tapering off as a director and moving on to more administrative roles. His production/distribution company, New World Pictures, picked up where AIP left off, producing high-quality, low-budget films. Although Corman was seldom involved in their actual production, the majority of his films for New World (and his later company, Concorde Pictures) evidence a distinctly Corman look. His humor is present in them, as is his penchant toward wry observations of our culture. This is best exemplified by his 1988 remake of his earlier *Not of This Earth* (1957).

The 1957 original starred Paul Birch as a vampire from outer space and featured Beverly Garland as his nurse, Jonathan Haze as a chauffeur, and Dick Miller, in a memorable turn, as a vacuum cleaner salesman. Notable for its humorous embellishments (at one point, the vampire accidentally consumes dog's blood), unpretentious yet capable direction, and genuinely creepy scare scenes, it is a film that fits comfortably into Corman's body of work. So does the 1988 remake directed by Jim Wynorski, which opens with a title sequence heavily laden with clips from earlier Corman films. This in itself is a joke: Corman, ever strapped by lean budgets, frequently reused footage from film to film, often lifting archival footage from older films for scenes in his own. The conspicuous use of these early scenes in the 1988 remake gently pokes fun at Corman's tightfisted inventiveness and lets the audience in on the fact that the film it is about to see will have the same kind of cheerfully cheap tone that gives Corman's work such lasting appeal.

Traci Lords, in the nurse role played by

Garland (whom Lords resembles), had won notoriety as an underage porn queen. This was her first "legitimate" part. While Lords has continued as an actress in various other films (with various levels of success), her casting in this film gives it a taste of the sensational that adds to the film's undercurrent of tabloid humor.

After more than a dozen years away from the viewfinder, Corman returned to directing with the 1990 *Frankenstein Unbound.* Adapted from the novel by Brian Aldiss, the film is a well-crafted "what if" detailing scientist John Hurt's time-warped appearance in 1817 Switzerland, where he makes the acquaintance of Lord Byron, Percy Shelley, and Mary Godwin (soon to become Mary Shelley, author of the classic *Frankenstein*). In addition to such august company, Hurt also runs into Dr. Frankenstein (Raul Julia) himself, who's having some trouble with his science project—the Monster's existential agonies and demands for a mate, combined with its short-tempered predilection for dismembering anyone who rubs it the wrong way, are sorely testing the venerable doctor's resources.

The film's tone harkens back to Corman's Poe cycle with its attention to period

Vincent Price and Elizabeth Shepherd go to blazes in *Tomb of Legeia* (1965), Corman's final Poe film. (Copyright © 1965 American-International Pictures)

detail, its lavish appearance, and its concern with heroes out of control. The physical appearance of the Monster is original and effective—particularly its stitched-together eyes of different colors and the mismatched visible sutures. This deviation from the familiar flat-headed, neck-bolted Karloff makeup, while a matter of necessity (Universal holds the copyright to the Monster makeup in the Karloff film and protects it fiercely), adds much to the film's reinterpretation of the story. This Monster is an angry, frightened creation, enormously strong (Dr. Frankenstein alludes to several improvements he's made on basic anatomy), and, at the same time, the thoughtful, emotional beast of Shelley's novel.

True to his characteristic economy of production, Corman's effects are lean and practical, yet inspired. The scene in which the Monster chases Frankenstein's fiancée (whose horses are no match for the Monster's new and improved speed) has a freakish, abnormal look that is genuinely frightening.

The film's downbeat conclusion is also in keeping with Corman's tendency toward philosophical subtexts. In addition to being a monster-on-the-loose/ science-fiction film, *Frankenstein Unbound* is a work that seriously questions technology and our culture's fascination with it.

In all of Corman's films, no matter how small the

scale or ludicrous the premise, one finds similar unforced elements of seriousness and thoughtfulness. Even in his overtly comic fearfilms like *The Little Shop of Horrors*, one finds Corman's sense of social concern—which, typically, is played out by a hero in disarray. *Little Shop*'s Seymour, amusingly befuddled as he is, still works as a figure of social alienation (not unlike Dr. Frankenstein) who falls deeper and deeper into a trap he's created for himself. The same is true of Corman's Poe film heroes: In all of these films, Vincent Price is a character who has retreated so deeply into his own mind and obsessions that he can ·no longer see his actions as wrong or misguided. No character in a Corman film, no matter how sketchily written or ironically played, is without personal flaws that make him seem all the more human. And it is this that makes Corman's films rise above their mechanically produced peers.

Certainly Corman's work falls into the category of exploitation film in the sense that it is tailored to appeal to a specific audience, one within a specific cultural context. In other words, they're films produced in response to a perception of what a specific group of people wants to see. But Corman's films are never exploitative in the sense of using people—audiences or cast members—for personal gain without giving anything back in return. As a result, his work has earned him the respect and admiration of many. And his humility and humor have earned him our affection. In an industry founded on illusion and weighed down by increasing budgets and unwieldy spectacles, Corman's work stands out for its freshness, its originality, and its lasting immediacy.

Roger Corman (Courtesy of Fred Olen Ray)

Filmography
1954: *The Monster from the Ocean Floor* (producer), *The Fast and the Furious* (producer, writer), *Highway Dragnet* (coproducer/cowriter); 1955: *Swamp Women* (director), *Five Guns West* (producer/director), *Apache Woman* (producer/director); 1956: *The Day the World Ended* (producer/director), *Oklahoma Woman* (producer/director), *The Gunslinger* (producer/director), *It Conquered the World* (producer/director); 1957: *Attack of the Crab Monsters* (producer/director), *Not of This Earth* (producer/director), *The Undead* (producer/director), *Rock All Night* (producer/director), *Thunder Over Hawaii*, a.k.a. *Naked Paradise* (producer/director); *Carnival Rock* (director), *Sorority Girl*

(producer/director), *Teenage Doll* (producer/director), *Viking Women and the Sea Serpent* (producer/director); 1958: *She Gods of Shark Reef* (director), *Machine Gun Kelly* (producer/director), *Teenage Caveman* (producer/director), *War of the Satellites* (producer/director), *I, Mobster* (producer/director), *Hot Car Girl* (executive producer), *Night of the Blood Beast* (executive producer), *The Cry Baby Killer* (producer); 1959: *A Bucket of Blood* (producer/director), *Attack of the Giant Leeches* (executive producer), *The Wasp Woman* (producer/director); 1960: *Ski Troop Attack* (director), *House of Usher* (producer/director), *The Little Shop of Horrors* (producer/director), *The Last Woman on Earth* (producer/director); 1961: *Atlas* (director), *Creature from the Haunted Sea* (producer/director), *The Intruder* (producer/director), *The Pit and the Pendulum* (producer/director); 1962: *Tower of London* (director), *The Premature Burial* (producer/director), *Tales of Terror* (producer/director); 1963: *Battle Beyond the Sun* (executive producer), *The Haunted Palace* (producer/director), *The Raven* (producer/director), *The Terror* (producer/director), *X—The Man with X-Ray Eyes* (producer/director), *The Young Racers* (producer/director), *Dementia 13* (executive producer); 1964: *The Secret Invasion* (director), *The Masque of the Red Death* (producer/director); 1965: *Tomb of Ligeia* (producer/director); 1966: *The Wild Angels* (producer/director); 1967: *The Trip* (producer/director), *The St. Valentine's Day Massacre* (producer/director); 1969: *How to Make It* (director/actor), *De Sade* (codirector, uncredited); 1970: *Bloody Mama* (producer/director); *Gas-s-s-s* (producer/director), *The Dunwich Horror* (executive producer), *The Student Nurses* (executive producer); 1971: *Von Richtofen and Brown* (director); 1972: *Boxcar Bertha* (producer), *Unholy Rollers* (producer); 1973: *I Escaped from Devil's Island* (producer); 1974: *The Godfather, Part II* (actor), *Big Bad Mama* (producer), *Cockfighter* (producer); 1975: *Capone* (producer), *Death Race 2000* (producer); 1976: *Cannonball* (actor), *Jackson County Jail* (executive producer), *Moving Violation* (executive producer), *Lumiere* (producer), *Eat My Dust!* (producer), *Fighting Mad* (producer); 1977: *Grand Theft Auto* (executive producer), *I Never Promised You a Rose Garden* (executive producer), *Thunder and Lightning* (actor); 1978: *Piranha* (executive producer), *Avalanche* (producer), *Outside Chance* (producer),

Deathsport (producer); 1979: *Rock 'n' Roll High School* (executive producer), *Fast Charlie, the Moonbeam Rider* (producer), *Saint Jack* (producer); 1980: *Battle Beyond the Stars* (executive producer); 1981: *The Howling* (actor), *The Territory* (executive producer), *Galaxy of Terror* (producer), *Smokey Bites the Dust* (producer); 1982: *Der Stand Der Dinge* (actor), *Forbidden World* (producer); 1983: *Suburbia* (executive producer), *Love Letters* (producer), *Space Raiders* (producer); 1984: *Swing Shift* (actor), *The Warrior and the Sorceress* (executive producer), *Deathstalker* (executive producer), *Streetwalkin'* (executive producer); 1987: *Hour of the Assassin* (executive producer), *Stripped to Kill* (executive producer), *Sweet Revenge* (executive producer), *Amazons* (producer), *Munchies* (producer), *Slumber Party Massacre II* (producer), *Big Bad Mama II* (producer); 1988: *Dangerous Love* (executive producer), *The Drifter* (executive producer), *Not of This Earth* (executive producer), *Watchers* (executive producer), *Crime Zone* (executive producer), *Dance of the Damned* (executive producer), *Daddy's Boys* (producer), *Nightfall* (producer), *The Terror Within* (producer); 1989: *Andy Colby's Incredibly Amazing Adventure* (executive producer), *Heroes Stand Alone* (executive producer), *The Lawless Land* (executive producer), *Stripped to Kill II* (executive producer), *Bloodfist II* (producer), *Lords of the Deep* (producer), *Masque of the Red Death* (producer), *Time Trackers* (producer), *Two to Tango* (producer), *Wizards of the Lost Kingdom II* (producer); 1990: *Back to Back* (executive producer), *Bloodfist II* (producer), *A Cry in the Wild* (executive producer), *Full Fathom Five* (executive producer), *Frankenstein Unbound* (producer/director/cowriter), *Streets* (executive producer), *Transylvania Twist* (executive producer), *Welcome to Oblivion* (executive producer), *The Haunting of Morella* (producer), *Overexposed* (producer), *Primary Target* (producer), *Silk 2* (producer), *Watchers 2* (producer); 1991: *The Silence of the Lambs* (actor), *Hollywood Boulevard II* (executive producer), *The Terror Within II* (executive producer); 1993: *Carnosaur* (producer); 1994: *New Crime City* (producer), *Caged Heart* (producer), *Revenge of the Red Baron* (producer).

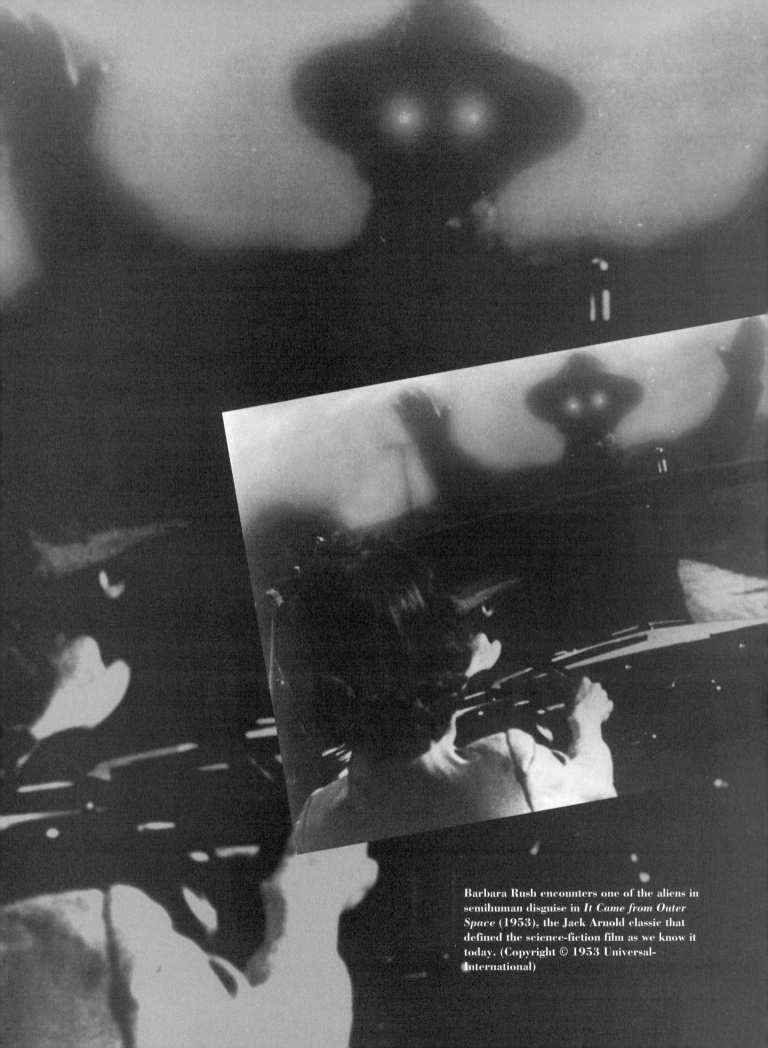

Barbara Rush encounters one of the aliens in semihuman disguise in *It Came from Outer Space* (1953), the Jack Arnold classic that defined the science-fiction film as we know it today. (Copyright © 1953 Universal-International)

BRUCE G. HALLENBECK

JACK ARNOLD

When Universal Pictures assumed its new corporate identity of Universal-International in 1946, it seemed to mark the end of an era. The celebrated Home of Horror's successful string of "monster rallies" seemed to be played out. Its legendary gallery of ghouls had all met and fought one another in film after film—except for the mummy, who shambled alone—and Abbott and Costello loomed in their futures. Universal, once the Home of Horror, was starting to look like an empty haunted house.

Then came the science-fiction boom of the 1950s, a phenomenon that began with two watershed films of very different types: the 1951 bloodthirsty-vegetable-from-outer-space opus, *The Thing,* and Eugene Lourie's prehistoric monster on the loose extravaganza, *The Beast from 20,000 Fathoms* (1953), with special effects by the young Ray Harryhausen. Just as Universal's *Dracula* and *Frankenstein* had set the pattern for most fearfilms of the thirties and forties, these two groundbreaking films, which combined traditional horror elements with science fiction, established a pattern for the fearfilms of the 1950s. Universal was quick to spot the beginnings of a new trend in all of this and immediately took the lead in exploiting it to the hilt with 3-D, a fascinating new process that seemed made for fearfilm because of its ability to make "things" jump off the screen into the audience's lap—the ultimate experience in confrontational, or in-your-face, cinema.

To reclaim its mantle as the Home of Horror, Universal needed the right vehicle to reestablish itself and a director who could step into James Whale's shoes and become its new genre master. It found the vehicle it needed in a Ray Bradbury story (written expressly for the screen) titled *It Came from Outer Space,* and the director it needed in Jack Arnold.

Like Whale before him, Jack Arnold was an unlikely choice for genre superstardom, since he had never expressed much interest in either science fiction or horror. Born in New Haven, Connecticut, in 1916, he learned filmmaking as a photographer in the U.S. Signal Corps during World War II. After the war, he moved into documentaries, then went to Hollywood to embark on a feature-film career, first as an actor, then as assistant director. Under contract to Universal, he made his feature film directorial debut in 1953 with the juvenile-delinquency drama *Girls in the Night. It Came from Outer Space,* produced by William Alland (the Val Lewton of 1950s sci-fi/horror), followed the same year.

A kinder, gentler variation of *The Thing, It Came from Outer Space* opens with a meteorlike spacecraft crashing in the Arizona desert, a setting much to Arnold's liking due to its forbidding and strangely claustrophobic barrenness. Scientist Richard Carlson tries to convince the authorities that aliens have landed and is greeted with understandable skepticism. Telephone linemen disappear, then reappear mysteriously changed—even Carlson's girlfriend (Barbara Rush) is "taken over" by the ETs. Like the alien creature in Steven Spielberg's blockbuster *E.T.* (1982), which Spielberg has admitted was strongly influenced by the Arnold film, the alien beings in *It Came from Outer Space* are not too attractive-looking, but they're not out to harm anyone, either. They just need help repairing their ship so they can move on and get home.

Scripted by Harry Essex and Ray Bradbury, who was credited only for his story contribution, *It Came from Outer Space* established the basic formula for Universal's fearfilms of the 1950s, but it went even further by defining the science-fiction film as we know it today.

The Fearmakers

It may look clichéd now, but it wasn't then; and it was Jack Arnold who, like James Whale before him, created the clichés.

Buoyed by the box office success of *It Came from Outer Space,* Universal encouraged Alland, Arnold, and company to follow it up with a monster show that might lend itself to a series in the tradition of its grand old *Dracula* and *Frankenstein* films. Thus emerged *Creature from the Black Lagoon* (1954), also in 3-D, in which Arnold replaced the first film's exotic desert setting with an equally exotic tropical one—and *Outer Space*'s kinder, gentler aliens with a sleek, streamlined, ferocious, and even "sexy" Gill Man, who quickly swam his/its way into the hearts of sci-fi/horror audiences everywhere.

The most famous scene in the film occurs when the Gill Man (played on land by Ben Chapman and underwater by Ricou Browning) swims beneath heroine Julia Adams in a manner critic John Baxter has called "a stylized representation of sexual intercourse." In fact, this scene was scripted (by Harry Essex and Arthur Ross) with no such sexual connotations at all. It was Arnold himself who supplied them when he rewrote the scene prior to shooting in an effort to add shadings to the creature's character—to make the creature less of a monster and more of a man and a symbol of loneliness and alienation.

In this film, too, Arnold made excellent use of locale, especially during the underwater scenes, which were filmed in Crystal Springs, Florida. In 3-D, these scenes were remarkably effective: Spearguns fired at the audience from the screen, and the entire theater filled with floating bubbles. The staging of these scenes remained the high-water mark (no pun intended) of underwater photography until the James Bond film *Thunderball* (1965), which boasted an exciting undersea battle staged by the Gill Man himself, second-unit director Ricou Browning.

Creature from the Black Lagoon evidences both the strongest and weakest elements of Arnold's style. On the plus side: powerful imagery and gripping, no-frills storytelling. On the minus side: one-dimensional characterizations of all but the monster star. The reason for this may have been that

Arnold always seemed more interested in images and themes than in his characters. Behind the sci-fi trappings of *Outer Space* lurks an obvious plea for understanding and tolerance—a rather daring concept in the early Cold War, pre–civil rights days of the 1950s. The first reaction of the townspeople, especially the authorities, to the aliens is to destroy

them because they're "different" and, therefore, threatening. This subtext, rare in sci-fi films at the time, was present in Bradbury's screen story. Rather than sublimating it in his direction, however, Arnold brought it boldly to the fore.

Creature from the Black Lagoon and its immediate follow-up, *Revenge of the Creature* (1955), also made a plea for tolerance. "Let's have some sympathy for the monster and his plight," Arnold urges us, echoing an idea that goes back to the original *Frankenstein* (1931) and *King Kong* (1933). *Revenge*, in fact, is basically a loose remake of *Kong* as the Gill Man is brought back to civilization in chains, escapes, and carries off the nearest blonde (Lori Nelson).

Revenge has some good moments, most of them due to Arnold's flair for atmosphere and to the exceptional underwater photography (the film was shot at Florida's Sea World). Although *Revenge*, too, was filmed in 3-D, it was released "flat" in most areas, losing most of its impact in the process as well as the claustrophobic feeling of being surrounded by water that Arnold and company had gone to such great lengths in both films to create. The almost surrealistic scene where heroine Lori Nelson, dressed in a white evening gown, clutches a buoy somewhere in the middle of the ocean as she awaits the creature's appearance sticks in the mind, however—and it may have served as the inspiration for the staging of the opening shark-attack scene in Steven Spielberg's *Jaws* (1975).

For its entry in the giant-bug sweepstakes, another trend of 1950s fearfilms, Universal again turned to Jack Arnold, whose *Tarantula* (1955) remains one of the most effective thrillers of its type, boasting some very good special effects for its time. In it, Arnold returned to the forbidding landscape of the desert. The subtle terrors of *Outer Space* were replaced by the most basic of 1950s monster-movie plots: a giant, hairy creature marauds the countryside, killing people until it is brought down by the military good guys. Also in the 1950s sci-fi tradition,

Grant Williams as Scott Carey, average man turned doll-sized survivor in *The Incredible Shrinking Man* (1957), the scariest—and best—of Jack Arnold's 1950s fearfilms. (Copyright © 1957 Universal-International)
"To God there is no zero. I still exist!" Grant Williams as Scott Carey in Arnold's life-affirming masterpiece, *The Incredible Shrinking Man* (1957). (Copyright © 1957 Universal-International)

THE INCREDIBLE SHRINKING MAN
starring Grant Williams and Randy Stuart
A Universal-International Picture

57/56

there are some peripheral monsters in the film to capture our interest: giant guinea pigs and a mutated mad scientist (Leo G. Carroll). But the real star is the titular bug itself, a truly megatarantula calculated to give arachnophobes everywhere a frisson or two. Like the Gill Man, it, too, exhibits voyeuristic tendencies—as it peers through a window to watch busty heroine Mara Corday undress.

A fast-moving desert menace film, and the obvious inspiration for Ron Underwood's 1990 homage to all such films, *Tremors*, *Tarantula* includes an early appearance by future superstar Clint Eastwood as the leader of the jet squadron that bombs the behemoth bug into oblivion. (Eastwood also has a bit in Arnold's *Revenge of the Creature*, as a lab technician who carries a rat in his pocket.)

Arnold received no director credit for one of Universal's best sci-fi/monster movies of the 1950s, *This Island Earth* (1955), the studio's first such film in color. Joseph M. Newman is credited as the director, but a number of key scenes, including the fiery finale, were staged by Jack Arnold instead. According to the film's costar, Jeff Morrow, who plays the kinder, gentler alien Exeter, Arnold was called in to direct the final scenes in the film, which take place on the doomed planet Metaluna, because Newman had fallen ill. Other sources suggest that Universal wasn't happy with Newman's work and turned to Arnold, the studio's resident "monster expert," to give the expensive but monster-less film a more exciting climax. Arnold delivered the goods—a rampaging mutant, another icon of fifties sci-fi/horror, that chases nubile heroine Faith Domergue around Metaluna's futuristic lab set before the planet explodes.

Arnold's finest genre film of the 1950s is undoubtedly *The Incredible Shrinking Man* (1957), a pet project of the director's that, in many ways, stands as his testament. It also contains the themes of loss of identity and intolerance dealt with in *Outer Space* and the subtext of alienation and loneliness of his two *Creature* films (the third and weakest film in the series, the 1956 *The Creature Walks Among Us,* was helmed by John Sherwood, Arnold's assistant); even Arnold's giant tarantula makes a repeat bow. There is also more depth to Arnold's characters in the film, especially the protagonist, Scott Carey (Grant Williams), an average middle-class guy whose life is forever changed when he is enveloped by

a peculiar mist while yachting. Following this experience, he rapidly begins to lose weight, then height—ultimately shrinking to the size of a doll, then to nothingness. Carey's final reflection on his plight ("To God there is no zero. I still exist!") as he shrinks yet again remains one of the most life-affirming moments in the history of sci-fi films.

Arnold and Richard Matheson, who scripted the film from his own novel *The Shrinking Man*, were clearly aiming for something more than run-of-the-mill sci-fi/horror here. In fact, the film doesn't play like science fiction at all; the apparently radioactive cloud that causes Carey to shrink is perfunctorily dealt with and quickly forgotten, much like the token explanation of the genesis of the zombie menace in George A. Romero's *Night of the Living Dead* (1968). The film can be more accurately described as a fable about mankind's collective loss of identity—a Kafkaesque nightmare come true.

Thanks to the exceptional trick photography and process work of Clifford Stine and the extraordinary oversized sets designed by Charles Baker, Fred Knoth,

and Jack Tait, the world of Scott Carey is completely believable—and it represents the most exotic, fearsomely isolated locale of all Arnold's films.

The film is also the scariest of Arnold's fearfilms. When Carey is reduced to doll size, everything in his world becomes terrifying, from the pet tabby that now towers over him like a hungry giant

The Metaluna monster attacks Faith Domergue as Jeff Morrow (left) and Rex Reason look on helplessly in the action-filled finale of *This Island Earth* (1955), directed without screen credit by Jack Arnold. (Copyright © 1955 Universal-International)

"MONSTER ON THE CAMPUS"
Starring ARTHUR FRANZ and JOANNA MOORE
A UNIVERSAL-INTERNATIONAL Picture
58/438

to the steps leading to the cellar—a labyrinth that stretches to hell. In fact, when Carey ends up in the cellar, unable to make his wife (Randy Stuart) hear him and come to his rescue, he does indeed seem to be in hell. By now the size of the tiniest insect, he is at the mercy of the most trivial thing—like the water drops from a broken pump, which threaten his existence as they explode around him like high-powered bombs. (The effect was achieved by dropping condoms filled with water.)

But the point Arnold and Matheson are trying to make is that despite his fate, Carey continues to fight. He doesn't give up. And the incredible lengths he goes to to survive—making what seems like a mile-long climb and then fighting a spider for some cake crumbs—are a tribute to his (read mankind's) tenacity and inner resolve.

A la David Cronenberg, the film is also a metaphor about disease and the corruption of the body. At first, there is denial ("This can't be happening to me!"), then the fight to survive, and finally acceptance.

But acceptance of what? Similar to Stanley Kubrick and Arthur C. Clarke, the cocreators of that other ambiguous masterpiece of filmed sci-fi, *2001: A Space Odyssey* (1968), neither Arnold nor Matheson have ever offered an explanation of the film's ending and Carey's sudden musings on his relationship to the universe. Perhaps by becoming as small as an atom,

Carey has begun to see his relationship with all living things in proper perspective—from their point of view, making *The Incredible Shrinking Man* perhaps the most moving ecological statement of all. Maybe he has simply come to the rather scientific realization that there is no difference between a tachyon and a galaxy.

Or perhaps he is, like all of us, just simply dying—and trying to come to terms with that bitter fact of life. The fact that we can still speculate on the meaning of the film's conclusion more than thirty-five years after it was made is a testament to its classic status.

Jack Arnold's artistry in the genre reached its zenith with this film. He made two other films in the genre afterward: *Monster on the Campus* (1958), an enjoyable if predictable variation on *Dr. Jekyll and Mr. Hyde*, and *The Space Children* (1958). Then he abandoned the genre altogether. Perhaps he felt, as James Whale did about *The Bride of Frankenstein* (1935), that there was no way he was ever going to top *The Incredible Shrinking Man*. Or, more likely, perhaps because the film was so well received and made so much money, Universal decided Arnold was now ready for more "important" projects. If so, he never found them. The largest critical and commercial big-screen hit he enjoyed in his postgenre period was *The Mouse That Roared* (1959), arguably the most overpraised of all Peter Sellers's comedies.

On the small screen, Arnold enjoyed an even

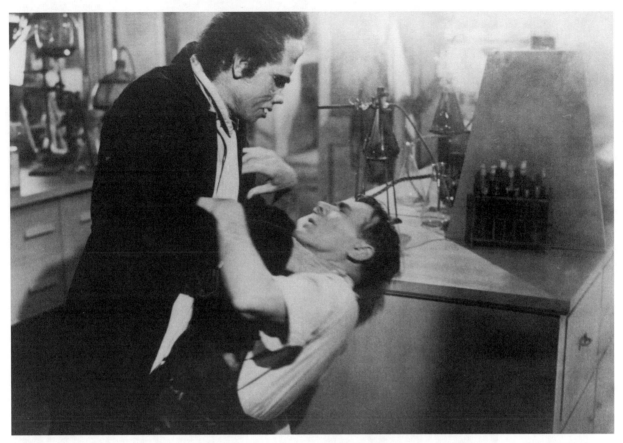

bigger success with *Gilligan's Island,* which he executive-produced in addition to directing several episodes. There was a lagoon in the series, but alas, no creature in it.

Toward the end of his life, Arnold spoke often of remaking *Creature from the Black Lagoon* as a state-of-the-art special effects extravaganza. Universal (now minus the International) made several false starts on the project. Unfortunately, it was not to be—at least not with Jack Arnold at the helm. He died in 1992 at the age of seventy-five.

Filmography

1928: *The Masked Angel* (actor); 1933: *Enlighten My Daughter* (actor); 1938: *Crime Ring* (actor), *Mr. Doodle Kicks Off* (actor), *Tarnished Angel* (actor), *This Marriage Business* (actor); 1940: *Danger on Wheels* (actor), *Enemy Agent* (actor), *Framed* (actor); 1941: *Lucky Devils* (actor), *Mexican Spitfire's Baby* (actor), *Tillie the Toiler* (actor); 1942: *Juke Box Jennie* (actor), *Junior G-Men of the Air* (actor), *You're Telling Me* (actor); 1950: *With These Hands* (documentary feature—producer/director); 1953: *Girls in the Night* (director), *It Came from Outer Space* (director), *The Glass Web* (director); 1954: *Creature from the Black Lagoon* (director); 1955: *This Island Earth* (codirector, uncredited), *Revenge of the Creature* (director), *The Man from Bitter Ridge* (director), *Tarantula* (director); 1956: *Outside the Law* (director), *Red Sundown* (director); 1957: *The Incredible Shrinking Man* (director), *The Tattered Dress* (director), *The Monolith Monsters* (cowriter); 1958: *High School Confidential* (director), *Man in the Shadow* (director), *The Lady Takes a Flyer* (director), *The Space Children* (director), *Monster on the Campus* (director); 1959: *The Mouse That Roared* (director), *No Name on the Bullet* (coproducer/director); 1961: *Bachelor in Paradise* (director); 1964: *The Lively Set* (director), *A Global Affair* (director); 1969: *Hello Down There* (director); 1974: *Black Eye* (director); 1975: *Games Girls Play* (director), *Boss Nigger* (director); 1977: *The Swiss Conspiracy* (director), *Sex and the Married Woman* (director); 1980: *Marilyn: The Untold Story* (codirector); 1985: *Into the Night* (actor).

For *House on Haunted Hill* (1959), Castle returned to basic genre themes, spicing them up with "Emergo!"

WILLIAM CASTLE

Like Tod Browning, William Castle contributed a body of work to the genre of fearfilm that remains notable but that might have been more distinguished had he restricted himself to producing his films and not chosen to direct them also. That the greatest critical and commercial fearfilm success of Castle's career was the classic chiller *Rosemary's Baby* (1968), a film Castle produced but left to the more talented Roman Polanski to direct, would seem to confirm this assessment.

Like Browning, Castle was a showman with a carnival pitchman's sensibility. Unlike Browning, however, Castle's sensibility wasn't rooted in the kind of "sucker born every minute" attitude Browning often seemed to have held toward his audience. Castle simply loved the show business of moviemaking more than the art, and his work reflects his attitude. The fearfilms he directed remain memorable— some even classic—more for the gimmicks he devised to exploit them and lure audiences— and for his cheerful rifling of suspense and shock techniques and plot elements from other, better films— than for any aesthetic qualities.

Born William Schloss in New York City in either 1911 or 1914 (accounts vary), the future fearmaker changed his surname to its English equivalent, Castle, in order to pursue an acting career more easily. He started out on the stage at age fifteen, then shifted direction behind the scenes a year later when Bela Lugosi tapped him as assistant stage manager for a road company tour of *Dracula*. In his autobiography, *Step Right Up! I'm Gonna Scare the Pants Off America*, however, Castle writes that he got hooked on horror even earlier, at age six, after seeing DeWolf Hopper in the original

"I wanted to work for myself, but I had to find something sure." The result: *Macabre* (1958), Castle's entrée into low-budget horror with a gimmick—in this case, an agreement to insure audiences against death by fright.

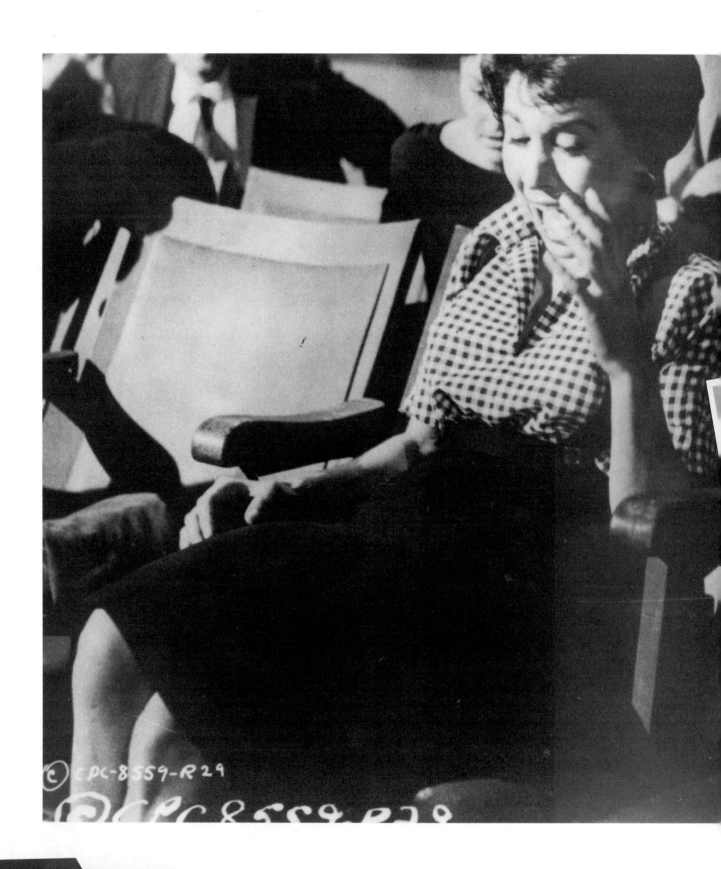

© CPC-8559-R29

WHEN THE SCREEN SCREAMS YOU'LL SCREAM TOO

...IF YOU VALUE YOUR LIFE!

PERCEPTO! newest and most startling gimmick on the screen!...

COLUMBIA PICTURES presents

The Tingler

starring **VINCENT PRICE**

with JUDITH EVELYN

DARRYL HICKMAN · PATRICIA CUTTS

Written by ROBB WHITE

Produced and Directed by WILLIAM CASTLE

A WILLIAM CASTLE PRODUCTION

GUARANTEED

Broadway production of Crane Wilbur's classic old-dark-house spoof, *The Monster*. In fact, Hopper starred in the 1933 revival of *The Monster*, at which time Castle would have been either twenty-two or twenty-five. The original Broadway production of Wilbur's play premiered in 1922 with Wilton Lackaye in the title role. (MGM filmed the play in 1925 as a vehicle for Lon Chaney.)

Castle's memory may simply have been faulty on this point, or perhaps he was just exercising his penchant for hyperbole. No matter. The play obviously had a formative influence on him, for Castle's subsequent shockers include most of the traditional ingredients of the old-dark-house school of fearmaking.

In fact, he even called one of his films *The Old Dark House* (1963)—a tepid remake of the classic 1932 James Whale film of the same name—which Castle undertook in association with Britain's reigning House of Horror, Hammer Film Productions.

In 1939, Columbia Pictures' chief, Harry Cohn,

brought Castle to Hollywood and put him to work as a dialogue coach. Castle quickly learned the techniques of filmmaking and made his directorial debut in 1943 with *The Chance of a Lifetime,* an entry in the studio's popular series of *Boston Blackie* detective dramas starring Chester Morris.

The following year, Castle directed Richard Dix in the first installment of a new series of detective films for the studio, titled *The Whistler* (1944), and he later directed three more entries in the series as well.

Castle directed a slew of B Westerns, gangster movies, costume dramas, and detective thrillers for Columbia and other studios over the next decade, developing along the way a solid reputation as an industrious, workmanlike, if somewhat pedestrian, contract filmmaker. Some of his early melodramas, particularly his entries in the *Whistler* and *Crime Doctor* series, remain effective examples of the B-movie art, directed in a fast-moving style markedly different from the slowly paced, unimaginative, TV sitcom-like direction of many of his subsequent shockers. Clearly, Castle's true genius as a filmmaker lay elsewhere than behind the megaphone.

By 1954, Castle realized that he was firmly established as a B-film director and that A-budget assignments were not going to come his way. If he was to elevate his status in the industry and become the minimogul he sought to be, he would have to do it on his own by creating his own independent production company. "I wanted to work for myself, but I had to find something sure," he said at the time.

He found it, as many fearmakers have done since, in Henri-Georges Clouzot's groundbreaking *Diabolique* (1955), which had just been released in the United States and was setting box-office records everywhere—a remarkable achievement for any film, but for a foreign-language film especially.

"There were lines all around the block and it took my wife and I days to get in," Castle said. "I decided then

Below: For *Mr. Sardonicus* (1961), the tale of a villainous nobleman disfigured by a permanent death's-head grin frozen onto his face, Castle conducted a "punishment poll" at the film's climax, allowing viewers to vote thumbs-up or thumbs-down on the villain's fate. From left to right: Ronald Lewis, Oscar Homolka, and the masked Mr. S. himself (Guy Rolfe). (Copyright © 1961 Columbia Pictures) Facing page: Jean Arless warms up for a "fright break" in *Homicidal* (1961), Castle's attempt to top Hitchcock's *Psycho* (1960). (Copyright ©1961 Columbia Pictures)

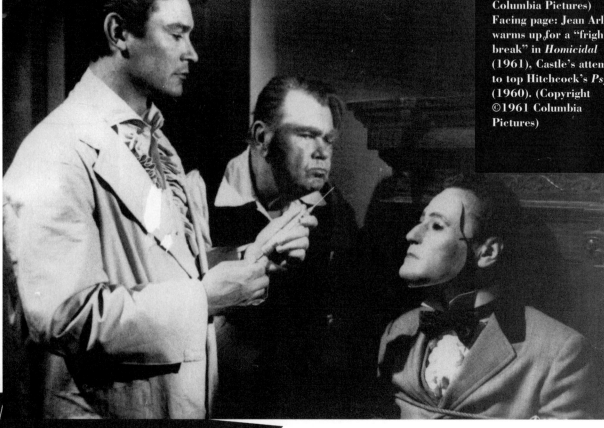

and there that I had a wide-open chance at something special. If a foreign horror picture with English subtitles could draw such a huge crowd, think what an all-English-speaking picture would do!"

Searching for a story that contained *Diabolique*'s crowd-pleasing ingredients of ghoulishness, suspense, and unexpected plot twists, Castle came across a novel called *The Marble Forest* by Theo Durant, the collective pseudonym of thirteen well-known mystery writers, each of whom had contributed an individual chapter to the book. The novel told the story of a small-town doctor whose daughter is kidnapped and held for ransom by a vengeful, unknown madman who buries the daughter alive in a local cemetery—the titular marble forest. As the doctor races around to unmask the perpetrator and find his daughter before she runs out of air, suspicion falls on one character after another in traditional detective-story fashion.

Similar to *Diabolique*, the story ends with a twist. There is no madman. The doctor planned the whole terrifying episode in an effort to drive his wealthy father-in-law into suffering a fatal heart attack so that he could claim his fortune.

Anticipating a hit on the order of *Diabolique*, Castle snapped up the rights to the book and brought in Robb White, a writer of children's books and part-time screenwriter, to do the screen adaptation, which, in an effort to make it even sound like *Diabolique*, they retitled *Macabre*. William Prince was given the role of the duplicitous doctor and Castle and White themselves financed the ninety-thousand-dollar budget of the film, which was completed and sold to Allied Artists for distribution in 1958.

Like many of Castle's detective movies of the forties, *Macabre* is an efficiently made little thriller, although the opening credits involving a cartoon hearse are groaningly sophomoric. After that, however, the film moves along at a relatively fast clip, creates a real sense of panic in the doctor's ordeal, and the ending actually does come as somewhat of a surprise. In terms of character development, richness of technique, shudders, and shocks, however, it was not in the same league with *Diabolique*. At a screening of the film prior to its release, Castle realized this himself. There was something missing, he told White. "It doesn't have that blood-curdling quality I tried to

get." To compensate, Castle devised a way to give the film "that blood-curdling quality" before the houselights even went down. He created a promotional scheme to lure prospective customers into believing that *Macabre* was the scariest movie ever made by offering to insure each one of them for one thousand dollars through Lloyds of London in the event of death by fright. The scheme worked like a charm and the film earned Castle, in his own words, "a small fortune." It also set the pattern for his future films in the genre, each of which would be built around some similarly outrageous come-on or promotional gimmick.

For his next fearfilm, *House on Haunted Hill* (1959), a throwback to the old-dark-house school, Castle devised "Emergo!" He supplied theater owners with a box and skeleton to be nailed up alongside the screen and maneuvered by means of a pulley. At one point in the film, the villainous protagonist, Vincent Price, manipulates a skeleton on wires to frighten his haunted-house victims. As the movie skeleton disappeared off-screen, the box alongside the screen opened up and the theater skeleton flailed about over the heads of the audience. The effect scared nobody, but it was outrageous and a lot of fun, and *House on Haunted Hill* was also a big hit.

Castle moved to Columbia for his next series of shockers, beginning with *The Tingler* (1959), also starring Vincent Price. This time, he had electrical buzzers placed under the seats in selected theaters literally to shock audiences at appropriate moments—a technique he ballyhooed in the film's advertising as "Percepto!"

For *13 Ghosts* (1960), he concocted "Illusion-O!"—which allowed audiences to see the movie's titular, and otherwise invisible, specters by donning special glasses supplied at the box office when they plunked down their ticket money.

For *Homicidal* (1961), his straight-faced parody of *Psycho*, he introduced an on-screen "fright-break"—a forty-five-second pause in which patrons could decide whether they were courageous enough to remain in their seats for the "horrific climax" or would opt to be cowards and split for the door.

For *Mr. Sardonicus* (1961), based on Ray Russell's takeoff of Victor Hugo's eerie tale of a man with a permanent death's-head grin frozen into his face, *The Man Who Laughs*, Castle again appeared at the film's climax to conduct a Punishment Poll, which allowed audiences to vote thumbs-up or thumbs-down on the villain's (Guy Rolfe) fate. Naturally, all voted thumbs-down and the film got back under way, meting

out justice accordingly.

For *Strait-Jacket* (1964), he created the memorable ad line, "Just keep telling yourself, it's only a movie!"—which Hallmark Releasing lifted to promote *Last House on the Left* (1972) and that many other distributors of horror films have since reused, as well.

For other productions, Castle had nurses stationed in theater lobbies to hand out bogus nerve-steadying pills to the weak of heart. He acted as usher, helping terrified patrons (most certainly planted) from their seats, and even offered rides to people who were nervous about walking home in the dark.

Taking a leaf from Hitchcock's book, Castle made himself a household name—among teenagers at least—by promoting himself as boldly as his films.

Hitchcock visibly connected himself with his work in the minds of audiences by doing uncredited walk-ons that audiences eagerly looked for. Castle went a step further by appearing on-screen before the credits to introduce many of his shockers ("Hello, I'm William Castle, the director of the motion picture you are about to see. . . ."), then returning at the climax to conduct his various fright-breaks and punishment polls. These appearances were obviously patterned on Hitchcock's droll intros and outros for his celebrated TV show. Castle was a much less droll performer, however, and his commentaries celebrating the world of ghouls, goblins, the weird, and the wonderful were more on a high school level of sophistication. The director also promoted the creation of a William Castle Fan Club, which he made oblique reference to from film to film in his precredit appearances by referring to "the last time we met." By 1963, newsletters announcing upcoming Castle releases and bearing the familiar logo of Castle's silhouetted figure sitting in a director's chair, glasses raised on his forehead and a cigar stuck in his mouth, were being sent out to 250,000 card-carrying members nationwide.

Castle
milked the *Diabolique*
formula from *Macabre* through *The Tingler*.
The latter even includes a scene straight out of
Diabolique: A devious husband sends his wife into
cardiac arrest by subjecting her to seeing a corpse
rising out of the family bathtub. Castle added his own
gimmicky signature, however, by filling the bathtub
with blood and shooting the sequence in color. The
rest of the film is in black and white.

Then *Psycho* came along and Castle found an
even more potent and lucrative formula to follow. In
the main, the perpetrators of the mayhem in Castle's
films were now revealed in his customary twist
endings to be tortured, fractured personalities like
Norman Bates's psycho rather than devious doctors
and husbands out for insurance money.

In film after film, Castle not only lifted plot
elements from the Hitchcock classic but individual
shots and set pieces. *In I Saw What You Did* (1965),
for example, Castle repeats the Hitchcock film's
celebrated shower murder, complete with screaming
violins, frenetic intercutting of shots of the murderer
and the victim, and blood swirling down the drain.
Strait-Jacket (1964), scripted by Robert Bloch, the
author of *Psycho,* and starring fading superstar Joan
Crawford as an alleged ax murderess (actually, it's her

psycho daughter, Diane Baker, who's behind it
all), combined elements from the Hitchcock
film with others from Robert Aldrich's smash-
hit psychothriller *Whatever Happened to Baby
Jane?* (1962). However, unlike Brian De Palma,
whose brazen mimicry of Hitchcock and other
filmmakers suggests a deep contempt for the
audience, Castle's equally brazen mimicry does
not strike one as contemptuous or mean-spirited,
but, rather, winning. It was part business move,
surely. But it also suggests Castle fully realized the
limits of his own talent and, wide-eyed film buff that
he was, wished he'd come up with the scene or idea
first. Unable to do so, he imitated it. It's as if he was
saying, "This is the best I can do."

Homicidal, the director's attempt to "top
Hitchcock's *Psycho,*" is probably Castle's
"masterpiece." The film is languidly paced and
endlessly talky, like most of the Castle-directed
shockers (Vincent Price's acerbic comments in *House
on Haunted Hill* do manage to give the incessant talk
in that film a delightful lift, however), and no *Psycho*
to be sure, but it earned Castle his best reviews. One
major news magazine gave *Homicidal* a better review
than *Psycho* and even placed the film on its annual
ten-best list.

For the release of *Psycho,* Hitchcock instituted a
policy that no one would be admitted into the theater
once the film had begun. Castle the showman reversed
this with his fright-break, which gave audiences the
chance to flee the theater during the film's closing
minutes if they felt too weak-hearted to withstand the
rest of the picture. In addition to this, Castle
structured the film itself around another gimmick
involving transvestism and dual personality, which he
sustained beyond the film's conclusion by tacking on a

The Fearmakers

special "curtain call" designed to mystify audiences even more. The gimmick worked, and continues to work, quite well.

Like *Psycho*, the plot of *Homicidal* (Robb White again scripted) centers on a mad female slasher who is actually a murderous male in disguise. In the film's double-whammy twist ending, however, it is revealed that he is really a she, after all. A young actress named Joan Marshall, making her screen debut (and apparently her swan song as well, as she hasn't been heard from since), was given the challenge of pulling the wool over our eyes as the deadly duo, and she pulls off the masquerade quite effectively. Her male character is a bit unusual-looking, but remarkably convincing, nonetheless. Castle gave Marshall the pseudonym Jean Arless. In the film's famous "curtain call," he has her two characters appear on screen side by side, leaving it up to us to decide whether Jean Arless is really a man or a woman.

Homicidal may have been the best of Castle's low-rent shockers. But *Rosemary's Baby* was the classiest fearfilm he ever had a hand in and remains the most influential of his career. He purchased the rights to the Ira Levin classic while the novel was still in galley form and he eagerly anticipated directing the film version as well as producing it.

Paramount had other ideas, however, and persuaded him to turn over the director's chair to Roman Polanski, who also wrote the script. The rest is fearfilm history. *Rosemary's Baby* was an enormous hit and made Castle a wealthy man in the bargain. As Polanski tells it, this was a shock the self-proclaimed shock master never quite got over. He certainly never repeated it. Castle directed only two more films, the mediocre sci-fi thriller *Project X* (1968) and a truly weird (but none-too-good) horror show called *Shanks* (1974), starring mime master Marcel Marceau. Neither film was a box-office hit. His last fearfilm was *Bug* (1975), a sci-fi tale about pesticide-spawned incendiary cockroaches. It, too, failed to repeat the success of *Rosemary's Baby* at the box office.

A consummate showman more revered today (and rightly so) for the outrageous gimmicks he concocted to promote his films than for the quality of the films themselves (most of which weren't very good to begin with and haven't aged particularly well), William Castle was by all accounts an ebullient man with a genuine zest for his chosen profession. Had he not died of a heart attack in 1977, in all likelihood he would today be one of fandom's most sought-after guest-star retirees—the B cinema's grand old "Sultan of Shock Schlock," a role Castle clearly would have enjoyed and probably would have played to the hilt to the immense merriment of us all.

Filmography

1943: *Chance of a Lifetime* (director), *Klondike Kate* (director); 1944: *The Whistler* (director), *The Mark of the Whistler* (director), *She's a Soldier Too* (director), *When Strangers Marry* (director); 1945: *The Crime Doctor's Warning* (director), *Voice of the Whistler* (director); 1946: *The Mysterious Intruder* (director), *The Return of Rusty* (director), *The Crime Doctor's Man Hunt* (director), *Just Before Dawn* (director); 1947: *The Crime Doctor's Gamble* (director); 1948: *The Lady from Shanghai* (co-associate producer), *The Gentleman from Nowhere* (director), *Texas, Brooklyn and Heaven* (director); 1949: *Johnny Stool Pigeon* (director), *Undertow* (director); 1950: *It's a Small World* (director); 1951: *Hollywood Story* (director), *The Fat Man* (director), *Cave of Outlaws* (director); 1953: *Serpent of the Nile* (director), *Conquest of Cochise* (director), *Slaves of Babylon* (director), *Fort Ti* (director); 1954: *Charge of the Lancers* (director), *Jesse James vs. The Daltons* (director), *Drums of Tahiti* (director), *Battle of Rogue River* (director), *Masterson of Kansas* (director), *The Iron Glove* (director), *The Saracen Blade* (director), *The Law vs. Billy the Kid* (director); 1955: *The Americano* (director), *New Orleans Uncensored* (director), *The Gun That Won the West* (director), *Duel on the Mississippi* (director); 1956: *The Houston Story* (director), *Uranium Boom* (director); 1958: *Macabre* (producer/director); 1959: *House on Haunted Hill* (producer/director), *The Tingler* (producer/director); 1960: *13 Ghosts* (producer/director); 1961: *Homicidal* (producer/director), *Mr. Sardonicus* (producer/director); 1962: *Zotz!* (producer/director); 1963: *The Old Dark House* (executive producer/director), *13 Frightened Girls* (producer/director); 1964: *Strait-Jacket* (producer/director); 1965: *The Night Walker* (producer/director), *I Saw What You Did* (producer/director); 1966: *Let's Kill Uncle* (producer/director); 1967: *The Busy Body* (producer/director), *The Spirit Is Willing* (producer/director); 1968: *Rosemary's Baby* (producer), *Project X* (producer/director); 1969: *Riot* (producer); 1974: *Shanks* (producer/director); 1975: *Bug* (producer).

Madeline Smith calms the Baron's latest and most bestial creature (Dave Prowse) in *Frankenstein and the Monster from Hell* (1973), Fisher's final installment in the long-running series and his cinematic swan song. (Hammer Films)

B R U C E   G .   H A L L E N B E C K

TERENCE FISHER

Fearfilm historians are only now beginning to give director Terence Fisher proper credit as the chief architect of the modern, post-Universal wave of horror films that began in the late fifties with the release of Hammer Films' groundbreaking *The Curse of Frankenstein* (1957). It's about time, too, for Fisher's contribution to Hammer's success and to the influential style of fear filmmaking the studio inaugurated cannot be overestimated.

Terence Fisher was born February 23, 1904, in London. He joined the merchant marine as a teenager but soon decided a life at sea was not for him. After knocking around at various jobs landside, he set his sights on breaking into the British film industry, with the goal of becoming an editor. He started out as a clapper boy and a few years later moved into the editing room, cutting a number of Will Hay comedies and other unspectacular low-budget B movies, often called "programmers." Eventually, he decided he wanted to move further up the cinematic hierarchy by becoming a director; following a training course in directing at Highbury Studios, he was assigned to helm his first feature, *Colonel Bogey* (1948).

Fisher's initial entry into gothic romance, the genre with which he would later become most associated, was the 1950 *So Long at the Fair,* a period mystery about a young woman (Jean Simmons) who is caught up in a conspiracy of silence over the disappearance of her brother (David Tomlinson) while on a trip to Paris during the 1899 Paris Exposition. As critic David Pirie noted of the film, which Fisher codirected with Anthony Darnborough, "it could easily have been reshot, sequence for sequence, as a vampire movie without making any difference in its basic mechanics."

In 1952, Fisher joined Hammer Films, the studio with which he would become most associated, to direct a number of thrillers featuring fading American film stars such as George Brent and Zachary Scott. The first real indication of the direction his career would ultimately take was Hammer's *Four-Sided Triangle* (1953), a sci-fi opus with a Frankenstein-like plot in which two scientists (John Van Eyssen and Stephen Murray), both in love with the same woman, create a living duplicate of her in a machine they've constructed in an old farmhouse.

Fisher's breakthrough came with *The Curse of Frankenstein,* made when he was in his fifties. Under the terms of his contract, he was owed another film by Hammer, and the next one up was the studio's planned remake of Universal's classic Karloff film. Hammer chief Sir James Carreras wanted the remake to adhere as closely to the original as possible without incurring the wrath of Universal's legal department, and he suggested that Fisher screen the older film as a refresher course. But Fisher politely declined, explaining later that he had seen an opportunity to do something completely different with the material and was determined to seize it.

Since nobody was sure whether the old Mary Shelley story was capable of scaring anyone anymore, the project had been initiated as "a bit of a giggle." In keeping with this approach, Jimmy Sangster's script emphasized the story's darkly humorous qualities in the James Whale tradition. Fisher's direction deemphasized these qualities, however, by encouraging his actors and everyone behind the scenes to play the story absolutely straight. There are still some vestiges of dark humor in the film, but on the whole, *The Curse of Frankenstein* is a fairly grim affair. It might have been even more grim had it been shot in black and white as originally planned. But here again, Fisher had his way: He persuaded the studio into giving him enough extra money to shoot the film in color. Indeed, *The Curse of Frankenstein* revels in color. The laboratory sets created by Hammer's resident art director Bernard Robinson absolutely radiate with lush reds and vivid blues. In an exterior scene depicting the death of a blind man and a little boy at the hands of the creature (Christopher Lee), Fisher anticipated Michelangelo Antonioni by insisting that the leaves on the trees be painted red ("the color of fear," he said) as a way of suggesting danger and subliminally heightening the suspense. Thus the "Hammer Style"—really the "Fisher style"—was born.

Upon release, the film was vilified by the British press for being overly violent and even sadistic—a charge that seems laughable today. Perhaps the critics, too, were expecting a more literal remake of the Whale film. What it got instead, however, was the story of a Byronic antihero (Peter Cushing) who tries to storm heaven by creating the perfect man. In doing so, Cushing's Baron Frankenstein himself became the story's most fearsome monster. Not only does he rob graves and gallows as Colin Clive did before him; he does things Clive would never have thought of doing—such as pushing an old man to his death from a staircase in order to rob his brain.

The box-office success of the film spurred Hammer to create a series of *Frankenstein* films with Fisher at the helm. (*The Evil of Frankenstein*, 1964, was the only entry in the series not directed by Fisher, and it remains markedly different from the studio's other *Frankenstein* films in both style and tone.) The immediate sequel, *The Revenge of Frankenstein* (1958), continued the adventures of the Baron (Cushing again) and introduced a theme that was close to Fisher's heart: society's ongoing and bitter struggle between its exploitative upper and exploited lower classes. The theme is not expressed subtly. As the film opens, we find the aristocratic Baron (using the fictitious name Dr. Stein) running a hospital for the poor, where he uses every opportunity to sever his patients' limbs and remove their organs to assemble his perfect man. Beautifully photographed by Jack Asher, Hammer's premier lighting cameraman, *Revenge* again featured the sumptuous sets, colorful costumes, and striking color effects that were now Fisher's and the studio's trademark.

Frustrated in his attempts to create the perfect man, Cushing's Baron briefly gave up this goal in Fisher's next entry in the series, *Frankenstein Created Woman* (1967). Moving beyond such mundane experiments as brain transplants, the Baron enters the metaphysical realm of soul transplantation by transforming an innkeeper's scar-faced and physically handicapped daughter (Susan Denberg) into a beautiful, sensuous creature. Unfortunately, he also gives her the soul of her guillotined lover, who orders her to kill the men who framed him for murder. In the end, she commits suicide.

On the face of it, the film's script by John Elder (pseudonym of Hammer producer Anthony Hinds) is completely absurd—a twisted retelling of the Hans Christian Andersen story *The Ugly Duckling*. But Fisher tells the story, which he called a tragic "adult fairy tale," absolutely straight, investing it with emotion not often found in genre films.

Fans of fearfilms in general and Hammer's *Frankenstein* series in particular found Cushing's kinder, gentler Baron in *Frankenstein Created Woman* to be somewhat of a letdown, however. So, in the next entry in the series, *Frankenstein Must Be Destroyed!* (1969), the character returned to his cold and brutal self. Devoid of any human compassion at all, he is, if anything, even more of a monster in this most downbeat of all Fisher Frankenstein films. Perhaps it was the nihilism of the late 1960s, but the film is devoid of any heroes at all. Even the film's youthful protagonists (Simon Ward and Veronica Carlson) support themselves by dealing in illegal drugs. By contrast, Freddie Jones's "creature," the tragic victim of yet another of the Baron's self-serving brain-transplant experiments, is the most

Fisher's breakthrough came with *The Curse of Frankenstein* (1957), when the director was fifty-four years old. You've got to hand it to the old boy. Pictured here: Peter Cushing and Robert Urquhart. (Hammer Films)

Clockwise from top: Christopher Lee awakens in *Horror of Dracula* (1958), the Hammer classic in which Fisher virtually reinvented the vampire myth. (Hammer Films) *The Revenge of Frankenstein* (1958), starring Peter Cushing, Francis Matthews, and Michael Gwynn (center) as a very human monster continued the adventures of the fiendish Baron. (Copyright © 1958 Columbia Pictures) The aging Anton Diffring goes to his fiery reward in *The Man Who Could Cheat Death* (1959), one of the most visually sumptuous of Fisher's gothic horrors. (Copyright © 1959 Paramount Pictures)

likable character in the film, and the most human "monster" in Fisher's series.

Fisher's final installment in the series, *Frankenstein and the Monster from Hell* (1973), placed Cushing's indefatigable Baron, masquerading under the name Dr. Victor, in charge of an insane asylum. As in *The Revenge of Frankenstein*, he stitches together his latest creature from the body parts of his patients. His results are no better, however. The creature (Dave Prowse) that emerges from all this surgery is a hairy Neanderthal beast with a fondness for mutilating victims with broken glass. In the poetic justice ending, the vengeful inmates turn the tables and mutilate the creature by literally tearing it limb from limb.

Working together, Fisher and Cushing created an interesting progression in the Baron's character from film to film. In *Curse* and *Revenge,* Cushing's youthful Baron is a man obsessed, who surrenders everything to his single overriding preoccupation: creating the perfect man. Except on one occasion when he dallies with a maid (whom he later kills when she tries to blackmail him into marrying her), he seems not even to have a libido. In fact, his attitude toward women, whom he basically sees as "interfering," is almost wholly misogynistic. In the later *Frankenstein Created Woman*, he turns somewhat mellow, as people often do in middle age, and even tries to atone for his misogyny (in his own misguided way) by giving the

disfigured peasant girl a new face and figure. Frustrated by a life of failure in *Frankenstein Must Be Destroyed!* he evolves into a character who is not only completely callous but also psychopathic, thus paving the way for *Frankenstein and the Monster From Hell* which finds him slightly senile and a lunatic literally in charge of his asylum, whose only reaction to the destruction of his latest creature is an offhanded, "Best thing that could have happened to him."

In addition to rethinking the Frankenstein myth, Fisher virtually reinvented the vampire myth in his classic *Horror of Dracula* (1958), the film he made for Hammer immediately following *The Curse of Frankenstein.* This film, Fisher and Hammer's first foray into vampire territory, redefined the genre for the modern generation, and its influence is still being felt today. It was a film that Fisher nurtured from script development all the way through to final edit, and it was, therefore, as close to a pet project as anything he

Andrée Melly as one of the alluring vampire women in Fisher's triumph of style over substance, *The Brides of Dracula* (1960). (Hammer Films)

ever did. Fisher altered Jimmy Sangster's screenplay considerably. For example, in the shooting script, Dracula (Christopher Lee) is introduced wearing a top hat and tails in the Bela Lugosi manner. Fisher opted instead for a much less flashy, though no less aristocratic, costume for the Count, whose regal bearing and polite manners in these opening scenes make his later eruptions into violence and bloodletting all the more startlingly effective. In addition, Fisher reversed other fearfilm clichés by having the ill-fated Jonathan Harker (John Van Eyssen) arrive at Castle Dracula on a beautiful sunny day rather than on the conventional dark and stormy night. The interior of the castle is neither covered in cobwebs nor infested with rats; rather, it is well kept,

sumptuously decorated, and vermin-free. Even the story itself, which turns the redoubtable Van Helsing (Peter Cushing) into as much of a gore hound as the Count, reverses the usual pattern. Shot in gloriously saturated Eastmancolor by Jack Asher (who was nominated for a British Academy Award for his work), Dracula's blazing red eyes, bloodstained fangs, and animalistic rages became the genre's new conventions virtually overnight.

Horror of Dracula (just *Dracula* in the U.K.) was a sensation the world over, consolidating Hammer's position as a producer of groundbreaking horror films and Fisher's reputation as a master of the genre. It remains the studio's and Fisher's masterpiece. But its sequel, *The Brides of Dracula* (1960), is not far behind. Some critics maintain that Fisher was only as good as his scripts. In fact, he was consistently better than his scripts, and *Brides,* the stitched-together work of three credited screenwriters, including Jimmy Sangster, is a good example of this. For one thing, there is no Dracula in the film, and the plot is full of holes and gaffes. So Fisher opted to turn the film into a triumph of style over substance. Ostensibly, the film takes place in Transylvania, but Fisher transformed the locale into a genuine country of the mind—a fairy-tale landscape of foreboding windmills, graveyards, seemingly enchanted forests, and ornate châteaus. Magnificently photographed by Jack Asher, the film possesses the most fantasticated atmosphere of any film Fisher ever directed.

Fisher's final vampire film was *Dracula—Prince of Darkness* (1965), the first of Hammer's Dracula films to resurrect the bloodthirsty Count, once again played by Christopher Lee. As with *Brides,* the script was again rather weak. In fact, it was basically a rehash of *Horror of Dracula;* the climax of the earlier film was even reused for the opening scene. The film's most arresting moments occur before the Count is actually revived, when four benighted travelers arrive at Castle Dracula, courtesy of a coach teamed by phantom horses, and Dracula's servant greets them with the memorable line, "My master died without issue . . . in the accepted sense of the term." Later, in an extraordinary ceremony with Christ-like overtones of resurrection, the servant murders one of the travelers and hangs his body upside down over Dracula's coffin, slitting the man's throat to let the blood spill onto the ashes to revive the Count— who, for once, reconstitutes without all his clothes on. Another potent sequence occurs subsequently when Helen (Barbara Shelley), one of the travelers, who has since become a vampire, is "staked" by a group of monks. The scene has all the elements of a gang rape as the religious fanatics zealously go about their business of exorcising the "evil" (read sensuality) from the hapless and helpless young woman. Shelley says that Fisher instructed her to play the vampire woman as a totally sensual being. "When you're a vampire," he told her, "you're neither heterosexual nor homosexual. You go after anything that's not nailed down."

Shortly after *Horror of Dracula* was released, Fisher directed a new version of Sir Arthur Conan Doyle's *The Hound of the Baskervilles* (1959), in which Peter Cushing played Sherlock Holmes as a Fisherian cross between Van Helsing and Baron Frankenstein— an eccentric, slightly mad genius determined to seek out evil and destroy it no matter who suffers in the process. It remains the best big-screen adaptation of Conan Doyle's durable tale, though it was not a box-office success—largely because genre fans expected a full-blooded horror film and got a gothic mystery, Fisher-style, instead.

Fisher's *The Mummy* (1959), while not in a class with some of his other remakes of Universal

Michael Gough, the real villain of the piece, unmasks the disfigured title character in *The Phantom of the Opera* (1962), one of Fisher's lushest and most romantic films, if not a particularly scary one. (Copyright © 1962 Universal-International)

classics, was nonetheless an exciting film (in fact, more exciting than the Karloff original) and, once again, a beautifully photographed one, in which Fisher once more delivered a twist that was purely stylistic. The film's contemporary scenes (circa 1890) are given an ethereal quality, whereas the scenes set in ancient

Egypt, which one would expect to have an ethereal atmosphere, are realistic and brightly lighted.

Fisher's *The Curse of the Werewolf* (1961) did for lycanthrope movies what *Horror of Dracula* did for vampire films. An "epic" that spans three generations, it has a marvelous circular quality, beginning and ending with the ringing of a church bell. The story of Leon (Oliver Reed), a bastard child who is born on Christmas Eve and thus condemned to become a werewolf, the film allowed Fisher the opportunity to indulge his romantic sensibilities even more than he had in his previous gothic horrors. When Leon feels loved, he doesn't transform into the titular beast. But when that love is denied him or when he is subjected to the coarseness and brutality of the world, he transforms and goes on a rampage that ends, inevitably, in his own destruction. Arguably the best werewolf film ever made, *The Curse of the Werewolf* ranks with Fisher's finest work. As does *The Phantom of the Opera* (1962), Fisher's ultimate statement on the gothic-romance formula. Fans and critics were disappointed with it at the time, but the film has since undergone much reassessment, and many now consider it to be one

of Fisher's lushest and most romantic films, if not a particularly scary one.

Fisher often used the phrase "the attraction of evil" to describe the thematic core of his work and the probable reason why his films enjoyed such widespread appeal. The theme runs consistently throughout his gothic romances and many of his other films, as well. For example, his female characters are strongly attracted to Dracula right off the bat (no pun intended); no hokey hypnosis is needed to get them to undo their nighties for the pointy-toothed bloodsucker. Perhaps an even more blatant example of this theme is found in *The Two Faces of Dr. Jekyll* (1960), Fisher's unique reworking of the oft-filmed Robert Louis Stevenson story. In it, the director once again delivered the unexpected by making Dr. Jekyll (Paul Massie) a bearded, scruffy-looking sad sack and his alter ego, Hyde (Massie also), an energetic, handsome man of the world—and the epitome of evil to boot, a fiend who murders both his best friend and his wife.

Although Fisher worked almost exclusively for Hammer, he ventured outside the studio on several occasions, and some of his non-Hammer films are equally enjoyable, if not quite as

Peter Cushing returned to his cold (or in this case hot) and brutal self in Fisher's *Frankenstein Must Be Destroyed!* (1969) with Freddie Jones. (Copyright © 1969 Warner Brothers)

groundbreaking. *Island of Terror* (1966), for example, is a tight little sci-fi thriller in the mold of Hammer's earlier Quatermass films and *X the Unknown* (1957). It features Peter Cushing as a scientist (again!) investigating a series of bizarre deaths on a remote island off the Irish coast. The perpetrators of all the mayhem turn out to be creatures spawned by Cushing himself in his experiments to find a cure for cancer. Despite an obviously foolish script, *Island of Terror* works remarkably well due to the solid performances Fisher elicits from his cast and the charming atmosphere of pubs, churches, and old manor houses—Fisher elements all—with which the film is imbued.

In his later years, Fisher found employment as a director increasingly difficult to come by because, as Fisher's Phantom, Herbert Lom, put it, he had become a "sweet old alcoholic." Fisher's taste for Guinness stout was apparently responsible for two consecutive motor accidents in which he stumbled into an oncoming car, breaking the same leg twice. Eventually, he was deemed uninsurable and directing offers ceased coming his way entirely. He died June 18, 1980, of cancer at the age of seventy-six, leaving a legacy of classic fearfilms behind him that may never be surpassed.

Filmography

1933: *Falling for You* (editor); 1935: *Brown on Resolution* (assistant editor); 1936: *Everybody Dance* (editor), *Good Morning, Boys* (editor), *Jack of all Trades* (editor), *Tudor Rose* (editor), *Windbag the Sailor* (editor); 1938: *Mr. Satan* (editor); 1939: *On the Night of the Fire* (editor); 1940: *George and Margaret* (editor); 1941: *Atlantic Ferry* (editor), *The Seventh Survivor* (editor); 1942: *The Flying Fortress* (editor), *The Night Invader* (editor), *The Peterville Diamond* (editor), *Tomorrow We Live* (editor); 1943: *The Dark Tower* (editor); 1944: *Flight From Folly* (editor), *One Exciting Night* (editor), *The Hundred Pound Window* (production assistant); 1945: *The Wicked Lady* (editor); 1947: *Master of Bankdam* (editor); 1948: *To the Public Danger* (short film, director), *Colonel Bogey* (director), *Song for Tomorrow* (director), *Portrait from Life* (director); 1949: *Marry Me* (director); 1950: *The Astonished Heart* (codirector); *So Long at the Fair* (codirector); 1951: *Home to Danger* (director); 1952: *The Last Page* (director), *Wings of Danger* (director), *Stolen Face* (director), *Distant Trumpet* (director); 1953: *Four-Sided Triangle* (director/cowriter), *Spaceways* (director), *Mantrap* (director/cowriter), *Blood Orange* (director), *Three's Company* (codirector); 1954: *Face the Music* (director), *The Stranger Came Home* (director), *Mask of Dust* (director), *Final Appointment* (director), *Children Galore* (director), *Murder by Proxy* (director); 1955: *The Flaw* (director), *Stolen Assignment* (director); 1956: *The Last Man to Hang* (director); 1957: *Kill Me Tomorrow* (director), *The Curse of Frankenstein* (director); 1958: *Horror of Dracula* (director), *The Revenge of Frankenstein* (director); 1959: *The Hound of the Baskervilles* (director), *The Man Who Could Cheat Death* (director), *The Mummy* (director), *The Stranglers of Bombay* (director); 1960: *The Two Faces of Dr. Jekyll* (director), *The Brides of Dracula* (director), *The Sword of Sherwood Forest* (director); 1961: *The Curse of the Werewolf;* 1962: *The Phantom of the Opera* (director), *Sherlock Holmes and the Deadly Necklace* (director); 1964: *The Horror of It All* (director), *The Gorgon* (director), *The Earth Dies Screaming* (director); 1965: *Dracula—Prince of Darkness* (director); 1966: *Island of Terror* (director); 1967: *Frankenstein Created Woman* (director), *Night of the Big Heat* (director); 1968: *The Devil Rides Out*, a.k.a. *The Devil's Bride* (director); 1969: *Frankenstein Must Be Destroyed!* (director); 1973: *Frankenstein and the Monster from Hell* (director).

A haunting image of Deborah Kerr from *The Innocents* (1961), Jack Clayton's film of the classic Henry James ghost story *The Turn of the Screw*, photographed by Freddie Francis. (The John McCarty Collection)

FREDDIE FRANCIS

Next to Terence Fisher, Freddie Francis was Hammer Films's most important and prolific directorial talent. He was also the most important and prolific director for Hammer's chief European fearfilm rival at the time, Max Rosenberg and Milton J. Subotsky's Amicus Productions.

One of the British film industry's most accomplished directors of photography (or lighting cameramen, as they are called "across the pond") before turning director, Francis was born in London in 1917. He studied engineering, then gravitated to the film industry, becoming an assistant stills photographer for Gaumont-British Studios in 1934. He moved up to the position of apprentice cameraman a year later and received his first credit as director of photography for the war film *A Hill in Korea* in 1956. His subsequent credits in this capacity include many of the best British films of the period, such as *Room at the Top* (1959), the haunting ghost story *The Innocents* (1961), based on the Henry James classic *The Turn of the Screw,* and Karel Reisz's updated version of the classic psycho thriller *Night Must Fall* (1964). He won his first Oscar for photographing *Sons and Lovers* (1960), and his second for his brilliant work on the Civil War film *Glory* (1989). He also did second-unit photography for several films peripheral to the genre in which he would later make his name as a director. For John Huston's *Moby Dick* (1956), he shot most of the on-location whaling scenes and supervised the extensive miniature work involved in realizing the climactic battle between the crew of the *Pequod* and the white whale. He later performed the same function for the climactic houseboat scene in Martin Scorsese's remake of *Cape Fear* (1991) in addition to serving as the film's director of photography.

Francis made the transition to director in 1961 with the obscure British farce *Two and Two Make Six.*

He also served as codirector of the horror/sci-fi film *The Day of the Triffids* (1963), though he received no screen credit. *Vengeance* (1962), arguably the best version of Curt Siodmak's oft-filmed (and quite mediocre) novel *Donovan's Brain,* was the first outright horror film to bear his name as director. In 1963, he began his long association with Hammer Films by directing one of the company's best "mini-Hitchcock's," a visually arresting psychothriller called *Paranoiac,* starring Oliver Reed. His keen cinematographer's eye and deft hand at keeping audiences guessing without leaving them confused made him a natural for this type of thriller, and the studio allowed him to follow it up with two more: the clever (if improbable) old-dark-house mystery *Nightmare* and *Hysteria* (both 1964), the weakest of the bunch, though it still manages to be quite gripping due to Francis's sure hand at suspense. For Amicus, he went on to direct one more psychothriller, *The Psychopath* (1966), a total knockoff of Robert Bloch's novel *Psycho,* scripted by Bloch himself—before turning almost wholly to gothic horror, a genre in which, like Terence Fisher, he seemed to be more comfortable.

The first of Francis's gothic horrors was *The Evil of Frankenstein* (1964), the third entry in Hammer's long-running series starring Peter Cushing. All the other entries in the series were made by Terence Fisher, and, as a result, *Evil* stands out as something of an anomaly. It ignores the plot threads of the first two films in the series (*The Curse of Frankenstein* and *The Revenge of Frankenstein*) altogether, and Fisher's consistent theme of Victorian hypocrisy is sorely missed. Matters are not helped by John Elder's perfunctory script, which consists mainly of a collection of old Universal *Frankenstein* movie clichés. Still, the film is hard to dislike, for Francis succeeds admirably in keeping the mundane plot humming along, and Cushing, as always, is in fine form as the Baron, although Francis has him downplay his villainy somewhat. In fact, he's a rather congenial chap this time around, given to good-natured quips. "He has a good brain and excellent eyes," the Baron remarks at one point of his latest creation. "I won't tell you where I got them, but I can assure you they're perfect."

Francis's next bout with one of Hammer's classic monsters came in 1968 when he directed *Dracula Has Risen from the Grave*, based on another (and much better) John Elder script. Visually, it remains one of the most gorgeous of the studio's many gothic horrors. It was set designer Bernard Robinson's last film for the studio before his untimely death, and it may be said that, under Francis's guidance, he went out in a blaze of glory. The rooftop sets where the film's Romeo and Juliet lovers (Barry Andrews and Veronica Carlson) meet for their

frequent trysts have a marvelous fairy-tale quality, like something out of Disney rather than Hammer.

It was Francis's idea to announce each of Dracula's (Christopher Lee) appearances with a none-too-subtle blood-red filter effect. Subtler and more effective is his treatment of sexuality, a prime ingredient of the vampire myth. Francis offers us two very different types of women in the film. Zena (Barbara Ewing) is an earthy barmaid who succumbs easily to Dracula's charms. Once

Facing page: Director Freddie Francis gives Veronica Carlson pointers for an upcoming love scene in *Dracula Has Risen from the Grave* (1968). (Courtesy Veronica Carlson)
Above: Francis began his long association with Hammer Films with one of the company's best psychothrillers, *Paranoiac* (1963), starring Oliver Reed. The film was loosely derived (without credit) from the Josephine Tey novel *Brat Farrar*. (Copyright © 1962 Universal-International)

bitten, however, she is denied her return as an undead. Instead, the Count has his servant (Ewan Hooper) burn her corpse in an oven. Dracula really has eyes only for Maria (Carlson), a virginal, fresh-faced beauty whose innocence is demonstrated by the fact that she still sleeps with stuffed animals and dolls. She's a woman-child who also happens to be the niece of the local monsignor (Rupert Davies), a cleric with whom the Count has a vengeful score to settle.

Religion—or, more accurately, the mystery of faith—is another important subtheme of the film. Vampire films have always been hugely popular in Catholic countries like Spain and Italy, and it was, perhaps, with an eye toward these markets that Elder and Francis conceived the story as a religious allegory. Paul (Andrews), the film's hero, is a professed atheist; Dracula's servant is a priest whom he has bent to his will; and the primary target of the Count's wrath, his sacrificial lamb, is the hated

Dracula is impaled on a huge silver cross and his evil is banished.

Religious imagery dominates the film, which begins in a church and ends with Dracula's impalement, in a Christ-like pose, on the aforementioned cross. In between, there is a trek up a mountainside to Dracula's castle, where the monsignor and soon-to-be-victimized priest perform an exorcism. The climb, accompanied by James Bernard's religioso score (even including church bells), is shot by Francis to suggest a mist-shrouded ascent to a slightly sinister heaven, a visual approach far different from any other entry in the studio's series.

The film is so rich visually that it's hard to pick one scene that stands out over another, though certainly Dracula's first appearance outside Carlson's window, bathed in blues, is an exceptionally beautiful fairy-tale image—one worthy of Cocteau, in fact. This fairy-tale motif, combined with the subtheme of the corruption of the innocent, is

monsignor, who has placed a cross on the door of Dracula's castle, ostensibly locking the fiend out of his own house. As the film progresses, Paul becomes more and more religious, finally reclaiming his lost faith entirely at the climax when

Above: Francis's *The Evil of Frankenstein* (1964), featuring wrestler Kiwi Kingston as the thawed-out Monster, consisted mainly of a string of old Universal *Frankenstein* movie clichés. Still, it's a hard film to dislike. (Copyright © 1964 Universal-International) Left: Christopher Lee in the crawling-hand episode of Francis's first horror anthology, *Dr. Terror's House of Horrors* (1965). (Copyright ©1965 Amicus Productions)

carefully sustained throughout. In one striking scene, Carlson literally embraces death as she lovingly puts her arms around Dracula's coffin. Later, as Dracula carries her off to his mountainside lair—he dressed in black; she in the whitest of nightgowns—Francis pushes the fairy-tale motif inherent in horror films about as far as any director ever has.

Francis further honed his skills as a fearmaker with Amicus's string of anthology films, beginning with the 1965 *Dr. Terror's House of Horrors*, which, like many of Amicus's early films, was scripted by the company's CEO, Milton J. Subotsky. The film consists of a series of short tales— a werewolf story, a vampire tale, a crawling-hand episode—linked by a surrounding story in which Dr. Terror (Peter Cushing) foresees the fates of various characters by using Tarot cards. The film is basically standard horror movie stuff, but the script is rather witty and Francis's direction is potently atmospheric. Some tales engaged Francis's imagination more than others, a characteristic of his subsequent anthology films as well, which include the wonderfully titled *Torture Garden* (1967), from a script by Robert Bloch; *Tales From the Crypt* (1972), his best film in this vein; and *Tales That Witness Madness* (1973).

Francis always considered his fearfilms to be "a bit of a giggle." *Crypt*, based on the famous EC Comics series of the same name, is definitely that. It's also the most consistently ghoulish and scary of his

Collector Peter Cushing makes a big mistake by acquiring the skull of the infamous Marquis de Sade in Francis's *The Skull* (1965), based on the short story by Robert Bloch. (Copyright ©1965 Amicus Productions)

anthology films. The opening story, "And All Through the House," is justly famous for introducing the idea of a killer Santa Claus to the horror film's bag of tricks. Francis's treatment of the story, which involves a psychopath who dresses up as Santa and terrorizes a woman (Joan Collins) who has just murdered her husband, strikes just the right balance between humor and horror that was so much a part of the EC Comics formula. But the film's final story, in which a sadistic director (Nigel Patrick) of a home for the blind is given his just desserts by his victims when they force him to run down a narrow unlighted corridor lined with razor blades, is the episode most people vividly remember.

Around this same time, Francis started working for his son Kevin's company, Tyburn Films. The younger Francis was determined to produce films in the Hammer style. *The Ghoul* (1975), directed by his father from a script by Hammer's John Elder and starring Hammer vets Peter Cushing and Veronica Carlson, was the first. The plot, essentially a reworking of Hammer's *The Reptile* (1966) with elements, such as the surprise murder of the female star midway through the film, borrowed from *Psycho* as well, revolves around an aristocrat (Cushing) who keeps his cannibalistic son (Don Henderson) locked in the attic until "feeding time." Like Francis's work for Hammer, the film boasts a vivid sense of atmosphere and a nice period flavor (it's set in the 1920s). Francis's follow-up for

Tyburn, *Legend of the Werewolf* (1975), is the stronger of the two vehicles, however. It, too, stars the venerable Cushing, this time as a French police pathologist who investigates a series of grisly murders and discovers they've been committed by a werewolf (David Rintoul). John Elder wrote the script, this time borrowing from Hammer's *The Curse of the Werewolf* (1961), which he also wrote. Francis's take on lycanthropy, however, is much less somber than Hammer's, largely owing to the good time he apparently

Above: For Amicus, Francis also directed *Psychopath* (1966), a total knockoff of Robert Bloch's novel *Psycho*, scripted by Bloch himself. (Copyright © 1965 Amicus Productions)

Right: Religion—or, more accurately, the mystery of faith—is an important subtheme of Francis's *Dracula Has Risen from the Grave* (1968), one of the most visually striking of Hammer's many gothic horrors. Shown here: Ewan Hooper as the tormented priest under Dracula's control. (Hammer Films)

Opposite page: Peter Cushing rises from the grave for revenge in *Tales from the Crypt* (1972), the most consistently ghoulish and scary of Francis's horror anthology films. (Copyright © 1972 Cinerama Releasing)

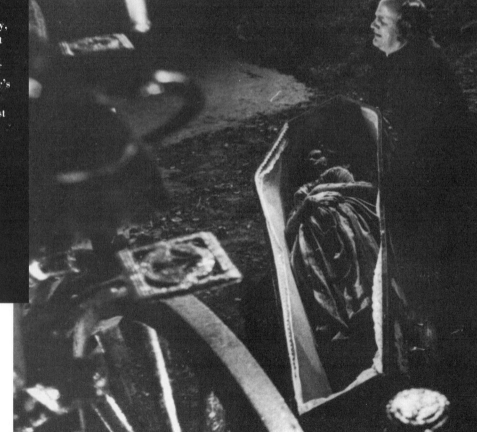

allowed Cushing to have infusing what could have been a cardboard stock character with large doses of eccentric humor. Graham Freeborn's werewolf makeup, on the other hand, is a blatant rip-off of Roy Ashton's work on the earlier film.

In the late sixties, Francis decided to develop a project of his own. The result was a black comedy called *Mumsy, Nanny, Sonny and Girly* (U.S. title *Girly,* 1969). Based on a British play, it recounts the whimsical adventures of a murderous family. Unfortunately, the film's freewheeling mixture of humor and horror proved to be a bit too strange for most audiences and it disappeared quickly from view. For the Francis completist, it's worth searching out, however.

Francis followed up *Girly* with what is probably his worst film, *Trog* (1970), the tale of an utterly nonsensical Neanderthal monster on the loose piece produced by B-movie veteran Herman Cohen and starring Joan Crawford. Francis's 1987 film *Dark*

Tower, made in Spain, does manage to give *Trog* some strong competition in the worst-film category, however. The story of a possessed office building, it was an obvious rip-off of Tobe Hooper's *Poltergeist* (1982). Despite a good performance from the very capable Jenny Agutter, the film is a meandering bore, which boasts scene after scene of people doing nothing but walking along corridors waiting for something spooky to happen. Francis was so displeased with the film that he had his name taken off the credits and substituted a pseudonym, Ken Barnett.

If these are his worst films, *The Skull* (1965) and especially *The Creeping Flesh* (1972) are arguably his best. The first is based on Robert Bloch's classic short story "The Skull of the Marquis de Sade." It stars Peter Cushing as a collector of black-magic artifacts who purchases the skull of the infamous nobleman from dealer Patrick Wymark. As one might expect, bizarre things quickly begin to happen; Cushing is possessed by the skull and eventually driven to murder.

The fascinating thing about *The Skull* is not so much the story, which is slight and fairly routine, as Francis's inventive treatment of it. The film contains many arresting skull point-of-view shots. And the last half of the film contains virtually no dialogue as the

skull glides through Cushing's house seeking victims. There is also a marvelous nightmare sequence in which Cushing is removed from his home and taken to a surreal courthouse where a phantom judge forces him to play Russian roulette. Francis heightens the tension in this scene with extreme close-ups of Cushing clicking off one chamber of the gun after another, at which point the nightmare dissolves into a phantasmagoria of floating skulls and walls that close in on Cushing, finally crushing him.

The even better *The Creeping Flesh* benefited from a more solid script (by Peter Spenceley and Jonathan Rumbold) that delves into H. P. Lovecraft territory. In it, scientist Peter Cushing unearths a prehistoric skeleton that is the source of mankind's evil instincts. Mistakenly believing it is the source of mankind's goodness, he injects his daughter (Lorna Heilbron) with a serum derived from the skeleton in the hopes that it will stifle her budding sexual appetite. Instead, she goes mad and, like her mother before her, becomes sexually insatiable and promiscuous—and eventually a murderess. The skeleton (whose flesh reconstitutes if the bones get wet) meanwhile rises up after being drenched in a rainstorm and stalks the countryside in hood and robe, looking very much like a medieval monk.

Francis uses much visual symbolism to suggest

the theme of sexual repression and the dire effect it had on the Victorian family. A subplot concerning the attempts of Cushing's half brother (Christopher Lee) to best Cushing in scientific standing—at any and all costs—is also reflective of another Victorian-era sensibility: public responsibility but private hypocrisy. Eventually, Lee declares Cushing and Heilbron insane and has them imprisoned in his own asylum, where Cushing recounts the events of the story in flashback. This gives the film a sort of *Cabinet of Dr. Caligari* quality: Is Cushing's tale literally true, or just the ravings of a lunatic?

Following the success of David Lynch's *The Elephant Man* (1980), which he photographed, Francis persuaded that film's producer, Mel Brooks, to give him the chance to direct one of his long-cherished projects, *The Doctor and the Devils* (1985), based on poet Dylan Thomas's unproduced 1940s screenplay about Dr. Knox and his involvement with the infamous grave robbers/murderers Burke and Hare. Despite some excellent performances, the completed film reeked of compromise, which Francis admits to. He had wanted to film Thomas's philosophical script as written, but Brooks insisted on a more traditional horror film and brought in playwright Ronald Harwood to do a substantial rewrite. The result was a film that wasn't horrifying

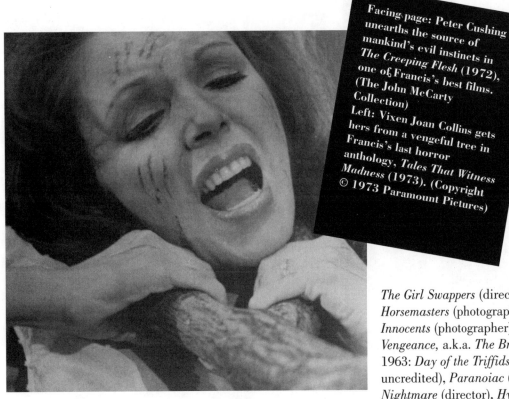

enough to satisfy most fearfilm fans or philosophical or poetic enough to do justice to Thomas's original conception. Ultimately, the film does not hold up to other treatments of the same tale—Robert Wise's *The Body Snatcher* (1945), based on the short story by Robert Louis Stevenson, and John Gilling's *The Flesh and the Fiends* (1959), which starred Peter Cushing as Knox.

Since the aforementioned disaster *Dark Tower*, Freddie Francis has devoted all of his energies to photographing the films of other directors. Rumor has it that Martin Scorsese, with whom Francis was associated on the remake of *Cape Fear*, may back a Francis-directed screen biography of Edgar Allan Poe. We shall have to wait and see.

Filmography

1956: *Moby Dick* (second-unit photographer), *A Hill in Korea* (photographer); 1957: *Time Without Pity* (photographer), *The Scamp* (photographer); 1958: *Next to No Time* (photographer); 1959: *Virgin Island* (photographer), *Room at the Top* (photographer); 1960: *The Battle of the Sexes* (photographer), *Never Take Sweets from a Stranger*, a.k.a. *Never Take Candy from a Stranger* (photographer), *Saturday Night and Sunday Morning* (photographer), *Sons and Lovers* (photographer); 1961: *Two and Two Make Six*, a.k.a. *The Girl Swappers* (director), *The Horsemasters* (photographer), *The Innocents* (photographer); 1962: *Vengeance*, a.k.a. *The Brain* (director); 1963: *Day of the Triffids* (codirector, uncredited), *Paranoiac* (director); 1964: *Nightmare* (director), *Hysteria* (director), *Traitor's Gate* (director), *The Evil of Frankenstein* (director), *Night Must Fall* (photographer); 1965: *Dr. Terror's House of Horrors* (director), *The Skull* (director); 1966: *The Psychopath* (director), *The Deadly Bees* (director); 1967: *They Came From Beyond Space* (director), *Torture Garden* (director); 1968: *The Intrepid Mr. Twigg* (short film, director), *Dracula Has Risen from the Grave* (director); 1969: *Mumsy, Nanny, Sonny and Girly*, a.k.a. *Girly* (director); 1970: *Trog* (director); 1971: *Vampire Happening* (director); 1972: *Tales from the Crypt* (director), *The Creeping Flesh* (director); 1973: *Tales That Witness Madness* (director), *Craze* (director); 1974: *Son of Dracula* (director); 1975: *The Ghoul* (director), *Legend of the Werewolf* (director); 1977: *Golden Rendezvous* (director, uncredited); 1980: *The Elephant Man* (photographer); 1981: *The French Lieutenant's Woman* (photographer); 1983: *Memed My Hawk* (photographer); 1984: *The Jigsaw Man* (photographer), *Dune* (photographer); 1985: *The Doctor and the Devils* (director), *Code Name: Emerald* (photographer); 1987: *Dark Tower* (director, uncredited); 1988: *Clara's Heart* (photographer); 1989: *Her Alibi* (photographer), *Glory* (photographer); 1991: *Cape Fear* (photographer).

After Polanski's highly publicized sex scandal, which resulted in his fleeing the United States, he surprised many by seeming to shift gears entirely and making the luminously beautiful *Tess* (1979), starring Nastassia Kinski. (Copyright © 1979 Columbia Pictures Industries, Inc.)

ROMAN POLANSKI

Polanski's talents are as undeniable as his intentions are dubious," wrote critic Andrew Sarris in *The American Cinema,* and, unlike many assessments in that classic handbook of film theory, time and a few bad pictures have done little to alter Sarris's verdict. At once the most accessible and most enigmatic of filmmakers to emerge from Poland in the 1960s, Polanski has always seemed to follow the career path of a seasoned pragmatist, balancing each personal project with a more overtly commercial one. Certainly this is how he started his filmmaking career in the West—making the exploitative "horror" thriller *Repulsion* (1965) in order to secure the backing to make his avant-garde *Cul-de-Sac* (1966). This modis operandi was probably the logical extension of his experiences as a Jewish youth during World War II when he hid out in the occupied ghetto of Warsaw, passing himself off as acceptably Aryan (often, according to Polanski, with the aid of a wax foreskin) to survive. Only now he was an artist passing himself off as a suitably down-to-earth commercial filmmaker. The difference lay only in the stakes.

Yet Polanski is merely pragmatic nor' by nor'west, as Shakespeare might have put it, since generally only the surface of his work changes, not his thematic concerns. If Polanski's popular-culture works—*Repulsion, Rosemary's Baby* (1968), *Chinatown* (1974)—succeed better with mass audiences than his more deliberately artistic works—*Cul-de-Sac, The Fearless Vampire Killers* (1967), *Macbeth* (1971), *What?* (1973), *The Tenant* (1976), *Tess* (1979)—it's not because they are thematically lighter in weight. Indeed, *The Fearless Vampire Killers, What?* and, to some degree, *Tess* come across on the surface as less deliberately "important" works than his popular entertainments.

Polanski earned his status as a premier fearmaker with his first English-language film, *Repulsion.* Fantasy and a horrific tone had permeated his preceding Polish short films, and his preoccupation with alienation and isolation were certainly evident in his debut feature, *Knife in the Water* (1962). *Repulsion,* however, was more deliberately horrific. It replaced the prosaic tensions of *Knife in the Water* with the visceral tensions of watching an alienated woman (Catherine Deneuve) sink further and further into homicidal madness and utter mental collapse.

To some degree, Polanski's approach in the film is not markedly different from that of Hitchcock's in *Psycho* (1960) or William Castle's in *Homicidal* (1961). But Polanski offered one supremely significant variation: his denial of an explanation. No cozy psychiatrist shows up at the end to explain it all in an effort to restore some sense of order to the chaos the audience has experienced. *Repulsion* is simply a journey into a personal hell without explanation or apology. True, there are clues to the nature of Deneuve's madness—notably the family photograph shown at the film's conclusion, which may or may not reveal signs of Deneuve's insanity to come. But there are no answers. And this is what makes the film much more unsettling than its forebears.

All of Polanski's work revolves around the pathological inability of his characters to engage in normal human interaction. *Repulsion,* for example, may be described as a study in decay (decay being a recurrent symbol in the film), as a study in madness, as a study into the numbing of the senses by modern society, and, perhaps most personally, as a study of the alienation of the displaced foreigner in an alien society. All these perfectly valid assessments, however, are tied to Polanski's central theme of not being able to connect with other human beings.

So fascinating and all-pervasive are Polanski's

thematic obsessions that his cinematic skill is often overlooked in most assessments of his work. However, it is Polanski's stylistic power as a filmmaker that allows his themes to come across with such force. What lingers in the mind about *Repulsion* is not so much the film's standard horror set pieces—specifically the murders—but subtler and more unsettling touches such as the scene where Deneuve walks past a car crash without noticing it because she is so turned in on herself, or her mixed revulsion at and fetishistic attraction to the razor of her sister's lover, or her fruitless attempt to wipe up the blood of a victim with a paperback novel.

With *Repulsion*, Polanski demonstrated that he was capable of delivering the commercial goods and yet could still impose his own personal vision on the material. Its success allowed him to make the unclassifiable *Cul-de-Sac*, another study of alienation and mental breakdown this time in the avant-garde style of playwright Samuel Beckett's *Waiting for Godot* (at one point the working title of the film was *If Katelbach Comes*).

More traditional horror abounded in *The Fearless Vampire Killers* (*Dance of the Vampires* in the U.K. and Europe), Polanski's first film in color and wide-screen presentation. Cursed with a somewhat tortured history thanks to executive producer Martin Ransohoff's postproduction tampering with the U.S. release print (it was drastically cut, voices were overdubbed, and an obnoxious cartoon was grafted onto the front of it), it took some years before the film could be correctly appraised by American audiences. It was well worth the wait, since Polanski's original confirmed what many suspected—that there was a genuinely great film lurking beneath Ransohoff's

bastardization. In many respects, it may be Polanski's greatest film.

Even more than the later *Tess* (which runs it a close second), this is Polanski's most breathtakingly beautiful film. Yet it is not just a pretty picture postcard. It's also a cockeyed rethinking of the vampire movie genre. And despite its status as a successful parody, it also does right by the genre. In fact, it breaks new ground by tackling certain issues relating to the genre that more straightforward horror films conveniently tend to sidestep—for example, the effectiveness (or lack thereof) of the crucifix on a Jewish vampire, the necrophiliac aspects of the vampire legend, and the subtext of homosexual panic that lies beneath the surface of many vampire tales (notably *Dracula*), with their images of men reacting in horror and revulsion to sexually aggressive women. *Vampire Killers* even takes this concept a step further by introducing an overtly gay vampire into the plot.

Perhaps Polanski's most trenchant reexamination of the vampire myth is his removal of the mask of hero from his Van Helsing character, Abronsius (Jack MacGowran). On the surface, Abronsius is a typical horror film vampire hunter, albeit an unusually addled one. But beneath the surface, his "hero," like Van Helsing before him, is a dangerous obsessive on a mission as questionable (from a motivational standpoint) as that of his vampire quarry—possibly even more questionable, since Abronsius has chosen his self-righteous path.

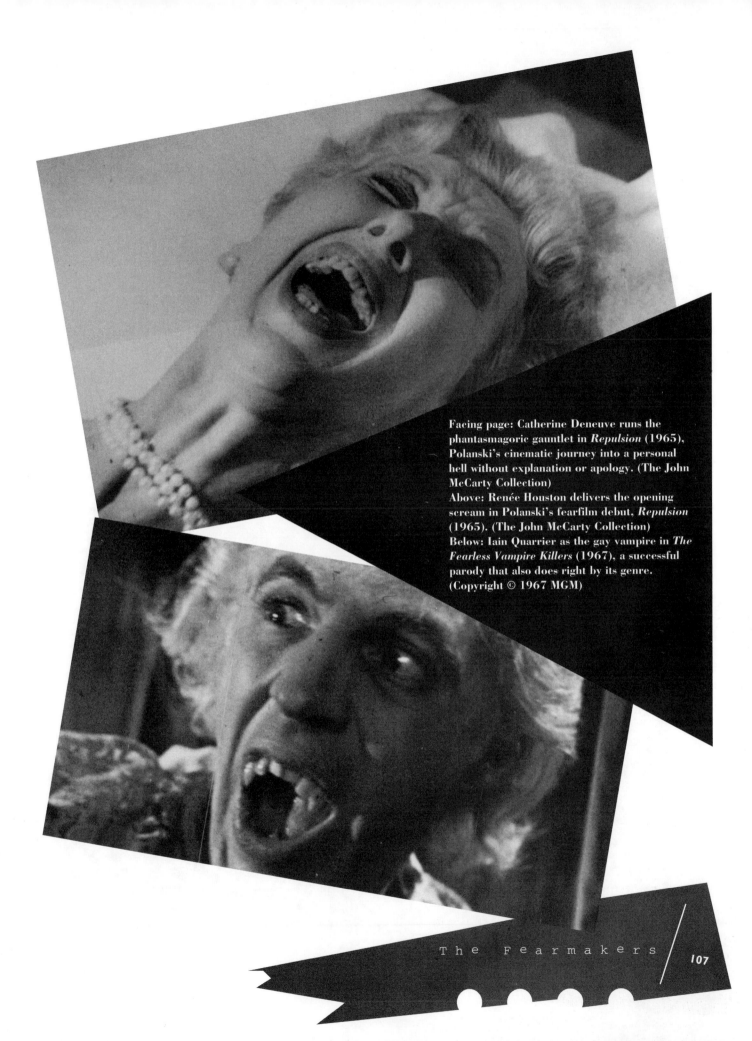

Facing page: Catherine Deneuve runs the phantasmagoric gauntlet in *Repulsion* (1965), Polanski's cinematic journey into a personal hell without explanation or apology. (The John McCarty Collection)
Above: Renée Houston delivers the opening scream in Polanski's fearfilm debut, *Repulsion* (1965). (The John McCarty Collection)
Below: Iain Quarrier as the gay vampire in *The Fearless Vampire Killers* (1967), a successful parody that also does right by its genre. (Copyright © 1967 MGM)

Abronsius's mission has turned him into a typically alienated and isolated Polanski character (even Abronsius's faithful assistant isn't really in synch with the man's mind-set or goal). Significantly, it is the vampire, Von Krolock (Ferdy Mayne), with whom Abronsius has the most in common, the only character with whom he shows signs of being able to connect. Rather than follow this course, however, he single-mindedly sets out to destroy Von Krolock, and, by doing so, he winds up carrying "away with him the very evil he sought to destroy."

These same themes pervade Polanski's first American film, *Rosemary's Baby,* although the film itself lacks the greatness of *Vampire Killers* on almost every level. Visually, *Rosemary's Baby* is relatively indifferent, apart from the brief sequence detailing Rosemary's coupling with Satan, which is a noteworthy attempt to present the fantastic events of the story in a realistic light. What believability that approach generates, however, is grotesquely undermined by the overpraised hamming of its gallery of old-guard character actors—Ruth Gordon, Sidney Blackmer, and Patsy Kelly—whose performances might have been a good deal of fun if the film itself had been similarly over the top.

This is not to say that *Rosemary's Baby* is not an accomplished piece of filmmaking. It is. As with *Vampire Killers,* Polanski took the devil worship mythology further than anyone had yet dared. The film seems a bit tame now, but its vivid depiction of satanic ritual was far nearer the mark than the decorous, albeit stylish, blasphemies of Edgar G. Ulmer's *The Black Cat* (1934) and Mark Robson's *The*

Abronsius (Jack MacGowran) and Alfred (Roman Polanski) practice staking a vampire on a pillow in *The Fearless Vampire Killers* (1967), Polanski's cockeyed rethinking of the vampire myth. (Copyright © 1967 MGM)

Seventh Victim (1943). Its greatest accomplishment, though, lies in the shrewdly subtle manner in which the script (a model of construction written by Polanski himself) piles up seemingly innocent details and coincidences to create an increasingly sinister mood.

After *Rosemary's Baby,* real life intruded into Polanski's world to an unprecedented and tragic extent with the death of his composer friend Christopher Komeda from a brain tumor and the murder of his wife, Sharon Tate, by the Manson family. Polanski's artistic response to this was an uncompromising and uncompromisingly bloody screen adaptation of Shakespeare's *Macbeth.* Like Orson Welles and Akira Kurosawa before him, Polanski turned Shakespeare's grimmest play into a wholly personal work that also did right by its source. As Welles had done with his 1948 version of *Macbeth,* Polanski stripped the play down to its barbaric

elements. But Polanski went a step further and completely uncovered the horror story that lay beneath the Bard's beautifully crafted lines. Welles's *Macbeth* is a masterpiece of film as theater. But Polanski's version is far more visceral, direct, and deliberately terrifying. His three witches are genuinely grotesque. His murders and mayhem as gruesome and graphic as the most unrelenting modern splatter movie. The line "Who would have thought the old man had so much blood in him?" comes across in Welles's version as black humor. In Polanski's, it is a horrific statement of fact.

At the time of its release, most critics were unable to see the film as anything but a reflection of the Manson murders. Despite Polanski's claims to the contrary, there may well have been a connection—at least on the level of personal catharsis. But this assessment ignores the fact that *Macbeth* is nothing

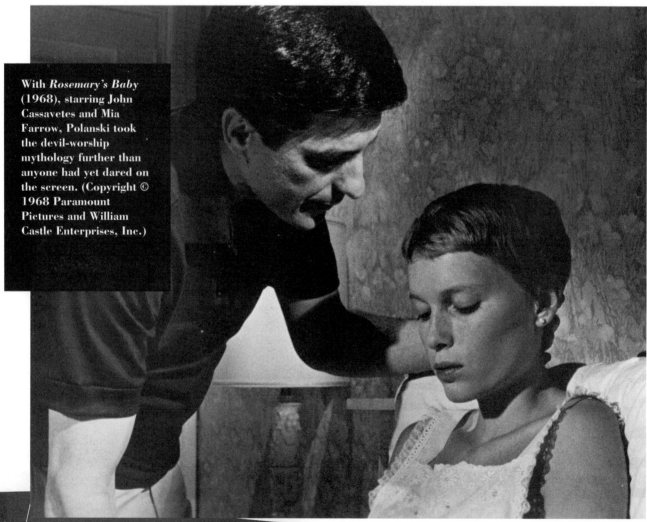

With *Rosemary's Baby* (1968), starring John Cassavetes and Mia Farrow, Polanski took the devil-worship mythology further than anyone had yet dared on the screen. (Copyright © 1968 Paramount Pictures and William Castle Enterprises, Inc.)

more, nor less, than a logical extension of Polanski's work up to that time. Shakespeare's themes appealed to him because they fit so well with his own. Nevertheless, the film did nothing at the box office, and even less for Polanski's career overall. His next project, the vastly misunderstood kinky comedy *What?* (a.k.a. *Diary of Forbidden Dreams*) fared even worse, receiving almost no distribution at all.

Polanski bounced back from these two successive commercial failures with a vengeance via *Chinatown*, a deliberately convoluted and perverted retake on the private-eye genre. Wholly successful as an entertainment and sliding neatly into Polanski's filmography, the film is brilliantly executed, flawlessly cast and acted, and as perverse as only a Polanski film can be. Nevertheless, it remains the director's least personal work. As far as Polanski the artist is concerned, *Chinatown*'s most important feature is that its critical and box-office success allowed him to make *The Tenant*.

Based on an interesting but not terribly accomplished novel by Roland Topor, *The Tenant* draws much of its tone from Kafka (as *Cul-de-Sac* drew from Beckett). It traces the story of an Eastern European immigrant (played by Polanski) who sublets a dreary apartment. The previous tenant had killed herself by jumping from the window. Trying vainly to fit in with both the neighboring tenants and the area in general, he slowly begins to take on the characteristics of his predecessor in what at first seems a subconscious effort to win their approval. What little personality of his own exists quickly degenerates, until he becomes increasingly suspicious that his predecessor had been deliberately driven to commit suicide by the neighbors and that they are in the process of doing the same to him. Ultimately, he plays out her life as if it was his own—jumping, not once but twice, from the same window and ending up just as she had, swathed in mummylike bandages, screaming in a hospital bed.

The complexity of *The Tenant* does not really survive being reduced to a simple synopsis, since much of that complexity, and the film's effectiveness, derives from subtle touches and nuances of mood that have no actual relation to the plotline. For example, the inevitability of not only the main character's fate but that of his predecessor is deftly suggested by his discovery that the woman he saw medically "mummified" in the hospital was keenly interested in Egyptology. It's almost as if her interest in ancient Egypt had drawn her into becoming a kind of mummy herself, while his desire to be accepted by his French neighbors draws him to become her. Similarly, the film's complete refusal to be concrete about the events it portrays is unsettling to the extreme. There is no doubt that the character played by Polanski is crumbling. But to some degree, he is being driven to this state. Yet we can never be certain whether any of this is deliberate on the part of the neighbors. It seems unlikely, since apart from their basic xenophobia (the film is no valentine card to the French people), there is no evidence of any motive to drive him to suicide. Nevertheless, the neighbors are sufficiently sinister and the atmosphere of the apartment so pervasively malignant that it is impossible to state with any degree of certainty that this is, in fact, the case.

After a highly publicized sex scandal resulted in his fleeing the United States in 1977, Polanski surprised many by seeming to shift gears entirely in making the luminously beautiful *Tess*. And yet was it such a shift? The basic premise of the story was, once again, the failure of human interaction. Polanski's approach to Thomas Hardy's novel was undeniably personal, and his stylistic use of landscapes in the film should have come as no surprise to anyone familiar with his magical snowscapes in *The Fearless Vampire Killers*.

Coming after the glories of *The Tenant* and *Tess*, his long-cherished project *Pirates* (1986) was something of a letdown. Perhaps the project was cherished just a little too long and had become stale by the time he got around to filming it. (The only problem with this theory is that *The Tenant* had a similarly lengthy gestation period.) The film is marred by the overblown acting of Walter Matthau, and, while he may resemble Polanski, French actor Cris Campion is not an effective replacement in the role that the director had intended to play himself had the film been made years earlier. Still, *Pirates* isn't quite the disaster it is sometimes painted to be. Typical of the director, it is visually striking—even sumptuous—and often the imagery recalls the surface obsessions of earlier Polanski films, especially his short subject *Two Men and a Wardrobe* (1958). Its greatest flaw is that it seems a relatively trivial work to have come from Polanski.

But regardless of its flaws, *Pirates* is a masterpiece compared with Polanski's next film, *Frantic* (1988). The story line has all the right ingredients—a man inadvertently trapped in an

The Fearmakers

In adapting *Macbeth* (1971), Polanski translated personal tragedy into a fearfilm that uncovered all the horror beneath the Bard's beautifully crafted lines. (Copyright © 1971 Columbia Pictures Industries, Inc.)

Polanski (left) slashes detective Jack Nicholson's nose as thug Roy Jensen holds him down in *Chinatown* (1974), the director's brilliantly crafted and perfectly acted retake on the private-eye genre. (Copyright © 1974 Long Road Pictures)

incomprehensible nightmare situation in a foreign land—but almost none of it works. Horribly miscast with an unlikable Harrison Ford in the lead and Betty Buckley (dressed like Nancy Reagan for some reason) as his kidnapped wife, *Frantic* tries hard to be suspenseful and frightening. Unfortunately, the material is too thin. Polanski's touches fail to integrate. Worst of all, we don't really care what happens to Ford's character and are hard-pressed even to understand his obsessive devotion to Buckley.

However, the artistic disaster of *Frantic* and, to a lesser extent, *Pirates* does not diminish Polanski's importance as an filmmaker—and fearmaker—with a unique and uniquely unsettling point of view. Many tend to dismiss his work as pointlessly defeatist. There is no argument that his films gravitate toward the hopeless, but it is wrong to suggest that this

gravitation is in any way pointless. Polanski's characters may be on one-way trips to various personal hells, but they go there kicking and screaming. All the characters continually try, however clumsily, to connect with other human beings, to break out of their isolation, and to free themselves of their alienation—although only Tess, of all Polanski's protagonists, achieves these goals (and is promptly arrested and hanged).

And what of the existence of the films themselves? Are they not the most eloquent evidence of Polanski's own unswerving, unstoppable devotion to connect with the rest of humanity? What better defense of them could there be?

Filmography
1954: *Pokolenie* (actor); 1957: *A Toothy Smile** (director/writer), *Breaking Up the Dance** (director/writer), *The Crime** (director/writer); 1958: *Two Men and a Wardrobe**; 1959: *The Lamp** (director/writer), *When Angels Fall** (director/writer), *Lotna* (actor); 1960: *Niewinni Czarodzieje* (actor); 1961: *The Fat and the Lean** (director/cowriter), *Samson* (actor); 1962: *Knife in the Water* (director/cowriter), *Mammals** (director/cowriter);

1963: *Les Plus Belles Escroqueries du Monde* (codirector/cowriter); 1965: *Repulsion* (director/cowriter); 1966: *Cul-de-Sac* (director/cowriter); 1967: *The Fearless Vampire Killers,* a.k.a. *Dance of the Vampires* (director/cowriter/actor); 1968: *Rosemary's Baby* (director/writer); 1969: *The Magic Christian* (actor); 1971: *Macbeth* (director/cowriter); 1972: *Weekend of a Champion* (producer/actor); 1973: *What?* a.k.a. *Diary of Forbidden Dreams* (director/cowriter/actor); 1974: *Chinatown* (director/actor); *Blood for Dracula,* a.k.a. *Andy Warhol's Dracula* (actor); 1976: *The Tenant* (director/cowriter/actor); 1979: *Tess* (director/cowriter); 1986: *Pirates* (director/cowriter); 1988: *Frantic* (director/cowriter); 1994: *Bitter Moon* (director/cowriter), *A Simple Formality* (actor); 1995: *Death and the Maiden* (director/cowriter).
　　　*short film

Polanski as the doomed title character in *The Tenant* (1976), one of the most unsettling fearfilms of his career. (Copyright ©Marianne Productions S.A.)

Lois Chiles and the hit-and-run victim from hell in *Creepshow 2* (1987), written by Romero.. (Copyright © 1986 New World Pictures)
Below: George A. Romero's work is unified by a blend of cynicism, conscience, and compassion. (Hollywood Book & Poster)

M I C H A E L   J .   C O L L I N S

GEORGE A. ROMERO

In 1968, George A. Romero forever changed the face of fearfilm with his groundbreaking *Night of the Living Dead.* The film has inspired dozens of imitations, kept millions of viewers awake at night, and paved the way for a new generation of cinema. Aside from its explicit violence and taut storytelling style, *Night of the Living Dead* proved to aspiring directors that one needn't have the backing of a major studio to produce work of enduring popularity. However indirectly, we have this film and Romero to thank for the blossoming of independent cinema that has taken place over the past twenty-five years.

But Romero's contribution to American film only began with *Night of the Living Dead.* Since that film, he has directed more than a dozen films and television shows, and his talent shows no sign of fading. Romero's distinctive style and his consistent concern for strongly acted, suspenseful situations place him among the better American directors both in and out of the genre he has chosen.

Born in the Bronx in 1939, Romero began making his first films, in 8mm, while still in his teens. He later studied art, design, and theater at the Carnegie-Mellon Institute of Art in Pittsburgh, where he graduated in 1961 with a B.A. Subsequently, he formed his own Pittsburgh-based company, Latent Image, to produce industrial films and television commercials. Then in 1967, he teamed up with another Pittsburgh advertising firm, Hardman

Associates, to produce a low-budget feature-length horror film that he hoped would serve as his ticket into the film industry. As a result, *Night of the Living Dead* took shape more as a portfolio piece than as a self-conscious entry into fearfilm. Owing to its popularity and marketability, the horror film has traditionally been the proving ground for unknown directors, since it's much easier to find a distributor for horror movies than it might be for a drama or a comedy. Romero's first film was a demonstration not only that he could direct a film but that his direction was versatile. The overwhelmingly suspenseful mood of the film also contains moments of dark humor ("They're dead . . . they're . . . all messed up"), romance, and tragedy. This blend of the horrific with the drama of everyday life immediately marks the film as one of lasting power.

Romero dislikes being tagged as a "message filmmaker." His films, though, do have messages, and it's hard to believe those messages end up in his films without Romero's knowledge or permission. *Night of the Living Dead,* like the majority of his films, has a bitter, cynical message, which, simply put, is this: People are too petty, too full of themselves, ever to survive.

After *Living Dead,* Romero made *The Crazies* (a.k.a. *Code Name: Trixie,* 1973), a dark film about the effects of chemical poisoning in a small Pennsylvania town. As in *Living Dead,* a feverish claustrophobia leads to distrust of organized control systems (the armed forces in this case) and the terrors of social upheaval. Wishing to expand his repertoire, Romero moved on to the defiantly unusual *Martin* (1978). Starring John Amplas in the title role, *Martin* is an innovative take on the traditional vampire myth. Yes, Martin does drink

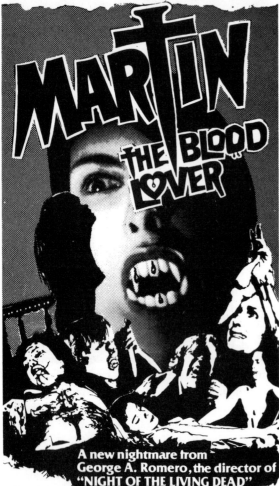

He could be the boy next door...

MARTIN
THE BLOOD LOVER

A new nightmare from
George A. Romero, the director of
"NIGHT OF THE LIVING DEAD"

IN COLOR

Introducing JOHN AMPLAS as "MARTIN"
Starring LINCOLN MAAZEL · CHRISTINE FORREST · ELYANE NADEAU
with SARAH VENABLE · TOM SAVINI · FRAN MIDDLETON · AL LEVITSKY
Produced by RICHARD RUBINSTEIN
Original Score: DONALD RUBINSTEIN · Photography by: MICHAEL GORNICK
A Laurel Film in Association with Barney C. Guttman   Braddock Associates 1977

Read the Stein & Day Book
A *Libra Films* Release

 **R RESTRICTED**
Under 17 requires accompanying Parent or Adult Guardian

blood, but it's unclear whether his thirst stems from supernatural craving or neurosis. Throughout Romero's films runs the theme of doubt in organized systems, whether they be mythic, supernatural, or social. Martin continually mocks his aging cousin, Tata Cuda (Lincoln Maazel), for believing in the folklore surrounding vampirism. Early in the film, Martin emphasizes his contempt for Cuda's superstitions by caressing a crucifix and eating garlic. As the dumbfounded Cuda looks on in shock, Martin tells him, "It's just a sickness—there isn't any magic." Martin's comment may refer to his own vampirism, or to Cuda's reliance on symbols and totems. Either way, the film offers us both Martin's fantasy life (in haunting, surreal black and white) and his real one (in color) as he goes about stalking his victims. In the vampire sequences, Romero's fondness for undermining his audience's expectations comes to the fore. Martin's visions are romantic, adventurous period pieces set in lush locations. In contrast to these lurid fantasies, the actual stalking of his victims against the banal backdrop of suburban America seldom goes easily; his victims fight, shout, and struggle. Martin's desire, he confesses to a radio talk-show host, is to have sex without "the blood part." Sadly, his first such encounter, in the arms of a depressed neighborhood housewife, leads to his undoing. When she commits suicide, Cuda imagines that Martin killed her, and, having sworn to destroy him if he ever did such a thing, Cuda unceremoniously pounds a stake into him.

Throughout *Martin*, Romero emphasizes his ongoing concern for the decay of social systems. The church to which Cuda belongs has burned down, and the new priest (played by Romero himself) is more interested in money and wine than in exorcism. The backdrop of Pittsburgh, where the film was shot, is one of urban blight; Martin roams around in neighborhoods destroyed by the failing economy of all American cities.

Romero's next picture was *Dawn of the Dead* (1979), a sequel to his first film. The scenario is a follow-up on the zombie invasion that began in *Living Dead*, when, in Yeats's classic phrase, "mere anarchy is loosed upon the world." The film opens in a TV station broadcasting news of the zombie menace that has gone increasingly out of control. As Romero crosscuts to a SWAT team raid on a tenement building, the audience is treated to the first of countless graphic scenes of zombie carnage. Accompanied by a TV station crew member and her helicopter-pilot boyfriend, two of the SWAT team escape to a mall, where the bulk of the film takes place.

Dawn of the Dead has a great many moments of dark comedy. The idea of the dead returning robotically to a mall where they once spent many happy hours is in itself a wry comment on consumer culture. And scenes of the living dead falling into fountains, stumbling on escalators, and clamoring for admission to department stores add to the film's overall tone of macabre humor. But underlying this satire, the film makes a more pessimistic statement concerning our culture and our society. As the four protagonists wall themselves inside the mall, sealing it off from zombie attack, their fortress becomes increasingly domestic. With the entire contents of the mall at their disposal, they run amok through the stores, indulging in the same fantasy of unlimited consumption parodied in the zombies' behavior. Soon the small space they've cleared for themselves resembles the same sort of suburban dream home that any other metaphorical "zombie" might desire. And with the immediate threat of the undead fought off for the moment, they become bored. As one of them succumbs to the bite of a zombie and becomes zombified himself, the party of settlers finds itself at a loss as to what to do next. Indeed, this hopelessness is the major framework of Romero's zombie trilogy, wherein goals as we've come to know them cease to exist. Money is useless. Nobody cares what car you drive. And staying alive means being constantly engaged in a fight against the undead. There is no place toward which one might aim, no peace anywhere.

Romero's cynical streak bares itself even more boldly during the film's climax, when outlaw bikers raid the mall. Our heroes, having defeated the immediate threat of the zombies for the time being, are now faced with something worse—their fellow humans. The weave of the social fabric, always under stress in Romero's films, rips entirely here as the fight for survival yields to a fight for plunder. This progression of events sums up the more dour political philosophy that once equipped with the means for survival, humanity will turn its attention to conquest simply for the sake of increasing its holdings.

Although the film's gleefully gory content may chase off some viewers, its serious, intelligent ideas about society and civilization in America and where each may be headed make the film impossible to dismiss. One can argue that even the excesses of

bloodshed and organ spilling serve the same purpose: In a film that makes such strong critical points about American culture, the treatment of violence is an essential theme. *Dawn of the Dead* is an epic view of a civilization in decline.

It's apt, then, that Romero followed *Dawn* with *Knightriders* (1981), which, although in no way a fearfilm, makes similarly strong and bitter comments on issues of integrity and personal value systems. Like Romero's other work, the film focuses on a world falling apart—in this case, a troop of motorcyclists acting out a medieval fantasy. The idyllic microcosm falls into disarray as the result of crooked, violent policemen, sleazy promoters, greed, and power struggles within the troop.

Creepshow, Romero's pastiche of 1950s EC horror comics, written by Stephen King, appeared in 1982. It's a demonstration of the dark wit and over-the-top

putrefaction that so distressed parents and teachers in the 1950s, when EC horror comics came under fire for ostensibly corrupting the youth of our proud land. An anthology film, *Creepshow*'s stories are united by one involving an angry father who throws his son's horror comic away with the warning "If I ever catch you reading this crap again, you won't sit down for a week!" Romero then follows this with the first tale, "Father's Day," a typically EC-ish story involving jealousy, rage, decadence, and the spectacularly rotten corpse of a vicious father. Romero's use of matting in these scenes to echo the stylized look of comic-book art is not only great fun but indicative of his sophistication as a filmmaker. The film is also thematically consistent with the rest of Romero's work; the social institutions of family, wealth, marriage, and class are again mercilessly criticized and parodied.

Perhaps the most memorable segment of

Creepshow is the final one in which E. G. Marshall, playing a ruthless tycoon obsessed with cleanliness (modeled on Howard Hughes), fights an escalating war against cockroaches that have invaded his high-rise apartment. Trapped in his stark white digs, Marshall goes slowly out of his mind to the jazzy strains of his Wurlitzer as increasing battalions of cockroaches descend upon him. Longtime Romero collaborator Tom Savini's final effects sequence in this segment of Marshall's body splitting open, disgorging thousands of cockroaches, is remarkable.

Day of the Dead, the concluding chapter of Romero's "zombie trilogy," hit screens in 1985. Although Romero has professed dissatisfaction with the film (budget limitations prevented him from pursuing the much grander idea he'd originally envisioned), it remains a solid, powerful piece of fear filmmaking. Set entirely in an underground bunker, the film concerns the escalating tensions between a military unit and a team of scientists. Our sympathies are entirely with the scientists. Most of the soldiers range from the imbecilic to the power-mad. Only two,

a helicopter pilot named John (Terry Alexander) and an electronics expert named McDermott (Jarlath Conroy), offer any hope that the military might be anything more than a legion of fools.

Day of the Dead is a much grimmer film than its predecessor. The relentlessly claustrophobic sets, the constantly simmering anger and distrust among the characters, and the apocalyptic finale offer little of the slapstick irony of the mall zombies. Even the droll characters of Bub (Howard Sherman), a behavioral-experiment zombie, and his tutor, Dr. Logan (Richard Liberty), a twinkly-eyed, avuncular neurologist, are presented in poignant terms. Logan, teaching Bub to follow orders and identify simple objects, becomes the film's father figure, despite his numerous gory experiments.

The only place in which any hope exists is the small compound occupied by John and McDermott, which is decorated to resemble a tropical vacation home. And theirs is a bleak hope indeed.

To the sound of tape-recorded ocean waves, the two live in philosophical acceptance of their conditions, making what they can of a dire situation. As above them the world they knew is completely overrun by the undead and all about them the living demonstrate their venal stupidity, John and McDermott comfort themselves by abandoning their harsh reality as much as possible and accepting that they cannot leave.

Ironically, the film concludes on a much happier note than Romero's other zombie films, as the heroine, Sarah (Lori Cardille), John, and McDermott escape to a real tropical island. The sole survivors of one of the last enclaves of "civilization," they have left behind the complete destruction and meaningless struggles of the mainland, and as the film concludes, theirs is the only promise of a new beginning.

Despite its richness of characterization and its complexity of message, the film fared less well than expected at the box office, and it has achieved much less attention than Romero's previous zombie films. Nevertheless, it remains a potent, affecting film, and one well worthy of recognition, however belated.

Since *Day of the Dead*, Romero has released two and a half features: *Monkey Shines* (1988), the first half of *Two Evil Eyes* (1990), the other half of which was directed by Dario Argento, and *The Dark Half* (1993). Perhaps his most conventional and accessible film to date, *Monkey Shines* is a suspense thriller about the relationship between a quadriplegic (Jason Beghe) and the capuchin monkey trained to help him achieve some degree of independence. The monkey is more unique than Beghe reckons on, however. The subject of an intelligence-heightening drug experiment, the monkey develops a near-telepathic bond with Beghe, becomes acutely sensitive to his mood swings, and acts out Beghe's anger and aggression toward others.

Monkey Shines is an accomplished, mature film, an emblem of Romero's sophistication in his chosen medium. But the film was a commercial flop, and as of this writing Romero has completed only one other film—an adaptation of Stephen King's novel *The Dark Half,* which was completed a few years before its 1993 release but held back by the financial collapse of its distributor.

The Dark Half continues Romero's trend toward increasingly intimate films. The story of best-selling novelist Thad Beaumont's (Timothy Hutton) battle with his recently materialized nom de plume, George Stark (Hutton also), *The Dark Half* is a well-produced, unnerving film in which Romero's dark wit is finely honed. Moments of brutality are jarringly juxtaposed with comic flourishes. For example, when a writer from *People* magazine turns up to do an interview on Beaumont and his troublesome alter ego, someone comments on the formerly stylish ponytail hanging down from the baseball cap the magazine writer wears on his head. The writer shortly thereafter removes the hat, revealing a glowingly bald pate—a standard and fairly mild sight gag. But later in the film, in a stunningly lighted and photographed set piece with nods to the stylistic hyperbole of occasional Romero collaborator Argento, George Stark catches up with the magazine writer and in the violent interlude that follows cuts off the ponytail, adding a sense of the absurd to what is otherwise a viscerally powerfully scene.

Above: Romero's most conventional and accessible film to date and a commercial flop, *Monkey Shines* (1988) starred Jason Beghe as a quadriplegic who becomes the victim of the capuchin monkey trained to help him. (Copyright © 1988 Orion Pictures Corp.)
Facing page: A dark parable of the undertow of social mobility: Timothy Hutton in Romero's *The Dark Half* (1993), which sat on the shelf for several years due to the financial collapse of its distributor, Orion Pictures. (Copyright © 1990 Orion Pictures Corp.)

Romero handles the broader subtext of the film—class anxiety—with his customary deftness and subtlety. The opening scene uses the medium of film with understated intelligence as it contrasts Beaumont's hardscrabble boyhood with the relative opulence of his current lifestyle. All the elements differentiating Beaumont from Stark are class indicators. Whereas Beaumont owns the traditional Jeep and Volvo of Yuppiedom, Stark drives a muscly Olds Toronado; whereas Beaumont is fashionably fit, Stark smokes and drinks. George

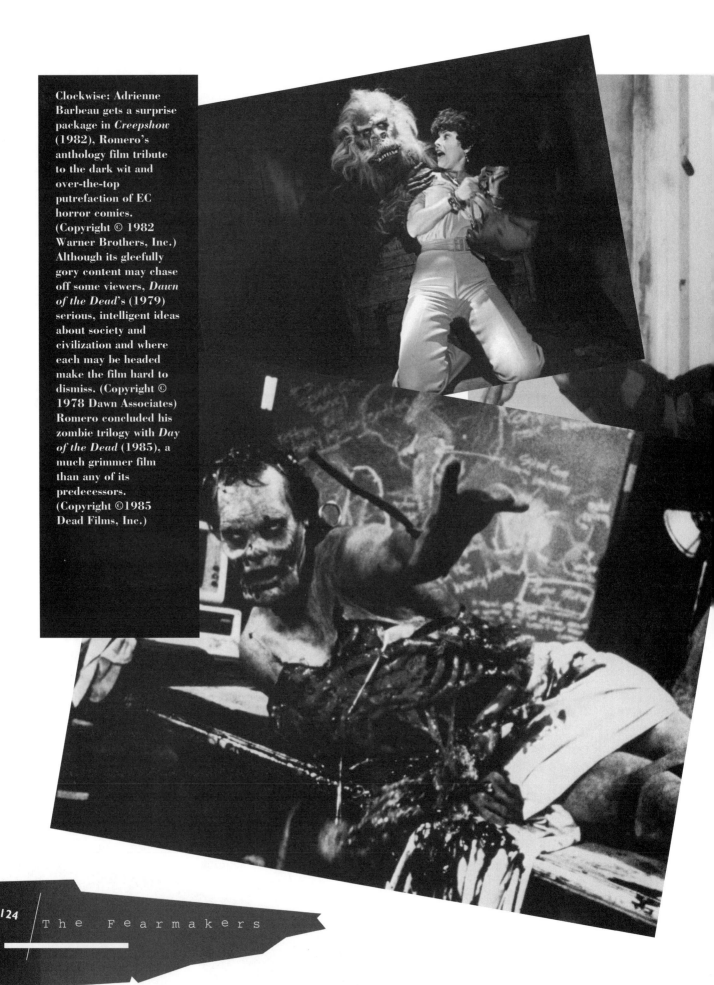

Clockwise: Adrienne Barbeau gets a surprise package in *Creepshow* (1982), Romero's anthology film tribute to the dark wit and over-the-top putrefaction of EC horror comics. (Copyright © 1982 Warner Brothers, Inc.) Although its gleefully gory content may chase off some viewers, *Dawn of the Dead*'s (1979) serious, intelligent ideas about society and civilization and where each may be headed make the film hard to dismiss. (Copyright © 1978 Dawn Associates) Romero concluded his zombie trilogy with *Day of the Dead* (1985), a much grimmer film than any of its predecessors. (Copyright ©1985 Dead Films, Inc.)

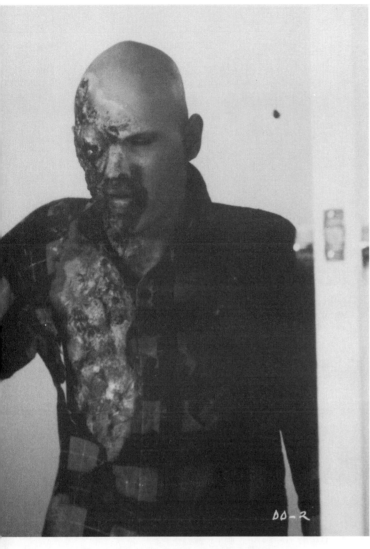

DO-2

Romero's dedication to independence may keep him outside the lavish budgets and extensive promotion available to Hollywood directors, but it allows him to craft his films with an intensely personal vision. In the current climate of film distribution, characterized by Hollywood's all-or-nothing gambles on huge budgets at the expense of smaller films, his work is refreshingly welcome.

Filmography

1968: *Night of the Living Dead* (director/cowriter /photographer/editor); 1972: *There's Always Vanilla* (director/photographer/editor); 1973: *Jack's Wife*, a.k.a. *Hungry Wives* and *Season of the Witch* (director/writer /photographer/editor), *The Crazies*, a.k.a. *Code Name: Trixie* (director/writer); 1978: *Martin* (director/writer); 1979: *Dawn of the Dead* (director/writer/coeditor); 1981: *Knightriders* (director/writer/coeditor); 1982: *Creepshow* (director/coeditor); 1983: "Trick or Treat"* (writer); 1985: *Day of the Dead* (director/writer), "The Devil's Advocate"* (writer); 1986: *Flight of the Spruce Goose* (actor), "Baker's Dozen"* (writer), "Circus"* (writer); 1987: *Creepshow 2* (writer); 1988: *Lightning Over Braddock: A Rustbowl Fantasy* (actor), *Monkey Shines* (director/writer); 1990: *Two Evil Eyes* (codirector/cowriter), *Night of the Living Dead* (executive producer/writer), *Tales From the Darkside: The Movie* (cowriter); 1993: *The Dark Half* (director/writer); 1995: *The Black Mariah* (director).

*Episode of the TV anthology series *Tales from the Darkside*.

Stark is more than just the dark half of Beaumont's successful literary id; he's the white-trash terrorist that stalked the conspicuous consumption of 1980s Yuppies like Beaumont, an unmonied past that refuses to die. Romero's film, beyond being an effective, absorbing thriller, is a dark parable of the undertow of social mobility.

Taken as a whole, Romero's body of work is unified by a blend of cynicism, conscience, and compassion. Romero's determined choices of characterization and casting are indications of his commitment to progressive ideas. In all of his films, there exists a pronounced concern for the cultural outsider. One is more likely to find women, African-Americans, and the disabled or disenfranchised in hero roles in Romero's films than in those of any other director.

The face of fear in *Tenebrae* (1982), which was butchered and

retitled *Unsane* for U.S. release. (Hollywood Book & Poster)

Background: Players and potential victims cavort Argento-style

in *Opera* (1987). (Hollywood Book & Poster)

WALTER L. GAY

DARIO ARGENTO

Born in 1943, Dario Argento, the son of Italian film producer Salvatore Argento, segued from his early career as a film critic to assistant to Italian shockmeister Mario Bava to full-time screenwriter (and cowriter— with Bernardo Bertolucci and Sergio Leone of the rightfully revered epic spaghetti Western *Once Upon a Time in the West,* 1968). He has since parlayed his phobias into a directorial career that marks him as the Italian cinema's reigning king of bloody terror.

Argento's fear filmmaking is skewed at best and full of contradictions. Horror-film characters have always been apt to run foolishly into dark attics or cellars, often with known killers or monsters lurking about. But Argento's characters are ten times as likely to commit such foolish acts, and much else, to propel the plots of his pictures from one shock scene to the next. His characters often share psychic bonds with animals, even insects.

Argento the film festival guest professes to love animals; but Argento the director kills them off on-screen with alarming frequency. Nineteenth-century criminology and pounding synthesizer scores often inhabit the same film. He usually keeps his chillers cold, distancing viewers from his characters emotionally, while using his fluid camera style to bring audiences and characters together physically— in some cases by taking the viewer right into the victim's eyeball or brain pan.

Popular and critical reaction to Argento's work is likewise divided. Some people, witnessing Argento's creeping camera, garish lighting, and convoluted story lines, accuse him of placing style over substance. Others rationalize his excesses as attempts to choreograph nightmares. Extreme reactions dismiss him as a no-talent hack or overpraise him as "the Italian Hitchcock." Argento may have his flaws, but provoking lukewarm reaction

is not one of them.

Nineteen-seventy saw the release of *The Bird with the Crystal Plumage,* Argento's directorial debut and the first of his string of *"giallo"* (or "yellow"—in Italy, the "color of fear") shockers. American writer in Rome Tony Musante sees a woman attacked by a crazed knife wielder in an art gallery. He alerts the police and they reward him by withholding his passport, stranding him in Rome. On the way back to his apartment from the police station, he almost has his head taken off by a meat cleaver, and he takes it upon himself to catch the killer with the help of his girlfriend (Suzy Kendall). One of the clues to the killer's identity is a macabre painting of a black-clad murderer attacking a young girl; the artist is a demented recluse who fattens felines for dinner.

Argento opens this flick with shots of the killer's black-gloved hands (à la Mario Bava's *Blood and Black Lace,* 1964) and emulates Hitchcock with lingering shots of several gleaming knife blades. Hitchcockian voyeurism is also introduced early on; in fact, this theme recurs in nearly every Argento picture. The gore is fairly restrained compared with the all-out massacres of his later *Inferno* and *Opera,* a remarkable degree of suspense is sustained throughout, and the title even makes sense by film's end.

Realizing that there was gold in "them thar *giallos,"* especially ones with black-clad killers and funny animal titles, Argento launched his second outing, *The Cat O'Nine Tails* (1971), which opens with a bungled break-in at a genetics lab, and soon escalates to homicide. Overbearing reporter James Franciscus and blind habitual puzzle solver Karl

Malden appoint themselves civilian detectives to try and catch the killer. Though the film drags in the middle, boredom is spelled by a slate of sick secondary characters and some delightfully dumb dialogue. For example, after the killer nearly asphyxiates Malden and tries to poison Franciscus, the latter remarks to his girlfriend, "They're playing a little rough."

Suspense mounts in the final third of the film when Malden's niece is abducted and Franciscus is locked inside a mausoleum. The murderer is unmasked in a literally bone-crunching climax, with the heroes fighting for their lives as the police close in; before the bloody battle is over, the killer reveals that an extra Y chromosome in his genes is what drove him to mania.

The Cat O'Nine Tails is much too long at 112 minutes, but Argento livens the pace up with a spooky cemetery sequence, several gory murders, and a rope-burn number that leaves viewers' palms stinging for weeks afterward. The film also boasts a likable

protagonist in Malden's character—an unusual departure from Argento's overall body of work.

Four Flies on Grey Velvet followed in 1971. Featuring Mimsy Farmer, Michael Brandon, and another throbbing Ennio Morricone score, the film relies on the outdated premise that a killer's image is imprinted on the retinas of his victims. Quite bloody and gruesome in its original form, the film was heavily trimmed by Paramount for U.S. release.

Argento's influence was felt early on, if only superficially. After *The Bird with the Crystal Plumage* turned a profit, other directors trotted out generally lame thrillers with titles in a similar vein, such as *Seven Deaths in the Cat's Eye* and *Scorpion with Two Tails.* With the possible exception of Lucio Fulci's grisly *Don't Torture a Duckling,* this subgenre offered little that was either new or shocking. But when titles began to reach such absurd extremes as *The Black Belly of the Tarantula,* the subgenre at least offered terror triviologists a few laughs.

In its original cut, Argento's *Deep Red* (1976) easily lives up to its name. A renowned psychic lecturing in Rome senses a killer in the auditorium and then is summarily murdered by the cleaver-wielding maniac. The butchery is witnessed by her neighbor, pianist David Hemmings, who, like any good Argento protagonist, immediately rushes to the murder scene unarmed. Hemmings takes it upon himself to solve the case—partly as a challenge to his intellect and possibly to get the best of some arrogant Roman cops. He also wants to match wits with dynamic journalist Daria Nicolodi. (Hemmings also evidences some outdated notions regarding women as the "gentler, weaker sex," which are dashed to pieces by the time the film is over.)

While retreading ideas from *Crystal Plumage*, Argento lays on gallons of gore this time around. Sundry knifings and hackings are augmented by a decapitation via elevator and the shocking sight of a victim's teeth being smashed out on a stone mantelpiece. The throbbing score was supplied not by Morricone this time but by a group called Goblin, which later scored George A. Romero's *Dawn of the Dead* (1979), a film Argento coproduced.

In his first four pictures, Argento veiled the identities of his killers by showing the black-garbed miscreants only in long shot, or by employing close-ups of the psychos' gloved hands and feverishly rolling eyeballs, or by not showing them at all, just the results of their handiwork. Until the eventual unmaskings, his murderers seemed to be more

Above: Like any good Argento protagonist should, amateur sleuth David Hemmings rushes to the murder scene unarmed in *Deep Red* (1976). (Hollywood Book & Poster)
Left: Cristina Marsillach strikes back at the crazed killer in the closing reel of *Opera* (1988). (Hollywood Book & Poster)

ghostly than flesh-and-blood real. Possibly taking a cue from this, Argento plunged headlong into the world of the supernatural with his next two films, beginning with *Suspiria* (1976), the first film of a projected trilogy about sorceresses living and killing in Rome, New York City, and Argento's fictional Friburg, Germany. Student Jessica Harper arrives at her Tanz Akademie in time to witness the bloody murders of two fellow students. With screwy Argento logic, the school remains open in spite of this. We quickly find out that the Akademie is the lair of the Mother of Whispers, and in no time our heroine is fighting for her life. Argento pulled out all the stops in this one, cranking up the Goblin sound track and employing garish-colored gels and flying cameras to create a dizzyingly nightmarish atmosphere. The influence of Roger Corman's *The Masque of the Red Death* (1964) and *House of Usher* (1960) is evident in Argento's ghastly red/blue/black color schemes and the film's holocaust of an ending, which makes up in pure pyrotechnics what it lacks in logic and narrative punch. Argento also set out to please the gorehounds by providing them with an open-heart slaying, the killing of a blind man, who is then partially devoured by his bewitched Seeing Eye dog, and a frequently imitated but never equalled "maggot storm."

The second installment in the "Three Mothers" trilogy was *Inferno* (1980). Costar Irene Miracle inadvertently unleashes evil forces as she investigates the legend of three witches who rule the world from their respective houses, all built by an architect named Varelli. Her search leads to a flooded cellar full of corpses and her eventual bloody death. Her brother (Leigh McCloskey), a music student living in Rome, comes to visit and, like Jessica Harper in *Suspiria*, finds himself in a hotbed of sorcery and violence. One character is attacked by wildcats. A sadistic antique dealer drowns cats by the sackful until he's deservedly shredded by rats, then hacked to death. A servant is found dead, his eyes ripped out, while another is burned alive. In one sequence sure to offend highbrows everywhere, a painful double knifing is accompanied by a chorus from Verdi's *Nabucco*. These proceedings, scored by Keith Emerson and lighted like *Suspiria*, are punctuated by some of the most frightening imagery in the Argento canon, including an alchemist's lair complete with bubbling cauldrons. That these diverse elements don't quite add up when the obligatory fiery finale rolls around may explain why Argento has yet to complete his trilogy.

As the violence in Argento's movies escalated, so did accusations that his films existed for the sake of their bloody violence alone. This criticism tended to overlook the fact that Argento lavished equal care on his lighting, music, and cinematography, if not always his scripts. In terms of screen slaughter, neither repelled critics nor adoring gorehounds had seen anything yet, however.

The title of his next film, *Tenebrae* (1982), refers to the novel written by its lead character, and to the darkness in man's

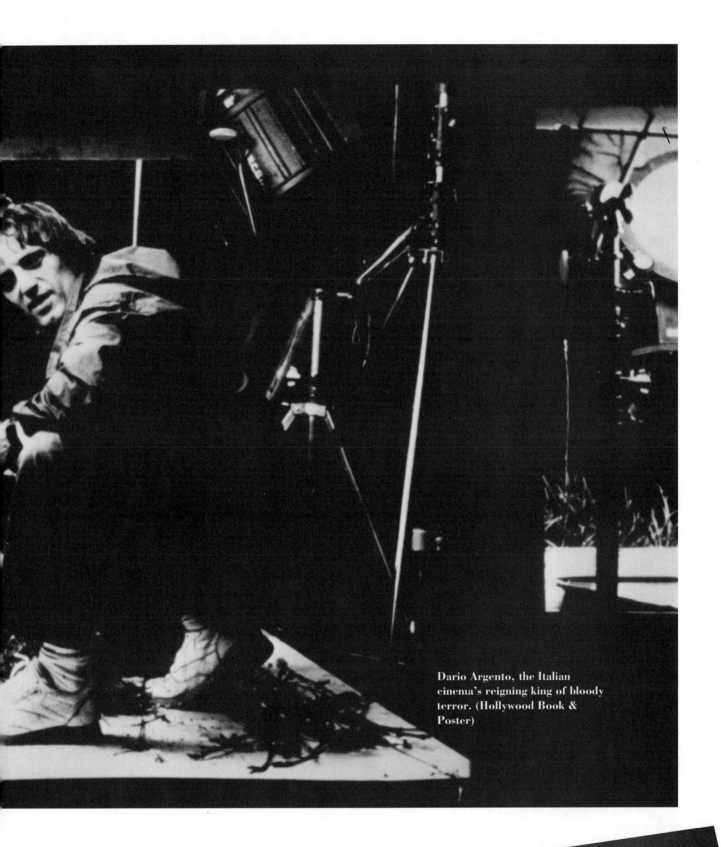

Dario Argento, the Italian
cinema's reigning king of bloody
terror. (Hollywood Book &
Poster)

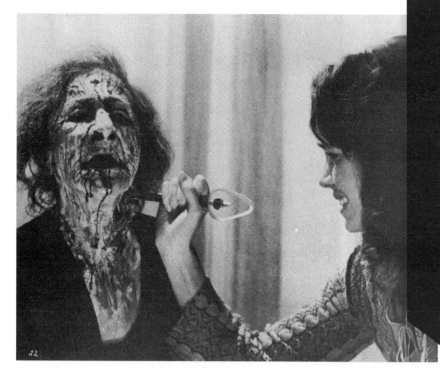

soul. Murders commence when writer Anthony Franciosa travels to Rome to promote the novel. Victims are slashed to ribbons and pages of the book are crammed into their mouths. Before long, we find out there are two killers at work, making for the messiest Argento movie to date. Uncut prints contain the now-infamous scene in which a woman whose arm has been cut off literally sprays her kitchen wall with her gushing blood. *Tenebrae* itself was butchered and retitled *Unsane* for U.S. release; true-blue Argento fans should accept no substitute for the unexpurgated original, however.

For the 1985 *Phenomena* (known in the United States as *Creepers),* Argento spent more than two months auditioning actresses to play the heroine, then settled on Jennifer Connelly. She plays an actor's daughter sent to a girls' school in Switzerland. Like Jessica Harper, she arrives during a wave of gruesome murders. Police have not found a single intact body, just the odd head or severed limb. Resident entomologist Donald Pleasence helps the police pinpoint the times of the murders by analyzing maggots in the body parts. Our heroine has always had an affinity for insects, we're told, and she soon goes into spells of sleepwalking where she can see through the eyes of insects. This doesn't win her any popularity contests with the teachers and other students, but it does enable her to get closer to the killer—and thus become next on his "hit" parade.

The American version is terribly disjointed—even for an Argento film—boasting the disappearance of an entire character. Fine Goblin music is riddled with snatches of heavy metal that don't fit the mood or on-screen action, despite Argento's insistence to the contrary. The original version contains scenes of attenuated hand impalement, face slashing, and a tonsil on the end of a spear. Perhaps the American release might have benefited from some of these trimmed tidbits. On the other hand, the original also contains more Jennifer Connelly. Even with his notorious disdain for actors, Argento generally manages to elicit professional performances from them, although not so of Connelly, who stands as his weakest, most colorless protagonist ever.

Argento has also been known to get behind the careers of up-and-coming fearmakers whose talents he admires. He did so with Lamberto Bava, the son of the great stylist Mario Bava, to whom Argento's own career owes a considerable debt, by producing Bava's *Demons* (1986), a gore for gore's sake extravaganza filmed in Berlin and Rome that starred another

Argento apprentice, Michele Soavi. Soavi later filmed a tribute to his mentor, the documentary *Dario Argento's World of Horror,* and two high-style/low-substance thrillers, *Stage Fright* and *The Church* (1989), the latter produced by Argento. Regrettably, Soavi then abandoned style as well as substance with the dreary *The Sect* (1990), a.k.a. *The Devil's Daughter,* which Argento wrote and produced.

Frustrated in his attempts to direct a stage version of *Rigoletto* (complete with vampire nobleman), Argento proceeded to make the word *opera* synonymous in the minds of his fans with visceral terror in his next film—appropriately titled *Opera* (1988). The film opens as a temperamental soprano starring in *Macbeth* gets peeved at director Ian Charleson's innovations and walks off the production. (Vanessa Redgrave was originally signed to play the part of the diva but took a similarly abrupt hike.) The diva is later knocked out of the picture entirely by a convenient accident, allowing understudy Cristina Marsillach to replace her. Two people close to Marsillach are summarily butchered, acts she is forced to witness, since the killer has tied her up and propped her eyelids open with strategically placed needles. The murderer also mashes one of Charleson's

pet ravens. During the final performance of the opera, however, the remaining ravens are set loose in the house and, in an incredible "swimming crane" sequence, bloodily zero in on the villain.

Released uncut in the United States as *Terror at the Opera,* the film will long remain legendary among fans of gory fearfilms because of its now-famous scene where the murderer slices open a victim's throat to obtain some incriminating evidence that's been swallowed. The film also boasts some of the most relentlessly suspenseful sequences of Argento's career, as well as a grim backstage atmosphere and some dizzying camerawork that even on the small screen may induce vertigo in viewers.

Argento's recent *Two Evil Eyes* (1990) remains a disappointment, however. It's an excessive inflating of two of Edgar Allan Poe's most overworked tales, "The Facts in the Case of M. Valdemar" and "The Black Cat." George A. Romero directed the *Valdemar* story while Argento helmed the updated second segment. Harvey Keitel plays Rod Usher, a gorehound photographer who might have shot

Left: Argento paid gruesome homage to Poe's "The Black Cat" (and numerous other Poe stories) in the excessively inflated *Two Evil Eyes* (1990), codirected by George A. Romero. (Hollywood Book & Poster) Facing page, above: Evil forces unleashed—from *Inferno* (1980), the second installment in Argento's "Three Mothers" trilogy, which began with *Suspiria.* (Hollywood Book & Poster) Facing page, below: Overbearing reporter James Franciscus and blind habitual puzzle solver Karl Malden appoint themselves civilian detectives on the trail of a Y-chromosome killer in *The Cat O'Nine Tails* (1971). (Hollywood Book & Poster)

the splatter "documentary" *Faces of Death* if somebody else hadn't already beaten him to it. His girlfriend, Madeleine Potter, adopts the titular black cat, and it's hate at first sight for Keitel and the feline. Keitel torments the cat, then throttles it to death, preserving the moment on Kodak film. Potter confronts him about this and is walled up in their apartment. Detective John Amos investigates, and there's plenty more gore before the abrupt ending.

Argento is an avowed Poe fanatic who, in an introduction to an Italian printing of Poe's work, tells more about Poe than anybody would want to know. He has also paid homage to Poe in his earlier films (check out the bricked-up cadaver in *Deep Red* and the *Rue Morgue*-like/ razor-wielding chimp in *Phenomena*). His *Black Cat* episode is lavish and full of the creeping, subjective point of view camera moves his fans have come to love. Still, one wonders why such a devotee of Poe chose to undertake one of the author's most familiar, overused, and shortest stories and pad it out to a languorous sixty minutes. Argento might better have filmed one of Poe's unmined properties instead. For example, given Argento's unparalleled ability to invoke the ghoulish and sinister—not to mention his penchant for funny animal titles— picture Poe's *Hop-Frog* given the Argento treatment. The prospect of such an opus truly boggles the mind.

Filmography

1967: *Cemetery Without Crosses* (writer); 1968: *Once Upon a Time in the West* (cowriter); *Today Me . . . Tomorrow You* (writer), *One Night at Dinner* (writer), *Sex Revolution* (writer), *Zero Probability* (writer); 1969: *Commandos* (writer), *Legion of the Damned* (dialogue supervisor), *Season of Loves* (story supervisor); 1970: *Five Man Army* (cowriter), *The Bird with the Crystal Plumage* (director/writer); 1971: *The Cat O'Nine Tails* (director/cowriter), *Four Flies on Grey Velvet* (director/cowriter); 1973: *Five Days in Milan* (director/cowriter); 1976: *Deep Red* (director/cowriter), *Suspiria* (director/cowriter); 1979: *Dawn of the Dead* (coproducer); 1980: *Inferno* (director/writer); 1982: *Tenebrae* (director/cowriter); 1985: *Phenomena* (director/cowriter); 1986: *Demons* (producer); 1987: *Demons 2* (producer); 1988: *Opera,* a.k.a. *Terror at the Opera* (director/producer/cowriter); 1989: *The Church* (producer); 1990: *Two Evil Eyes* (codirector/coproducer/cowriter), *The Sect* (writer/producer); 1994: *Trauma* (director/cowriter).

Craven's *Deadly Blessing* (1981) again pitted city people against another bunch of rural reprobates.

WES CRAVEN

One autumn day in 1972, the town of Westport, New York was invaded by a motley crew of guerilla filmmakers. The ringleaders were local boy Sean S. Cunningham, a producer with a theater background, and a thirty-three-year-old Cleveland-born ex-professor of humanities turned sometime soft-core porn and documentary film producer/director/editor named Wes Craven. Their mission was to film a sleazy rape/revenge opus tentatively titled *Night of Vengeance,* which they expected to play briefly, then disappear into cinematic oblivion. Neither of them, however, knew that their nasty little feature, ultimately retitled *Last House on the Left,* would make history as one of the most infamous fearfilms of all time.

Craven's prior filmmaking experience consisted of playing a zombie in as well as directing a segment of a low-budget Roy Frumkes horror film called *Tales That Will Rip Your Heart Out.* The film was never released, although snippets from it later found their way into the intro of *Dr. Butcher, M.D.* Regrettably, Craven's zombie wasn't among them. Subsequently, Craven was taught the art of film editing by musician Harry Chapin; he then partnered with Sean S. Cunningham to make the soft-core porn documentary *Together* (1970). The film earned a tidy profit for the Esquire Theatre chain whose parent company, Hallmark Releasing, offered Craven and Cunningham some more money to make a grisly horror picture with an accent on brutal sex and violence. Craven retreated to Long Island for several weeks to write the script, which he loosely based on Ingmar Bergman's *The Virgin Spring* (1959), although his script strayed pretty far afield from its art-house origins.

At the time, Craven was incensed by the American public's casual acceptance of the inhumanity and wanton violence of the Vietnam War.

He resolved to drop violence into movie viewers' laps by portraying humans at their lowest, most barbaric level. (No doubt his experience as a teacher of college students came in handy as preparation.)

The result, *Last House on the Left,* practically choked audiences with its scenes of gruesome bloodletting and carnage. The heroines are two carefree teenaged girls played by Sandra Cassel and Lucy Grantham. Cassel is the only child of a rich doctor and has led a fairly sheltered seventeen-year existence. Grantham, on the other hand, is from a tough urban background and wise to the ways of the world. They set out for a rock concert by a group called Bloodlust and run into two escaped felons (played by David Hess and porn director Fred Lincoln), who had been aided in their escape by Hess's bastard son (Marc Sheffler) and Hess's woman, Jeramie Rain (the former Mrs. Richard Dreyfuss), who, we are told, kicked a police dog to death during the jailbreak. A night of abuse follows, in which Grantham gets the worst of it. Then the gang packs the unconscious girls into the trunk of their car for a country drive. After some more abuse and torture, Grantham escapes and takes off into the woods. Three of the gang corner her in a rural cemetery and butcher her. Hess then rapes Cassel, who, resigned to her fate, walks into a pond and is shot down. Later, the gang holes up in the home of a doctor and his wife— Cassel's parents, as fate would have it. Mom and Pop soon learn who their visitors are and what they've done, and it's vengeance time in the *Last House on the Left.*

Along with its sleazy atmosphere and rampant violence, the film showcased Craven's flair for snappy dialogue, wacky comedy amidst the carnage, and mobile camerawork. It also revealed the director's ongoing cinematic fondness for home-style booby traps and nightmare sequences. But it's the carnage

that people remember, even though the film was considerably toned down from its very inception. During postproduction, Craven himself felt he'd gone too far and decided to drop some of the more extreme scenes of violence on the cutting room floor. The test-market prerelease prints, variously known as *Krug and Company: Equal Opportunity Destroyers* and *Sex Crime of the Century*, ran ninety-one minutes and contained much more comic patter between resident dumb cops Marshall Anker and Martin Kove. The test-market prints also boasted one scene that traumatized the entire cast and crew—in which Jeramie Rain reels out Grantham's intestine and fondles it. The film's distributor, American-International, was so aghast that it insisted the film be cut to secure an R rather than an X rating from the MPAA. Happily, a few unlaundered pre-MPAA prints escaped onto the exploitation circuit and were seen by a few people before nearly all prints were further bowdlerized by scared theater owners. As of 1992, two legal versions of *Last House* have been released domestically on video, the eighty-two-minute R-rated version and the "complete unedited" version, which

had been cobbled together from several prints by Craven and Roy Frumkes. Though this version offers a glimpse of Grantham's entrails, it falls far short of ninety-one minutes and is by no means complete.

If imitation is the sincerest form of flattery, then *Last House on the Left* has indeed been highly praised. Mario Bava's heavily censored *Twitch of the Death Nerve* was reissued as *Last House on the Left, Part II*, even though it was filmed in 1971 and had nothing to do with Craven's film. Evan Isle's *New House on the Left* (1974) featured the same basic plot as Craven's film except that the action takes place on a passenger train chugging through Germany. The most blatant rip-off to date, however, is *The Fun*

Above: Retired cop Russ Grieve is turned into barbecue by the cannibalistic desert clan as his horrified family looks on helplessly in *The Hills Have Eyes* (1977), a high point in Craven's career. (The John McCarty Collection)
At left: It's vengeance time in the *Last House on the Left* (1972), which practically choked audiences with its scenes of gruesome bloodletting and carnage. (Hollywood Book & Poster)
Facing page: *Swamp Thing* (1982), featuring Dick Durock as the leafy lover and Adrienne Barbeau as his objet d'amour, nicely retained the look and feel of its comic-book origins. (Copyright © 1981 United Artists Corp.)

House, a sleazy little number filmed by Victor Janos circa 1972 about the making of a snuff movie; it was retitled and rereleased as *Last House on Dead End Street* in 1979 with the memorable ad line "It's only a movie . . ."—a line that was coincidentally used with great success to ballyhoo the Craven film.

There were "murder movies" before *Last House,* of course, but these ranged from stylized *"giallos"* like Mario Bava's *Blood and Black Lace* to laughable, gory geek shows like *Blood Feast* and *The Undertaker and His Pals.* None had the gritty "you are there" feel of *Last House,* an aspect enhanced by the film's low ninety-thousand-dollar budget, grainy 16-mm blowup photography, and terrible shooting conditions; nor were any of them as successful as Craven's film.

Craven moved on to *The Hills Have Eyes* (1977), the zenith of his career so far. In the film, retired cop Russ Grieve and his family are stranded in the desert, where they are set upon by the local cannibal clan living in the surrounding hills. This awful brood was based on the murderous Sawney Bean tribe that slaughtered travelers in seventeenth-century Scotland before being snuffed out by King James VI and his troops. The "white bread" tourist family takes quite a beating before retaliating, but once the survivors start fighting back, there's no stopping them. Their weapons include a hatchet, a .45 automatic, and some typically devious Craven-style booby traps—one baited with their own dead. The line between civilization and barbarism disintegrates before the crimson conclusion, a finale that has the survivors—like the vengeful mom and pop in *Last House*—devastated by their own capacity for slaughter and savagery.

In all respects, *The Hills Have Eyes* is much more slickly made than *Last House*—and more fun for many viewers. While it's extremely gruesome in spots, the accent is more on scares and atmosphere than blood. Additional terror stems from the script's reversal of conventions. For example, in most normal families, it would be the killer who would be considered the black sheep. In Craven's inbred hill family, however, it is Janus Blythe's Ruby who attains this lowly status by demonstrating civilized traits and compassion for her victims. While realistic and

believable, *Hills* does lack the painful "slaughter verité" of *Last House*. Clad in bone necklaces and animal skins, the villains resemble mythical ogres rather than the thrill-killers next door of the earlier film. Nevertheless, the film was justifiably hailed as a terror classic by the Museum of Modern Art.

Craven has interspersed his work in features with several fearfilms made for television, but perhaps because of the censorship restrictions and other limits of the medium, most of Craven's TV work has been lamer than the proverbial Peg-Leg Bates. However, his 1978 *Stranger in Our House* was a better-than-average teleflick. Here, professional eyelash-batter Linda Blair comes to realize that her visiting cousin, Lee Purcell, is a sorceress.

Freddy Krueger (Robert Englund) cuts up for the camera in *A Nightmare on Elm Street* (1984), Craven's must influential film. (Copyright © 1984 New Line Cinema)

Craven's next theatrical film, *Deadly Blessing* (1981), pitted city people Maren Jensen, Susan Buckner, and Sharon Stone against another bunch of rural reprobates, but all resemblance to *The Hills Have Eyes* ends there. While *Hills* was tightly scripted and compact, *Blessing* is a loose hodgepodge of slasher and supernatural elements that never quite add up. Still, it's worth seeing for its spook-house atmosphere, unsettling undertones of religious sadism and repression, and the intense turns of Ernest Borgnine and Michael Berryman as a pair of religious fanatics—one considerably more "devout" than the other. The film

also includes one of those out-of-left-field shock epilogues that have infested fearfilms since Carrie came out of her grave. This twist was excised from British prints, however, probably to the film's advantage.

Craven's *Swamp Thing* (1982) featured the popular DC comics superhero who made his literary debut in the 1971 issue of *House of Mystery*. The sad tale of a scientist in the bayous who is transformed into a half-human/half-plant avenger, the film retained the look of its comic-book origins and translated well to the big screen, largely due to its talented, noncondescending cast, which included Louis Jourdan and Adrienne Barbeau (as one of Craven's most resourceful heroines).

Craven's long-awaited *The Hills Have Eyes, Part II* emerged in 1985. It also emerged less violent, less thrilling, less everything than its predecessor. Scarcely worth watching, the film delivered one exceptional shock scene, however, in which blind Tamara Stafford blunders along a mine shaft strewn with the dismembered corpses of her friends. What a shame the rest of the movie failed to measure up to this single scene. While certainly not the worst fearfilm ever made, *Hills, Part II* ranks right up there with *Howling II* and several other you-name-it IIs, IIIs, IVs, Vs, and VIs as one of the most needless sequels ever made. Most of the film consists of flashback footage from the original film (even the

family pooch gets his own flashback!). Filmed in 1983, it was put on the shelf until 1985. Better it had stayed on the shelf.

Craven's most influential film, *A Nightmare on Elm Street* (1984), didn't sit on the shelf, but it was literally years in the making. Craven had tried in vain to pitch the story to producers, but most turned a deaf ear on him, feeling that the tide was turning against screen horror. New Line's Robert Shaye finally agreed to produce it, however, and the script nobody wanted became one of the most successful fearfilms of the eighties.

The now-familiar tale centers on a group of teenagers who share a common nightmare in which they are stalked by a disfigured creature named Freddy Krueger, who sports razor-edged knives on his gloves. Not content to kill his victims in their sleep, the fiend even crosses over into their waking life. This results in a life-and-death battle in which reality and nightmare become indistinguishable.

The film's abundant gore is surreal rather than "in your face" real, and there are many subtle chills, as well. A dark-veiled apparition oozes from the wall over heroine Heather Langenkamp's bed; a fugitive flees up a solid staircase that suddenly turns to rubber cement. The much-discussed shock epilogue imposed upon Craven by the producers owes the obvious debt

Filmed in 1983 but not released until 1985, Craven's eagerly awaited *The Hills Have Eyes, Part II*, with Michael Berryman reprising his role as one of the deadly desert rats, should have remained on the shelf. (Hollywood Book & Poster)

to *Carrie*, but it's still a neat wrap-up to this first outing in the adventures of the venerable Freddy Krueger, who went on to storm through myriad sequels Craven had nothing to do with.

Solid characterization sets *Elm Street* apart from most other teens-in-jeopardy fearfilms of its era. Even the least of Langenkamp's friends has more depth than your average "dead teenager" movie protagonist. Stubborn cop John Saxon as Langenkamp's father and Ronee Blakley as her alcoholic mom are presented not as paper targets or generic stupid parents but as real people with real flaws. In fact, it is their anger and folly that is responsible for Krueger's nocturnal reign of terror.

Craven's next film, *Deadly Friend* (1986), was an updated version of Terence Fisher's *Frankenstein Created Woman* with teenagers. Whiz kid Matthew Laborteaux moves with his homemade robot to a university town to pursue his advanced studies. There are quite a few lowbrows in evidence, even for a college burg (must be all those football scholarships). Also on hand are Richard Marcus as an abusive, murderous father and late screen loudmouth Anne Ramsey as a misanthropic neighbor. For solace and comfort, Laborteaux falls back on the robot, affable tenth-grader Michael Sharrett, and especially love interest Kristy Swanson. However, like the brookside idyll in *Last House* and the scientist's great moment of discovery in *Swamp Thing*, these joys are fragile and fleeting. The robot is destroyed in a sadistic Halloween prank and Swanson is murdered by her unredeemably evil father. Sharrett is drawn into love-struck Laborteaux's plot to resurrect Swanson by implanting robot circuitry into her brain. ("What a pacemaker is to the heart, this unit is to the brain!" says our hero in all sincerity.) Swanson comes back, decidedly dead, and the neighborhood no-goodnicks (including Ramsey, who loses her head to a basketball) start dropping like flies in an Ortho factory.

Craven went from this misfire to one of his masterpieces, *The Serpent and the Rainbow* (1988), a supernatural thriller based on the nonfiction exploits of anthropologist Wade Davis that Craven shot almost entirely on location in Haiti and the Dominican Republic. In Craven's largely fictionalized script, Bill Pullman plays a skeptical anthropologist sent to Haiti by a large pharmaceutical company to bring back a drug allegedly used for "zombification," since they believe it could revolutionize the science of anesthesiology. Pullman searches for the drug, scoffs at "local superstition," falls in love with Cathy Tyson, and comes under the iron hand of voodoo priest Zakes Mokae, who also doubles as head of President Duvalier's dreaded secret police, the Tontons Macoute.

The Serpent and the Rainbow gets off to a slow start, but it is rife with the authentic atmosphere of the Magic Island that made Jacques Tourneur's *I Walked with a Zombie* a horror classic—even though the latter was filmed entirely on a Hollywood soundstage. Ace acting is another of the film's assets. Feisty Tyson remains one of Craven's most engaging heroines, while Mokae is one of those rare villains you truly love to hate. Venerable British horror film second stringer Michael Gough adds a solid touch of class as a Boston professor and Paul Winfield is appropriately sneaky as the proprietor of a voodoo nightclub. Pullman is especially praiseworthy as he believably metamorphoses from smug, sneering invader of Haiti's underworld to cringing victim to enlightened avenger.

Typically, Craven followed up the excellent *The Serpent and the Rainbow* with an inferior effort, *Shocker* (1989), a poor entry among the many "executed killer" thrillers released in the late 1980s.

Facing page: Typically, Craven went from a misfire, *Deadly Friend* (1986), to a masterpiece, *The Serpent and the Rainbow* (1988), a supernatural thriller starring Bill Pullman. It was filmed on location in Haiti and the Dominican Republic. (Copyright © 1987 Universal City Studios, Inc.)
Right: Big Mitch Pileggi and Janne Peters get toasted in *Shocker* (1989), one of the poorest in a spate of 1980s "executed killer" thrillers. (Copyright © 1989 Universal City Studios, Inc.)

Big Mitch Pileggi is menacing, at least in the film's first half, as hulking serial killer Horace Pinker. There's also a fair amount of tension early on, along with lip-biting gore scenes, as Pinker is brought to justice and zapped in the electric chair. Then he uses the electricity to escape the chair and flees through the power lines and TV channels to resume his reign of terror. Peter Berg, survivor of a previous Pinker massacre, pursues the cathode-ray criminal through various old game shows and sitcoms ("Gee, Wally, is Craven trying to destroy his credibility here or what?" "Gosh, it sure looks that way, Beav.") to the interminable noise/light show finale, which serves mainly to keep an army of technicians and effects artists from more worthwhile motion-picture endeavors.

Craven redeemed himself two years later with *The People Under the Stairs* (1991). Ghetto youngster Brandon Adams reluctantly accompanies two neighborhood toughs on a break-and-enter mission into their slumlord's mansion. Getting in is a challenge; getting out is nearly impossible. Once inside, the burglars find the nasty owners (*Twin Peaks'* Wendie Robie and Everett McGill) are living off the less fortunate in more ways than one. Adams forms some desperate alliances with A. J. Langer's Alice, whom Robie and McGill are disciplining into a "perfect child"; Sean Whalen's Roach, a tormented

escapee who lives in the walls of the house; and the titular prisoners in the mansion's cellar. It's up to this ragged band of victims to topple the Ron and Nancy look-alikes' evil empire.

People fuses the time-honored concept of the "wicked stepmother" concept with Craven's familiar predilections for home-style booby traps and nightmare sequences. The house itself is one big booby-trap, wired with explosives and rigged with electronic doors of solid steel. It's also one big bad dream, seemingly designed by the same deranged architect responsible for the labyrinthine yet claustrophobic cabin in Sam Raimi's *The Evil Dead.* The nightmare increases a thousandfold when McGill, clad in a steel-studded leather suit and brandishing a shotgun, blasts apart the walls of his own kingdom to murder the fugitives.

Craven's contribution to the fearfilm genre consists of a few influential films easily cashed in on and cannibalized by others—and, in the case of *The Hills Have Eyes,* by himself. *Last House* aside, he has been kinder and gentler to women in his films than most of his peers. Despite the sadism inflicted upon Cassel and Grantham in *Last House,* or possibly in atonement for it, Craven has created more dynamic, intelligent screen heroines than all his fearfilm colleagues put together. Better yet, he doesn't patronize women, as witness the unique and memorable female villains in *Deadly Blessing, The*

Hills Have Eyes and *The People Under the Stairs.*

Given the up-and-down roller-coaster nature of Craven's career, his next picture will probably be a stinker. On the other hand, this talented, albeit erratic, director may break the pattern and give us a 1990s fearfilm on a par with *The Hills Have Eyes, Swamp Thing, A Nightmare on Elm Street,* or *The Serpent and the Rainbow.*

His fans can only wait, and hope.

Filmography

1969(?): *Tales That Will Rip Your Heart Out* (codirector/actor); 1970: *Together* (assistant producer); 1971: *You've Got to Walk It Like You Talk It or You'll Lose That Beat* (editor); 1972: *It Happened in Hollywood* (editor), *Last House on the Left* (director/writer); 1977: *The Hills Have Eyes* (director/writer/editor); 1978: *Stranger in Our House,* a.k.a. *Summer of Fear* (director); 1981: *Deadly Blessing* (director/cowriter); 1982: *Swamp Thing* (director/writer); 1984: *Invitation to Hell* (director), *A Nightmare on Elm Street* (director/writer); 1985: *The Hills Have Eyes, Part II* (director/writer); 1986: *Deadly Friend* (director); 1987: *Flowers in the Attic* (writer), *A Nightmare on Elm Street 3: Dream Warriors* (executive producer/writer); 1988: *The Serpent and the Rainbow* (director); 1989: *Shocker* (executive producer/director/writer/actor); 1990: *Bloodfist II* (codirector, uncredited), *Night Visions* (director), *The People Under the Stairs* (director/writer); 1992: *Nightmare Cafe* (TV series, producer/director); 1994: Wes Craven's *Nightmare on Elm Street: The Real Story* (producer/director).

BRIAN DE PALMA

If one were to inform a critic of Brian De Palma's that the director had just been canonized by the Pope, knighted by the Queen of England, and elected President of the United States, the critic's response would inevitably be "Yes, but he's so derivative of Hitchcock!"

It seems that in spite of everything De Palma has accomplished in his career within fearfilm and outside it, his critics remain determined to ignore him because he "borrows" from other filmmakers, primarily Hitchcock. They act as if they had caught him red-handed at something De Palma believed he was "getting away with."

In his 1992 return to the fearfilm genre, *Raising Cain,* De Palma includes a scene in which the murderer attempts to dispose of the body of his wife by sinking her car in a swamp. The scene is right out of Hitchcock's *Psycho.* As in the Hitchcock film, the car sinks partway then comes to a stop while the murderer and the audience hold their breath wondering whether the car will begin sinking again. De Palma's version is different, however. The woman is not really dead. As the car resumes sinking, she regains consciousness and, in a state of panic and horror, begins pounding on the rear window of the car, crying for help in the futile hope that someone will rescue her from her watery grave. All in all, that sequence is only a small part of *Raising Cain,* but it is typically singled out by De Palma's critics as an outright steal that he got caught at and

that sums up the entire film. In fact, De Palma just seems to be having a bit of fun with the sequence—and he's fully aware that we all know where it came from.

More serious charges of plagiarism have been leveled at other De Palma films such as *Dressed to Kill* (1980) and *Body Double* (1984). The former shares with *Psycho* a transvestite murderer. Both films feature an important female character, played

Left: John Lithgow played three characters, all of them unbalanced, in De Palma's 1992 return to fearfilm, *Raising Cain.* (Copyright ©1992 Universal City Studios, Inc.)
Above: Amy Irving in the famous and much imitated shock epilogue of *Carrie* (1976). (Copyright © 1976 United Artists Corp.)

by a name actress, who is murdered surprisingly early in the story. (*Body Double* also features a lead performance from Melanie Griffith, the daughter of Hitchcock leading lady Tippi Hedren.) And both contain a lengthy and somewhat technical explanation of the killer's psychosis following his/her capture. In *Body Double,* much of the story revolves around a struggling actor, played by Craig Wasson, who amuses himself watching a beautiful female neighbor through a telescope while house-sitting. The scantily clad neighbor does a sensuous dance in her bedroom window every evening. Like Jimmy Stewart in Hitchcock's *Rear Window* (1954), Wasson gradually becomes aware that a murder plot is developing. And, as in *Vertigo* (1958), he becomes obsessed with the idea that another woman he encounters is somehow linked to the victim.

As derivative as some of these plot elements are, De Palma basically uses them as starting points, and the similarities are, in many ways, quite superficial. Many other directors derive ideas from other films and filmmakers or base their work on preexisting source material and proceed to impose their individual stamp

on the finished piece, and yet they are not considered plagiarists. Look at all the versions of *Dracula*, for example. No one accuses the makers of these films of stealing from one another, or from Bram Stoker, for that matter. With *Psycho*, Hitchcock created a similar prototype. And *Dressed to Kill* is a variation on that prototype.

De Palma's critics don't just use the plagiarism

argument to denounce him. They also point to his flashy cinematic style and constantly moving camera as sleight-of-hand (sleight-of-eye?) tricks designed to conceal the fact that he has nothing to say—in other words, that he's all form and no substance. The fact is, however, that there is usually a method to De Palma's camera madness.

Born in Philadelphia in 1941, De Palma was not bitten by the filmmaking bug until after he'd gone to college (Columbia University), and the early features that served to launch his career, *Greetings* (1968) and *Hi, Mom!* (1970), reflect the cinema verité approach to filmmaking very much favored by East Coast colleges and film schools at that time. Prior to *Greetings,* De Palma had made one feature-length Hitchcockian thriller, *Murder à la Mod* (1968), which foreshadowed the direction his work would take in the seventies and eighties. But it was with the release of *Sisters* (1973) that his fixation on the work of Alfred Hitchcock came to the fore.

Sisters was the film that put De Palma on the map with fearfilm enthusiasts, and along with his next genre film, *Phantom of the Paradise* (1974), seemed to announce the arrival of a promising new talent. It is easy to see why. *Sisters* possesses an odd quality. It has a grainy documentarylike look that enhances the credibility of some of the plot's more bizarre twists and turns. The film's images are invariably dreamlike yet are shot with a shaky handheld camera to make them seem real and to create a sense of disorientation in the viewer, not unlike the feeling one gets from having a nightmare.

The titular sisters are Siamese twins who were surgically separated at birth. One grows up to be an attractive and seemingly normal young woman (Margot Kidder); the other, a murderess. In fact, only one twin survived the operation; the resulting trauma and guilt created a split personality, and it is this that allows her to keep the other twin alive. This theme of dual identities, or two sides to the same person, would become a dominant element in most of De Palma's fearfilms from then on.

In *Phantom of the Paradise*, De Palma reworked the venerable horror classic *The Phantom of the Opera* into a rock-music setting. William Finley writes a rock opera based on Goethe's *Faust* and submits it to villainous promoter Paul Williams, who steals the music and gets Finley sent to prison on a bogus drug charge. Finley escapes and finds the recordings of his music in Williams's warehouse. In attempting to

In *Phantom of the Paradise* (1974), De Palma reworked the venerable *The Phantom of the Opera* into a rock-music setting. (Copyright © 1974 Twentieth Century-Fox Film Corp.)
Facing page: De Palma's bloody entry into the genre: *Sisters* (1973). (Copyright © 1973 American-International Pictures)

Left: With *Obsession* (1976), starring Geneviève Bujold, De Palma began to attract the notice of mainstream critics, not just the college and midnight-show crowd. (Copyright © 1976 Columbia Pictures Industries, Inc.)

Below, left: Mom from hell Piper Laurie becomes the victim of her put-upon daughter's telekinetic wrath in *Carrie* (1976), De Palma's first big success. (Copyright © 1976 United Artists Corp.)

Facing page: De Palma's *The Fury* (1978), starring Kirk Douglas, was an odd pastiche of blood-and-guts horror and parapsychology. It remains an anomaly in the director's fearfilm career. (Copyright © 1978 Twentieth Century-Fox Film Corp.)

destroy them, he gets caught in a record-pressing machine and his face is hideously disfigured. Thereafter, he dons a bizarre mask and costume and begins haunting the promoter's theater, the Paradise, to exact his revenge. Again, De Palma's fascination with the idea of dual personality is in evidence.

By the mid 1970s, De Palma had moved onto bigger-budgeted fearfests such as *Obsession* and *Carrie* (both 1976)—the former featuring relatively big-name stars (Geneviève Bujold and Cliff Robertson), the latter based on a novel by the then-up-and-coming horror superstar Stephen King. No longer the exclusive darling of the college and midnight-show crowd, he was beginning to attract the notice of mainstream critics, as well. He was also beginning to put some flesh on his characters.

In *Sisters* and *Phantom of the Paradise*, his characters were largely two-dimensional—pawns in a game of cinematic style. In *Obsession*, we begin to care about De Palma's characters as people. This is even more true of *Carrie*. As we watch Sissy Spacek's struggle to win acceptance from her high school peers and the affection of a boy (William Katt) she admires, we empathize with her completely, and this makes the tragic ending of the film all the more powerful.

The film opens with the now-famous scene of Spacek showering after gym class. A bloody discharge runs down her leg as she experiences her first period. The other girls laugh at her terrified reaction and throw tampons at her. Punished by a teacher for their lack of sensitivity, they decide to get even with the hapless teen by dumping a pail of pig's blood on her as she and Katt are crowned king and queen of the prom—an honor that has been arranged for just this purpose. As the horrified Carrie once again finds herself "bathed in blood," she unleashes her

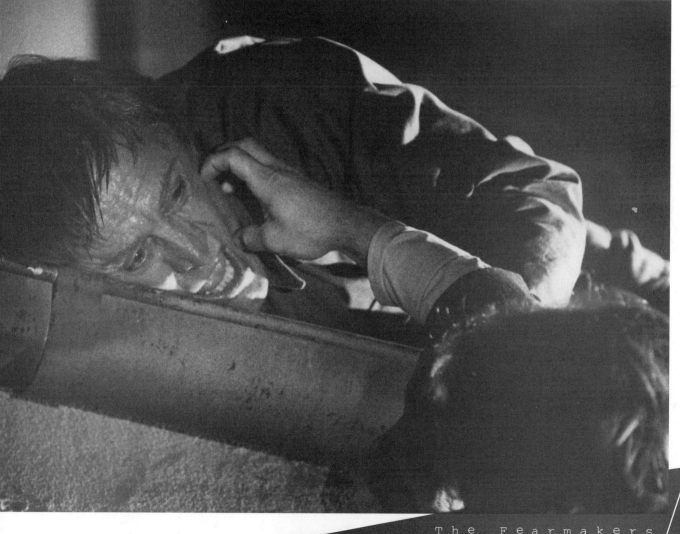

telekinetic powers to exact retribution on the entire student and faculty population. Here again, we are treated to a character possessed of a dual personality as the sweet, put-upon Carrie transforms into a monstrous avenging angel.

De Palma's next film, *The Fury* (1978), remains somewhat of an anomaly in the director's fearfilm career—an odd pastiche of blood-and-guts horror and parapsychology that has some fine moments to be sure but seems to fall completely outside De Palma's thematic interests. Perhaps the weak story line of the source novel (by John Farris, who also wrote the script), in which parapsychology already blurs the lines between reality and dream, diffused De Palma's vision. Or perhaps he just did the film for the money. In any case, with his next fearfilm, *Dressed to Kill*, he returned to form. In addition to the now-familiar dual-personality theme, the film evidences another significant De Palma theme: the idea that the lines separating our waking and dream lives are not as clear

and distinct as we might like to believe. In *Dressed to Kill*, these states become interchangeable. De Palma had hinted at this before, most notably in *Carrie*'s now-famous shock epilogue, but here he explores the idea more fully.

De Palma opens and closes *Dressed to Kill* with dream sequences. Significantly, in both sequences, we assume that what we are observing is actually happening. In fact, both scenes are actually nightmares experienced by the lead characters. De Palma catches us completely off guard with these dream sequences because the "waking" scenes in the film often have dreamlike (or nightmarelike) overtones, as well. For example, consider the scene in the subway station where the hooker heroine (Nancy Allen) is accosted by a gang of street-smart hooligans. As she runs away and they chase her, a train races by. De Palma cuts to a medium shot of Allen running as the camera stays with her. The train fills the background, moving faster than she is. But because

Movie sound-effects man John Travolta searches for the perfect scream in *Blow Out* (1981). (Copyright © 1981 Filmways Pictures Corp.)

the train is going in the opposite direction, we have the illusion that Allen, for all her effort, is moving backward as well, which is very much a dreamlike sensation. It is this dreamlike quality in some of the film's waking scenes that encourage us to accept the actual dream sequences as reality.

In *Dressed to Kill,* De Palma pushes his theme of dual personality to the limit. The psycho of the piece, Michael Caine, is a soft-spoken therapist who transforms into a razor-wielding blond murderess in his off moments. He is a classic split personality, just like Margot Kidder in *Sisters:* two distinct personalities sharing the same body—taking turns, as it were. But De Palma takes his preoccupation with duality to another level in *Dressed to Kill,* for nearly all the characters in the film assume more than one identity to achieve different objectives. For example, hooker Allen is sweet and coy to her female pimp, yet tough and authoritarian to her stockbroker. Bored housewives lustfully pursue strangers, staid

psychologists turn into raving psychos, and even teenagers are not who they appear to be.

With *Blow Out* (1981) and *Body Double,* De Palma continued his exploration of the blurred lines between reality and illusion. In both films, the main characters are involved in moviemaking; the illusion/reality juxtaposition is not between their waking and dream realities but between their film work and personal lives.

Blow Out features John Travolta as a movie sound-effects man working on a low-budget horror film. He needs a convincing scream to dub in for a murder scene. While out recording nocturnal ambient sound effects, he witnesses a car accident and records the horrifying incident on audiotape. The car careens from a bridge into the water below, presumably due to a tire blowout. Travolta rescues Nancy Allen, a passenger in the car, but the driver perishes.

Later, Travolta learns that the dead man was an influential politician and that his death was no accident. An elaborate conspiracy plot unfolds, in which Allen is targeted for death. He tries to save her but fails, coincidentally recording her final scream as she is killed. In what may be one of the most cynical endings in all cinema, Travolta uses the sound for the scream effect he'd been seeking. In other words, he incorporates his personal tragedy into his professional work; as a result, the lines between the two become blurred.

Craig Wasson in *Body Double* faces a much different personal and professional problem. He's been assigned to play the part of a vampire in a low-budget horror film, but the overpowering sense of claustrophobia he experiences while reposing in the vampire's coffin causes him to freeze up and prevents him from going through with the scene. As a complicated plot involving murder and mayhem unfolds, he is forced to overcome his fear of enclosed spaces; when he successfully does this, he is able to resume his vampire role and complete the scene with his phobia in check.

De Palma reinforces this theme throughout. For example, the film begins with a shot of a landscape that we assume is real. But it turns out to be a painted backdrop for the vampire movie that's being shot. The film's title, which refers to the practice of substituting a secondary performer for the lead performer in shots (such as nude scenes) the lead balks at doing, reinforces not only the blurred reality theme but De Palma's ongoing preoccupation with dual identity. Ultimately, De Palma seems to be saying, We are as consistent as the world around us—and he shows us repeatedly that

both we and our reality are illusory and terrifying.

In addition to being thematically consistent, De Palma is consistent in his ability to create exciting images—images that provide us with a visceral thrill. He is a director firmly in command of his medium. Consider the climactic scene in *Blow Out* of Travolta racing through the parade-filled streets to save Allen's life. De Palma uses a breathtaking array of intercut shots to build a ferocious visual and visceral momentum. His bird's-eye-view shots of the streets from above are particularly dazzling.

Recall as well the bravura museum sequence in *Dressed to Kill.* For more than fifteen minutes, we are treated to what is essentially a silent movie as the camera glides about the rooms and hallways of the museum while bored middle-class housewife Angie Dickinson ardently pursues the man, literally, of her dreams—her romantic fantasy come true.

Brian De Palma on the set of *Blow Out* (1981) with costars John Travolta and Nancy Allen. (Copyright © 1981 Filmways Pictures Corp.)

These are just a few of the many scenes in De Palma's body of work that illustrate he is possessed of genuine technical skill as a moviemaker. In addition to his thematic concerns, there is an energy and visual imagination to his work that's very different from the work of Hitchcock and other directors he is accused of imitating so slavishly.

Filmography
1960: *Icarus** (director/writer/photographer/ editor); 1961: *660124, The Story of an IBM Card** (director/writer/photographer/editor); 1962: *Wotan's Wake** (director); 1968: *Murder à la Mod* (director/writer/editor), *Greetings* (director/cowriter/editor); 1969: *The Wedding Party* (coproducer/codirector/cowriter/editor); 1970: *Dionysus in '69* (codirector/cophotographer/coeditor); *Hi, Mom!* a.k.a. *Blue Manhattan* and *Confessions of a Peeping John* (director/cowriter); 1972: *Get to Know Your Rabbit* (director); 1973: *Sisters* (director/ cowriter); 1974: *Phantom of the Paradise* (director/cowriter); 1976: *Obsession* (director/cowriter, uncredited), *Carrie* (director); 1978: *The Fury* (director); 1979: *Home Movies* (coproducer/codirector); 1980: *Dressed to Kill* (director/writer); 1981: *Blow Out* (director/writer); 1983: *Scarface* (director); 1984: *Body Double* (producer/director/cowriter); 1986: *Wise Guys* (director); 1987: *The Untouchables* (director); 1988: *The Great O'Grady* (actor); 1989: *Casualties of War* (director); 1990: *Bonfire of the Vanities* (producer/director/actor); 1992: *Raising Cain* (director/writer); 1993: *Carlito's Way* (director).
    *short film

Hooper's bizarre gang of backwoods rednecks
and cannibals/killers in the groundbreaking
The Texas Chainsaw Massacre (1974).
(Copyright © 1980 New Line Cinema)

TOBE HOOPER

At one time one of the most promising—and influential—of all contemporary fearmakers, Tobe Hooper has experienced a career slip in recent years even greater than John Carpenter's. His last theatrical feature as of this writing, *Spontaneous Combustion* (1990), was denied a theatrical release and went straight to video. Since then, Hooper has turned more and more to directing for television, a medium whose relatively timid standards of what can and cannot be shown (even on cable) are not at all compatible with Hooper's fearmaking talents when they are working at full throttle.

Unlike that of John Carpenter, Tobe Hooper's floundering career stems not from his inability to find a distinctive artistic voice for himself, but from his inability to find a continuing outlet for an artistic voice that is already quite distinctive. At bottom, Hooper is, like George A. Romero, a regional filmmaker. Romero has chosen to make most of his films in his native Pittsburgh to avoid major studio control over them, and he doesn't place specific emphasis on their regional settings. Hooper's best films, however, are inexorably linked to the specific geographic region in which they are set—the nightmarish (in Hooper's view) backwater of the rural South, where he grew up and where he made the groundbreaking *The Texas Chainsaw Massacre* (1974).

Whenever Hooper has strayed too far from this milieu in his work, his films have tended to lose their individuality and their edge, because the rubes and rednecks, bubbas, and gun- or chainsaw-toting backwoods bad guys who people Hooper's particular brand of regional cinema are not incidental to that cinema; they are intrinsic to it. Hooper knows of which he speaks, and even his most bizarre and extreme evocations of this landscape are not much exaggerated.

The Texas-born (in 1943) Hooper was captivated by the showbiz world of illusion and shock at a young age and began performing magic tricks onstage before paying audiences while still a child. He gravitated toward filmmaking in his teens and started making his first horror films in 8 mm during high school. After graduation, he got a job making documentaries for a local TV station, while turning out experimental

Tobe Hooper (left) and cinematographer Daniel Pearl somewhere in the wilds of Texas shooting *The Texas Chainsaw Massacre* (1974). (Courtesy Edwin Neal)

short films of his own during
his spare time. He made his first feature, *Eggshells,* in
1969, but it received scant distribution, a fate that did
not befall his second venture into feature filmmaking,
the notorious *The Texas Chainsaw Massacre.* Funded
by a slew of investors, the film was an enormous
success, earning an estimated $3 million back on its
shoestring budget of less than $250,000—although
legal shenanigans on the part of the film's investors
kept most of the profits out of the pockets of Hooper
and everyone else who'd sweated blood over a long
series of nerve-fraying weeks to get the film in the
can.

Hooper and his writing partner, Kim Henkel,
had loosely based the film on the same case that
inspired Hitchcock's *Psycho,* the twisted tale of
Wisconsin killer/cannibal Ed Gein. Hooper even
provides an opening title card stating that the movie is
based on an actual case, and he includes the names of
several victims. The names are fictitious, however, for,
like *Psycho,* the film bears very little resemblance to
the Gein case—except for its charnel-house
atmosphere, ghoulish farmhouse setting littered with
bones and mummified flesh, and the cannibalism of
its killers, here multiplied to three (or four, if you
count the meat-loving clan's aging, skeletal patriarch,
who is too weak to kill any longer but still has a yen
for it).

Into this stew of depravity, wherein a group of
young vacationers runs up against the brutal
meat-loving clan of backwoods degenerates with dire
results, Hooper and Henkel stirred a considerable
amount of ghoulish black humor of the kind found in
the notorious EC horror comics published by William
M. Gaines in the 1950s, a seminal influence not only
on Hooper but on George Romero and most other
fearmakers of their generation. The result was a totally
mad movie—a glimpse into a rural chamber of horrors
and sickness that makes Hitchcock's Bates motel and
its overlooking Victorian mansion seem tame and
healthy by comparison. It is a film that continues to
deliver in the shock department to this day, despite
scores of bloodier and more sensational imitations that
have followed in its wake.

Critics lambasted *Chainsaw* for its graphic
violence, when, in fact, the filmmakers had learned
quite a bit from Hitchcock by not showing too much of
it. Beginning with the opening title card and ominous
narration (by John Larroquette), a ruse aimed at
implanting fear in the minds of viewers right from the
start, the film actually contains relatively little graphic
gore. Only once do we see the titular mechanism
touch flesh—and very briefly at that—when the
apelike Leatherface (Gunner Hansen) falls in the road
while chasing the heroine (Marilyn Burns) and
accidentally cuts himself. The film certainly contains

THE FUNHOUSE

The inimitable William Finley strikes home in *The Funhouse* (1981), Hooper's first major studio fearfilm. (Copyright © 1981 Universal City Studios, Inc.) Not as grisly or off-the-wall as his previous films, *The Funhouse* (1981) nevertheless boasted a raw-edged atmosphere of seediness and derangement that marked it as Hooper's work. (Copyright ©1981 Universal City Studios, Inc.)

its share of mayhem, but its most extreme violence remains imagined on the part of the audience. Hooper lets the film's title and the whirring sound of the chain saw do the work for him.

In the 1980s, the Museum of Modern Art raised eyebrows by granting *Chainsaw* lasting respectability as a genre classic, installing it, along with Romero's *Night of the Living Dead,* in its permanent collection. This may be a last for Hooper, since his post-*Chainsaw* work has been quite spotty. But there have been a few high points along the way—and one bull's-eye scored—whenever Hooper, the only member of the *Chainsaw* cast and crew who was propelled to a Hollywood career by the film, has seen fit to return to his roots.

Hooper moved to Hollywood to make his next film, *Eaten Alive* (1976), another tale of rural rancidity in the vein of *Chainsaw* that likewise mixed outrageous horror with bizarre black comedy in the EC horror comics tradition. The story of a

THE FUNHOUSE

scythe-wielding motel owner who feeds his employees, guests, and an errant pet puppy to a giant gator that serves as one of several other roadside attractions, the film was shot entirely on a Hollywood soundstage, and it makes very effective use of stylized sets and lighting to create an overpowering atmosphere of mental and physical decay.

As bizarre as the events in the film are, they are not without a basis in reality, for the plot is suggestive of a 1937 mass murder case that occurred in Texas and about which Hooper and his coscreenwriters (including fellow Texan Kim Henkel) were surely aware. The case involved a backslappin' good ole boy named Joe Ball, the proprietor of a honky-tonk on the back roads of San Antonio named the Sociable Inn, where Ball made use of gators kept in the swamp out back to dispose of several waitresses in his employ when they aroused his jealousy by getting too chummy with the customers. Eventually, Ball was caught and sent to the slammer, to the shocked surprise of everyone in the area, for none of the residents believed Ball, of all people, capable of such monstrous acts. He was, after all, a World War I Medal of Honor winner—and onetime heroes don't do such things, do they? The irony of this was not lost on Hooper, who perversely cast Neville Brand, the most decorated hero of World War II after Audie Murphy, as the Ball figure in *Eaten Alive.*

Hooper's third feature failed to attain the notoriety and success of *Chainsaw,* however, due to its

limited release. It thereafter fell into a black hole with regard to rights and distribution, reemerging over the years under several different titles, including its original one, which is also shared by several Italian-made cannibal flicks. The alternate titles are *Starlight Slaughter, Horror Hotel Massacre,* and *Death Trap.* Imperfect though it is, it remains a potent second act in Hooper's unofficial "Gonzo With the Wind" southern gothic trilogy, which would conclude in 1986 with *The Texas Chainsaw Massacre 2.* It is essential fearfilm viewing for that reason alone.

After *Eaten Alive* disappeared from theater screens, Hooper found himself without a ready market for his violent essays in southern-fried madness and regrouped by taking on his first mainstream assignment, a TV miniseries based on Stephen King's overstuffed vampire novel: *Salem's Lot* (1979). A ratings winner, the telefilm landed Hooper the opportunity to direct his first fearfilm for a major Hollywood studio, Universal. The result was *The Funhouse* (1981), the tale of a group of teenagers who

test their mettle by staying after hours at a very dark carnival where they encounter the murderous mutant offspring of the carnival's sinister owner (Kevin Conway) and must fight to the dawn for their survival.

Plagued by incessant production and special-effects problems during the shoot, Hooper found his job on the block when the film began to go over budget, but he managed to keep the studio wolves at bay and complete the film as he envisioned it. Despite an uneven script, continually rewritten as production rolled, the film that emerged was a potent follow-up to *Chainsaw* and *Eaten Alive*, with stylistic ties to both of them. While not as grisly or totally off-the-wall as its two low-budget forebears, *The Funhouse* offers a similarly twisted take on down-home family values and boasts a raw-edged atmosphere of seediness and derangement that clearly mark it as the work of the same director. And the final sequence, in which the monster is finally trapped and killed by the surviving chill-seekers, remains one of the most intense in Hooper's oeuvre.

A box office success, *The Funhouse* revived Hooper's cinematic fortunes considerably—but only briefly. Granted an even larger budget and a prestigious cast that included Nicol Williamson, Oliver Reed, Sterling Hayden, and others, he moved to England to make his next fearfilm, *Venom* (1982), a far-fetched thriller about some international terrorists who take several people hostage in a London town house, only to find that a deadly snake has been trapped inside the besieged building with them. Recent history repeated itself, however, when the film ran into production problems and cost overruns. But this time, Hooper failed to weather the storm; he was replaced after a few weeks of shooting by British director Piers Haggard.

Out of work and back in California, Hooper got a call from Steven Spielberg, a big fan of *Chainsaw,* who came to Hooper's rescue with an offer the struggling director couldn't refuse. Busy making his gentle-alien fantasy, *E.T.,* Spielberg asked Hooper to direct a second script the mogul had in the hopper: *Poltergeist*

Facing page: A megabudget major hit about unquiet spirits from the other side. *Poltergeist* (1982) should have sent Hooper's stock soaring, but it didn't. (Copyright © 1982 MGM and Amblin Entertainment) Left: Stolid Scotland Yard inspector Peter Firth proves utterly useless against the space vampires as they reduce London to near rubble in *Lifeforce* (1985). (The John McCarty Collection)

(1982), a megabudget special-effects extravaganza about unquiet spirits from the other side who terrorize a suburban family whose home has been erected over a sacred Indian burial ground by some greedy real estate developers.

A monster box-office hit, *Poltergeist* demonstrated that Hooper could deliver a mainstream Hollywood-style horror film with a PG rating instead of an R, and it should have sent his stock in Tinseltown soaring. But throughout the production, rumors circulated that Spielberg had found disfavor

with Hooper's work and directed the film himself. Hooper denied that Spielberg had usurped control of the film (as did Spielberg himself) and he steadfastly maintained that *Poltergeist* was entirely his own work. But there's no doubt that with its overemphasis on technical razzle-dazzle, suburban California rather than rural South atmosphere, and repeated shots of characters being awed rather than sawed, *Poltergeist* looks and sounds much more like a Steven Spielberg film than a Tobe Hooper one.

Perhaps in an effort to put the controversy to rest

once and for all by demonstrating that he could deliver a big-budget FX-oriented fantasy film like *Poltergeist* without the guiding hand of a Steven Spielberg, Hooper moved completely away from the outrageous, horrific, and blackly humorous rural thrillers with a raw edge that had established his reputation and went into the science-fiction business.

The first of his two back-to-back SF films after *Poltergeist* was *Lifeforce* (1985), a loose

out of people. Soon all of London is in danger, but there's no Professor Quatermass to help them out of the extraterrestrial jam this time around—just Peter Firth's stolid Scotland Yard inspector, who proves entirely useless as John Dykstra's special effects reduce the city to near rubble.

Bereft of the fascinating speculations into the origins of the vampire myth contained in Wilson's novel, *Lifeforce* is enlivened only by its excellent special effects and frequent exploitative shots of Ms. May walking around in her birthday suit. The film lacks the excitement, sense of menace and even the intellectual verve of such low-budget British SF opuses of the fifties as Hammer's Quatermass series and *X the Unknown* (1957), to which it attempts to pay homage.

The same is true of Hooper's next SF extravaganza, *Invaders from Mars* (1986), an elaborate remake and update of one of the most fondly remembered and seminal fearfilms of

adaptation of Colin Wilson's novel *The Space Vampires*, made in England for Cannon Films. Dan O'Bannon and Don Jakoby wrote the screenplay, which deals with an astronaut (Steve Railsback) who discovers an alien life-form in the tail of Halley's comet and brings it back to earth. Turns out the alien (Mathilda May) is actually a vampire with a fondness for walking around in the buff and sucking not only the blood but the life

Facing page: Louise Fletcher attempts to stop Hunter Carson from fleeing the Mr. Potato Head Martians in Hooper's expensive remake/update of *Invaders from Mars* (1986). (Copyright © 1986 Cannon Films, Inc.)
Above: James Karen, Christopher Allport, Karen Black, and Hunter Carson try to figure out some Martian technology in the ill-conceived *Invaders from Mars* (1986). (Copyright © 1986 Cannon Films, Inc.)

the baby-boomer generation. Ill-conceived from beginning to end, Hooper's version of the 1953 William Cameron Menzies classic about a little boy who witnesses from his bedroom window the landing of an alien spacecraft and finds his parents, friends, and teachers taken over by the alien invaders soon after—until he wakes up and realizes it's all been a nightmare—completely lacks the superbly realized perspective of being viewed through a child's eyes that made the Menzies film so chilling when it came out and so enduring to us today.

Poorly reviewed and poorly attended, *Lifeforce* and *Invaders from Mars* did little to help Hooper emerge from the shadow of the Spielberg/*Poltergeist* controversy. Lacking the confrontational power of his early works, they could easily have been made by any one of a dozen directors just as effectively—or ineffectively as the case may be. Perhaps sensing this, too, and feeling his career slipping away from him, Hooper finally decided to go back once more to his roots with his next, and best, film, *The Texas Chainsaw Massacre 2* (1986).

In fact, Hooper had been toying with the idea of a *Chainsaw* sequel for years, but the rights to the first film were mired in litigation for many years. For assistance on the screenplay, Hooper turned to maverick screenwriter and fellow Texan L. M. Kit Carson, whose wife, Karen Black, and son, Hunter Carson, had starred in Hooper's *Invaders from Mars*. Carson proved to be an excellent choice as a collaborator. Subversive, funny, horrific to the extreme, and laced with satiric poison, Carson's unique script for *Chainsaw 2* remains one of the few modern horror-film screenplays deserving of publication.

The film picks up the story of the cannibal clan several years later, after the boys have closed up their backwater barbecue stand and headed for the big city, where they've turned their special recipe for barbecue and chili into a rolling success. Now they pick off their "secret ingredients" on remote bridges and other isolated spots where they can be easily snared. The walls come crashing in, however, when Dennis Hopper, the vengeance-seeking Texas Ranger relative of the character played by Marilyn Burns in the first film, tracks the slicers to their lair with the help of a female disc jockey and sets out to give them a taste of their own recipe for success.

With a sense of outrage rare in American films (particularly horror films) of the era, *Chainsaw 2* takes on the American landscape—particularly the landscape of the rural South—of the Reagan era in which it was made. From its opening scene of two bored rednecks pumping bullets into passing road signs from their speeding car (an all-American pastime, it seems) to its nightmarish finale in an abandoned survivalist fun camp called the Texas Battlefield Amusement Park ("It's what everyone wants! *NamLand!*" proclaims Chop-Top, the entrepenurial vet with a plate in his head who hopes to resurrect the place), *Chainsaw 2* is a truly frightening chronicle of the American dream gone sour.

Cultism, greed, America's gun culture, sexual repression, and the era's obsession with the past—as reflected in Jim Siedow's character, the leader of the meat-loving clan, who is determined to hold the family together and cling to the "older, better" ways—are just some of the targets of the filmmakers' wrath. Considerably more up front in its excesses than its predecessor had been, *Chainsaw 2* even takes on its predecessor—and, implicitly, the thirty-year movement toward more splatter in the horror film and other genres—by going so far over the top that even hardcore fans of ultraviolent movies were taken aback

and compelled to reassess their attitudes toward such fare. Perhaps not liking the message, they shot the messenger, for *Chainsaw 2* was not the success the first film was, even though it's a much richer film and Hooper's masterpiece to date.

A conventional sequel, *Leatherface: The Texas Chainsaw Massacre III* (1990), whose mechanical horrors and plot ignored all that had gone before in *Chainsaw 2*, followed three years later. For whatever reason, Hooper had nothing to do with it, and his modest output since—some episodes of the short-lived TV series *Freddy's Nightmares*, a spin-off of the *Nightmare on Elm Street* films, the regrettable SF opus *Spontaneous Combustion*, and an episode of the *John Carpenter's Body Bags* anthology for HBO— have been of little note.

Filmography
1965: *The Heiress** (director/writer/editor); 1966: *Down Friday Street** (director/writer/editor); 1967: *A Way of Learning** (director/writer/editor); 1969: *Eggshells* (director/producer/writer); 1970: T*he Heisters** (director/writer/editor); 1971: *The Windsplitter* (actor); 1974: *The Texas Chainsaw Massacre* (director/coproducer/cowriter); 1976: *Eaten Alive*, a.k.a. *Death Trap, Horror Hotel Massacre,* and *Starlight Slaughters* (director/cowriter); 1979: *Salem's Lot* (director); 1981: *The Funhouse* (director/cowriter, uncredited); 1982: *Poltergeist* (director); 1985: *Lifeforce* (director); 1986: *Invaders from Mars* (director), *The Texas Chainsaw Massacre 2* (director/producer); 1990: *Spontaneous Combustion* (director/cowriter).

*short film

Then came *Halloween* (1978) with newcomer Jamie Lee Curtis, the film that catapulted Carpenter to fame and spawned a tidal wave of "mad slasher" flicks. (Copyright © 1978 Compass International Pictures)

At right: Ugly right-wing aliens take over the earth in Carpenter's wanting mixture of political allegory and wrestling, *They Live* (1988). (Copyright © 1988 Universal City Studios, Inc.)

JOHN CARPENTER

John Carpenter's career as a premier fearmaker got off with a bang: His influential *Halloween* (1978) was one of the most financially successful films ever made outside of the Hollywood studio system, and it launched the controversial cycle of "mad slasher" movies that dominates the horror and fearfilm scene even into the nineties.

After *Halloween,* Carpenter seemed to be on a roll. But with the failure of *The Thing* (1982), his problematic but compelling big-budget remake of the 1951 classic, Carpenter's career has slipped into the doldrums. Like so many other younger generation fearmakers, he has fallen into the trap of turning out FX-oriented drivel for big studios in need of product. His latest theatrical

film as of this writing, *Memoirs of an Invisible Man* (1992), is a good case in point. The film is based on the H. F. Saint novel of the same name, a novel with a serious political subtext about being rendered invisible by the Reagan/Bush era—a theme Carpenter's film version shies away from. A comic take on the classic James Whale/Claude Rains tale of invisibility, the film appears to have been made solely to address a technical challenge Whale and his FX crew of the thirties found impossible to bring off, opting instead to skirt around it—namely, showing what happens to food when it is digested in an invisible man's stomach. Granted his biggest budget in years and backed by state-of-the-art FX, Carpenter and his crew ingeniously (and amusingly) show us what happens—over and over again. But so what? Audiences apparently found themselves asking the same question, and the film, a commercial disaster, disappeared from theaters in a single week.

The son of a music teacher (who occasionally played back-up for Roy Orbison, Brenda Lee, and other professionals), Carpenter initially thought of pursuing a career in music himself, but he changed direction due to his even stronger love of movies—though he has kept his hand in by composing the minimalist but often effective scores to many of his own films. A film-school graduate (USC), he is a bona fide member of the movie brat generation; he grew up on movies and feasted especially on the monster and SF movies of the 1950s. He still calls seeing Jack Arnold's *It Came from Outer Space* one of the formative experiences of his life.

Like most of his fellow film-school-grad movie brats, Carpenter makes movies mainly about the movies he loved most or was most influenced by while he was growing up. His debut feature, *Dark Star* (1974), which he began in college with fellow classmate Dan O'Bannon and later expanded for theatrical release with the help of *Blob* producer Jack H. Harris, rollickingly lifted from and satirized a slew of Carpenter's favorite SF movies and rocket operas, ranging from *Buck Rogers* serials to *Dr. Strangelove* and *2001: A Space Odyssey*, with a few auspicious dollops of effectively handled suspense tossed in for good measure. While no

doubt reflecting his own beliefs, even the antitotalitarian, anti-right-wing-conservative political commentary that occasionally emerges in his work is drawn from other films, as well—notably Hammer Films' distinguished Quatermass series by Nigel Kneale and Don Siegel's *Invasion of the Body Snatchers*. Unlike some of his movie-brat colleagues of similar bent, however, Carpenter makes no secret of his sources of inspiration. Instead of putting his own name on the Nigel Kneale-inspired screenplay of his 1987 film *Prince of Darkness*, Carpenter adopted the pseudonym Martin Quatermass. And he candidly refers to his 1988 film *They Live* as his version of *Invasion of the Body Snatchers* for the Reagan era.

Carpenter followed *Dark Star* with his first outright fearfilm, the independently financed *Assault on Precinct 13* (1976). It remains one of his best thrillers and certainly his most prescient, in light of such recent events as the terrifying 1992 burning of South Central Los Angeles following the Rodney King verdict. *Assault* is set in the same gang-infested, burned-out, bombed-out, despair-ridden location.

Assault is essentially a reworking of Howard Hawks's *Rio Bravo* (again, Carpenter makes no attempt to conceal this; in fact, he shares screen credit as the film's coeditor under the name John T. Chance, the character played by John Wayne in the Hawks film) and George A. Romero's *Night of the Living Dead* (1968). It tells the story of a disparate group of people—a young cop (Austin Stoker) and his policewoman partner (Laurie Zimmer), several soon-to-be-transferred prisoners, including the acerbic Darwin Joston, and assorted other types—who are trapped in an abandoned police station and are besieged by some vengeful gang members. The performances range from the mediocre to the dreadful and the characterizations are paper-thin, but the film's a grabber that sustains suspense from start to finish, and at times, it is shockingly unpredictable—such as the scene where an innocent bystander, a little girl eating an ice cream cone, is randomly and brutally gunned down in a drive-by shooting by one of the gang members.

Carpenter segued from the nail-bitingly effective *Assault on Precinct 13* to the even better TV movie *Someone's Watching Me* (1978), which he both wrote and directed. Unfortunately, it, too, suffers from thinly drawn characters and several mediocre performances, especially that of leading lady Lauren Hutton.

Hutton moves to the big city to escape a love affair gone sour. She settles into the high-rise (the film's original title) apartment of her dreams, a multiwindowed affair that allows her a clear view of everyone in the surrounding complexes—and them an equally clear view of her. One of the residents, a malevolent Peeping Tom with a telescope and a tape recorder, bugs her apartment and launches a campaign of terror to drive her to a breakdown. Used to being hassled by men, Hutton refuses to be intimidated, however, gets a telescope of her own, and bravely launches a counterattack.

As is obvious, Carpenter's script borrows heavily from Hitchcock's classic *Rear Window*, but in one scene the director effectively manages to upstage even the master. After discovering that her nemesis is watching her from the apartment virtually across the way, Hutton stations a friend (Adrienne Barbeau) at the telescope and, equipped with a walkie-talkie so the two can communicate, ventures into the peeper's apartment. After milking Hutton's Grace Kelly-like tour of the apartment for as much suspense as possible, Carpenter has her look through the peeper's telescope into her own place. To her (and our) shock, she sees Barbeau being assaulted by the phantom peeper, but unlike James Stewart in the Hitchcock film, she is unable to do anything about it. This reversal of our expectations comes as a surprise Sunday punch that effectively knocks us for a loop.

Then came *Halloween* (which Carpenter had actually made before *Someone's Watching Me*), the film that catapulted the director to fame among fearfilm fans and spawned a bloody tidal wave of similar "mad slasher" flicks that has not yet subsided and that still has critics gnashing their teeth over the phenomenon and gleefully sharpening their knives to eviscerate every such film that comes along. It is ironic that Carpenter's film, which led the pack and contains virtually all the controversial elements critics of such films find so dismaying—the linking of promiscuous sex with violent retribution, the puritanical message that "good" girls don't die but "loose" ones deserve to, and so on—escaped the critics' wrath. Even Siskel and Ebert, the premier detractors of such films, felt *Halloween* to be a skillfully made thrill show and a class act with "genre classic" written all over it.

of Curtis's virginal Little Red Riding Hood. In short, *Halloween*'s trendy blood and gore and visceral shocks are modern, but its core and structure are as old as Grimm's fairy tales.

Carpenter puts it another way. He calls *Halloween* "an old country fair haunted house movie" in which all the scares are skillfully "programmed." Indeed they are. *Halloween* has racked up an impressive profit worldwide (approximately 150 times its production cost) and has since spawned four sequels, none of which Carpenter directed. Deciding not to repeat himself, at least not overtly, he opted to move on to his next project, *The Fog* (1980), a film that replaced *Assault on Precinct 13*'s police station under siege and *Halloween*'s "country fair haunted house" with a haunted coastal community set upon by a ghost ship whose crew was murdered a hundred years ago for the gold on board. Now they have returned, looking very much like a collection of Romero's zombies, to seek vengeance on the descendants of those who perpetrated the deed.

The Fog is not without high points. The scene in which the zombies slither across the roof of an isolated radio station to get at gal deejay Adrienne Barbeau is creepy indeed. But too many of the scares are telegraphed. The characterizations are again paper-thin. And cowriter Carpenter, who consistently seems unable to find a way to conclude his films satisfactorily, opts for a *Carrie*sque shock epilogue that sinks what is otherwise an effective, if mundane, ghost tale.

Following *Escape from New York* (1981), a violent comic-strip adventure about a futuristic Manhattan turned into a maximum security prison, Carpenter made his first film for a major studio and the film that remains his best to date (though it, too, is plagued by some major deficiencies): his remake of *The Thing* (1982).

In fact, Carpenter's *The Thing* is not an outright remake of the esteemed elder horror/SF classic at all. And although Carpenter had numbered the 1951 film among his favorites and wanted to do a remake, he was not the producers' first choice. Kim Henkel and Tobe

The cleverest element of *Halloween,* which may account for its success, is that it has things both ways. Like *Psycho*, it broke ground by giving fear seekers no longer frightened by the antediluvian antics of the Frankenstein Monster and Dracula a different and more terrifying monster to rock them back in their theater seats. But Hitchcock's maniac on the loose, Norman Bates, was a contemporaneous monster inspired by a real-life psychopath. Carpenter's masked, unkillable slaughterer of baby-sitters, Michael Myers, was a combination of producer Howard Hawks's deadly, thinking vegetable in *The Thing* (at one point in *Halloween*, the heroine, Jamie Lee Curtis, and her soon-to-be-terrified charges glimpse a scene from the Hawks film on television) and an updated version of the Big Bad Wolf in pursuit

Hooper, the auteurs behind *The Texas Chainsaw Massacre*, were assigned to the project before him. But when their script failed to meet with the studio's approval, Carpenter and writer Bill Lancaster (Burt's son) were given the task instead. They accomplished the job by going back to basics—the original John W. Campbell, Jr., novella upon which producer Howard Hawks's film was loosely (*very loosely*) based.

Campbell's paranoid tale of a deadly alien life-form that has the ability to absorb other life-forms and replicate them completely was a perfect metaphor for the postwar political witch-hunt mentality of the late forties and early fifties. Ironically, Campbell concocted and published the tale (under his pseudonym Don A. Stuart) in 1938, long before America's witch-hunting began, and his inspiration

was not political, but personal—a traumatic experience rooted in his early childhood. It seems that Campbell's doting mother had an identical twin sister who was always rather critical of the boy and terribly cold toward him, as well. Since he couldn't tell the two women apart whenever the sister visited, he never knew what to expect when he encountered one or the other of them, affection or coldness. And it was this unsettling experience that led to his writing the story—which he aptly titled *Who Goes There?*

The original film jettisoned the identity-questioning subtext of the story, which had gained so much political relevance at the time, and refashioned his ferocious Thing into a creature that survives on blood and has the protective ability to heal or reconstitute itself if wounded or maimed.

Harry Dean Stanton and Kurt Russell take on roving gangs of convicts inside the massive walled-in prison that is New York in 1997 in Carpenter's *Escape from New York* (1981). (Copyright ©1981 Avco-Embassy Pictures)

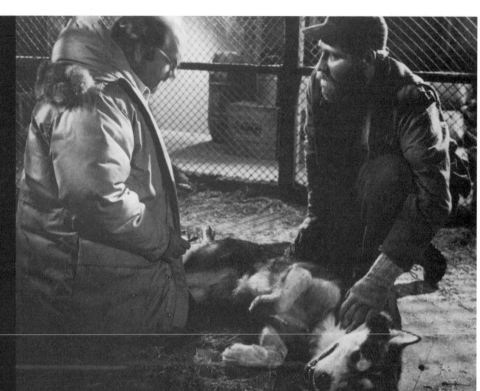

Scientists Wilford Brimley and Richard Masur examine one of the early victims of the Thing—from *The Thing* (1982). (Copyright ©1982 Universal City Studios, Inc.)
Below: Unlike the 1951 Howard Hawks film, Carpenter's problematic but compelling version of *The Thing* (1982) lost sight of the human side in favor of horrific FX such as this. (Copyright © 1982 Universal City Studios, Inc.)

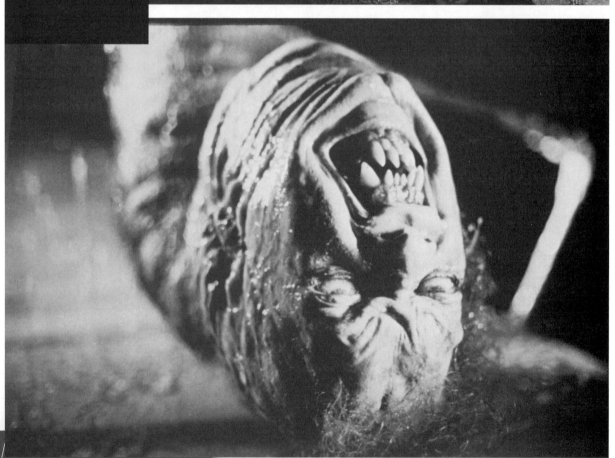

Concentrating instead on the Thing's seeming unstoppability and fleet-footedness ("Where is it?" rather than "Who goes there?") and the individual reactions of a diverse group of Arctic research scientists and military types confronted by the Thing in a remote outpost surrounded by snow and ice, Hawks created one of the most claustrophobic tales of terror and viscerally effective fright films ever made.

As its opening credit makes clear, the remake is John Carpenter's *The Thing*, not Hawks's film re-created. It is a much more faithful rendering of Campbell's story, bolstered by some of the most amazing special effects ever put on the screen (courtesy of FX coordinator Rob Bottin). The film contains some remarkable sequences: the breathtaking opening shot where the Norwegian survivors of an earlier battle with the Thing attempt to shoot down a husky (the Thing in disguise) as it runs to another research station for safety and to seek new victims; the husky/Thing's horrific initial transformation as it tries to absorb the life-forms of the other dogs with which it has been caged; the grisly investigation of the decimated Norwegian research station where the Thing was thawed out and first got loose; Kurt Russell's testing of his colleagues' blood samples with a hot wire to find out who's still human and who isn't (a tense scene taken straight from Campbell's novella).

But Carpenter's version is severely flawed, as well. The film loses total sight of the human side of the story in favor of horrific FX, with the result that it is more shocking than suspenseful or frightening. And after a while, even the impact of the shock effects wears off. There are so many of them, we grow numb. In addition, Carpenter's characterizations are again much too shallow to foster much sense of identification. Worse still,

the characters are not only unlikable (even Kurt Russell, the ostensible hero) but, unlike Hawks's well-drawn and believable team of scientists and military types, wholly uncredible. Who in their right mind, we keep asking ourselves, would give such a bunch of foul-mouthed, ill-tempered, gun-happy, stoned-out, squabbling fools the responsible job of running a sophisticated scientific research station?

Once again, Carpenter also fails to bring his story to a well-rounded conclusion. After beginning with a bang, his film regrettably concludes with a whimper. Unlike Campbell's story and Hawks's film, Carpenter's *The Thing*, having nowhere else to go at the conclusion, just simply *ends*. Perhaps Carpenter's strategy was to leave the door open for a sequel. But this is not likely to happen, since the film was a box-office flop. Its flat ending coupled with the director's reliance on high-tech special effects at the expense of virtually everything else killed the film with the critics and even many of Carpenter's most ardent supporters, who desperately believed it would be his genre masterwork.

In view of Carpenter's increasingly dismal contributions to fearfilm since *The Thing*, this unfortunately has so far proven to be the case.

Alexandra Paul looks on in bewilderment as Keith Gordon seethes over the destruction wrought upon his pristine '58 Plymouth Fury by some high school bullies in Carpenter's anemic version of Stephen King's *Christine* (1983). (Copyright © 1983 Columbia Pictures Intnernational, Inc.)

Rock musician Alice Cooper as one of the possessed street people in *Prince of Darkness* (1987), Carpenter's tale of Satan's reemergance in the modern world. (Copyright © 1987 Universal City Studios, Inc.)

Perhaps reacting to critics' charges that he had overindulged in freakish FX and gross-out shocks in *The Thing*, Carpenter firmly slammed on the breaks with his next film, *Christine* (1983), an anemic adaptation of a Stephen King novel about a nerdy high school loner (Keith Gordon) who falls for a haunted 1958 Plymouth (and vice versa) and restores the dilapidated auto to shape, with dire consequences for all his high school enemies and, ultimately, for himself, as well.

There are echoes of Hawks's *The Thing* in the technically ingenious scenes where the deadly, all-but-destroyed car supernaturally reconstitutes itself, and there is more focus on character than is usual in a Carpenter film. But Carpenter's carefully restrained approach worked against this film rather than for it, and *Christine*, too, was a box-office bomb. By willfully leaving out all the scares, bloodletting, and ghoulishness present in King's novel, Carpenter miscalculated and turned out a film that pleased no one but the MPAA ratings board.

The director returned to form with his next horror movie, the extravagant (but hollow and interminable) kung fu adventure cum ghost story and monster tale *Big Trouble in Little China* (1986). But he fared no better with critics or with fans, and the big-budget film was a commercial disaster. Made for less money, Carpenter's next film, *Prince of Darkness* (1987), didn't win over the public, either. A tale of Satan's reemergence in the modern world with wrong-headed scientific help, the film mixed Nigel Kneale–like metaphysics and social commentary with scare tactics derived from *Halloween* and *Assault on Precinct 13* (the film *Prince* most resembles), with tepid results in both cases. *They Live* (1988), in which the earth has been taken over by right-wing aliens who dominate us humans by playing on our capacity for greed and social apathy and who can be identified as aliens only if viewed through special sunglasses, rifled the work of Nigel Kneale (specifically Kneale's *Quatermass II*) and *Invasion of the Body Snatchers* for inspiration. But after establishing his bizarre political allegory, Carpenter proceeded to do nothing with it, and the film meandered off into endless set pieces of gunplay and, worse still, *wrestling!* Carpenter again wrote the script, but this time he decided not to call attention to the fact with a pseudonym that was an obvious homage; instead, he hid behind the anonymous name of Frank Armitage.

Carpenter has not had a sizable box-office hit since *Starman* (1984), his romantic SF comedy-drama entry in the post-*E.T.* lovable alien sweepstakes. And his name no longer appears above the title of his films as it once did. He clearly has a career problem. Can he resolve it and come back? Hard to tell, for his problem is not a lack of talent, nor is it a lack of feeling and regard for the genre in which he likes to work. Carpenter's problem is that he wants to be a working director, like his artistic mentor, Howard Hawks, moving from project to project (some chosen, some assigned), creating a distinctive signature along the way. If one film's a bust, well, those are the breaks, and it's back to the soundstage next week. But the Hollywood of today is much different from the way it was in Hawks's time—and has changed greatly even since Carpenter himself got started in the business. "Send me back to the forties and the studio system," he has said, comprehending his dilemma. "I would have been happiest there."

Filmography

1966: *Firelight** (director/writer/editor); 1970: *The Resurrection of Bronco Billy** (editor); 1974: *Dark Star* (producer/director/cowriter/music); 1976: *Assault on Precinct 13* (director/cowriter/music); 1978: *Zuma Beach* (cowriter), *The Eyes of Laura Mars* (cowriter), *Someone's Watching Me* (director/writer), *Halloween* (director/cowriter/music); 1979: *Elvis* (director); 1980: *The Fog* (director/cowriter/actor/music); 1981: *Escape from New York* (director/cowriter/music), *Halloween II* (coproducer/cowriter/music); 1982: *The Thing* (director); 1983: *Christine* (director/music), *Halloween III: Season of the Witch* (coproducer/music); 1984: *Starman* (director), *The Philadelphia Experiment* (executive producer); 1986: *Big Trouble in Little China* (director/music), *Black Moon Rising* (writer), *The Boy Who Could Fly* (actor); 1987: *Prince of Darkness* (director/writer/music); 1988: *Halloween 4: The Return of Michael Myers* (music), *The House on Carroll Street* (actor); *They Live* (director/writer/music): 1989: *Halloween 5* (music); 1990: *El Diablo* (cowriter) 1991: *Blood River* (writer); 1992: *Memoirs of an Invisible Man* (director); 1993: *John Carpenter Presents Body Bags+* (co-director/host); 1994: *Meltdown* (writer); *In the Mouth of Madness* (director/writer).

*short film
+anthology film for Showtime cable network

David Cronenberg sets up a scene in which a giant talking insect gets demolished in *Naked Lunch* (1991), his free adaptation of William S. Burroughs's surrealistic literary classic. (Copyright © 1991 Recorded Pictures, Ltd., and Naked Lunch Productions)

Facing page: Peter Weller as William Lee, a writer whose imagination plunges him into a nightmarish world of spies, junkies, witches, and shape-changing typewriters, in *Naked Lunch* (1991). (Copyright © 1991 Recorded Pictures, Ltd., and Naked Lunch Productions)

KEN HANKE

DAVID CRONENBERG

David Cronenberg may be the one fear filmmaker spawned by the genre in recent years about whom the word *genius* could be applied with some degree of accuracy. His work, ranging from *They Came from Within* (1976) to *M. Butterfly* (1993), while subject to the typical variances in quality inherent in any oeuvre, has proved remarkably consistent, lasting, and both stylistically and thematically progressive.

After abortive attempts at majoring in science and literature at the University of Toronto, Cronenberg turned his attention to filmmaking. His first film, the short subject *Transfer* (1966), told of the unnatural bonding of a patient to his psychiatrist—a theme more fully explored, fantasticated, and elaborated upon in his later feature *The Brood* (1979). His next, another short, called *From the Drain* (1967), while not clearly linked in direct fashion to his subsequent work, is nonetheless suggestive of his over-the-top sense of visceral horror with its murderous slime monster "from the drain."

His sixty-five-minute art film *Stereo* (1969), made on a grant from the Canadian Arts Council, foreshadowed *Scanners* (1981) with its emphasis on ESP, while his sixty-three-minute "short" *Crimes of the Future* (1970), with its mysterious plague that

causes sufferers to bleed fluid from their noses and eyes and that somehow compels others to attempt to ingest this liquid, has much in common with *They Came from Within* and *Rabid* (1977).

Cronenberg found his professional outlet through the auspices of then-low-budget horror filmmaker Ivan Reitman. It was through Reitman, along with financing from the Canadian Film Development Corporation, that he was able to make his debut feature, *They Came from Within*. It is not a great film. The acting is variable. Much of it is rather styleless, the cinematography rarely more than serviceable. Similarly, the dialogue is

often awkwardly constructed. However, none of this matters much in light of the concept itself, and Cronenberg's wide-eyed, all-stops-out presentation of that concept, which involves scatological-looking parasites (created by an obsessive, but not mad, scientist to stimulate sexuality) invading a posh high rise.

The tendency to view Cronenberg's work—especially his early work—with an eye toward its high quotient of gore is probably inescapable, but meaningless and unfortunate nonetheless. *They Came from Within*, for example, is intrinsically disturbing to a far greater degree than its gore set pieces. Its genuine power lies in the material.

To some extent, it is tempting to view

disturbing quality. Unlike a traditional zombie or a crazed killer, Cronenberg's horrors are inescapable because, ultimately, they do "come from within."

More stylistically assured and generally better made and acted, *Rabid* does not, unfortunately, deliver the same punch as *They Came from Within*. It is not, however, without its merits, and it signposts the great Cronenberg films to come. Its basic premise of a female (Marilyn Chambers), the victim of an experimental skin-grafting operation by a (this time) more mad than obsessive Cronenberg scientist, turning into a nightmarish horror that sprouts a vampiric penislike growth is clearly the reversed forerunner of the character played by James Woods who sprouts a vaginal opening in the more

Cronenberg's work in bold lines as a kind of "cinema of conspiracy." *They Came from Within* can be interpreted as the story of an obsessed scientist's conspiracy to undermine society by increasing sexual promiscuity. But this interpretation fails to hold water for long, since the scientist tries to stop the fruits of his labor once he realizes where it is leading. More important is the reason behind the scientist's conspiracy, since his work is but a reaction to a more insidious (and perhaps unintentional) larger conspiracy that dehumanizes humanity by placing it in grotesquely sterile, characterless high-rise "luxury" apartment complexes such as the one in which the film takes place. In other words, one conspiracy feeds off another, until they work down to the most personal conspiracy of all—the sabotage of one's own body. This is without question the most consistent theme in Cronenberg's work and the source of its unrelentingly

accomplished *Videodrome* (1983), and it offers our first solid glimpse of Cronenberg's apparent fascination with gender blurring.

With *The Brood*, Cronenberg was on surer ground. Blessed with better-than-average actors, including Oliver Reed and Samantha Eggar, and a far more disturbing plot and theme than those of *Rabid*, the filmmaker came into his own. Production values are higher and the cinematography of Mark Irwin and the music score by Howard Shore (both of whom would quickly become part of Cronenberg's behind-the-scenes stock company) were miles ahead of his earlier films.

Whatever merits *They Came from Within* and *Rabid* had, warmth was not among them. For all their power, they were cold works peopled by characters boasting very little personality, charm, or sympathy. They're vessels through which the ideas of the films flow but are not important in themselves. While not exactly Capraesque, *The Brood* offers far more human characters.

The film's allegorical presentation of child abuse as a sickness that feeds off itself is shrewdly achieved. Psychiatrist Reed taps into a method (called psychoplasmics) of externalizing patient Eggar's pent-up rage, causing the birth of the titular brood (in a typical Cronenberg touch, these bizarre creatures are clothed in Dr. Denton's). What Reed has not counted on is that this embodied rage might be used by Eggar as a means for revenge. The results are, not surprisingly, murderous and generally destructive.

While it may not be possible to feel more than an abstract sympathy for the film's ostensible hero

For a film best known for its "exploding head" effect, Cronenberg's next film, *Scanners,* is probably the single most upbeat film in his body of work. Where *The Brood* tapped into child abuse and the perils of radical-hip psychotherapy, *Scanners* took its cue from the use of Thalidomide in the 1950s that produced a number of seriously deformed babies. In the film, however, the drug is called Ephemerol, and its side effects are even more insidious because they are

From left to right: Cronenberg's sixty-five-minute art film *Stereo* (1969) foreshadowed *Scanners* (1981) with its emphasis on ESP. (Moving Image and Sound Archives)

(Art Hindle, who plays Eggar's husband), considerable feeling is generated for both Reed and Eggar. Reed's character, while off on a wrong and dangerous track, is not in the least bit villainous; in fact, his attempt to rescue Hindle and Eggar's daughter (Cindy Hinds) from the killer brood is a heroic act. As the mother of the brood, Eggar is not especially likable, but her plight is understandable and clearly not of her own making. Rather, it is the result of Eggar's childhood trauma at the hands of her mother and then Reed's efforts to break the evil chain that cause Eggar to visit similar abuse on her own child. That Eggar has essentially mutated into something even worse than an abusive mother is dwarfed by the film's final image of her daughter sprouting the telltale marks of the beginning of yet another brood. Not only has the patient not been cured; the chain remains unbroken.

invisible. Rather than producing deformed children, Ephemerol produces telepathic offspring (scanners) with remarkable powers. Much like *They Came from Within, Scanners* offers a double take on the conspiracy

Crimes of the Future (1970) dealt with a mysterious plague that causes sufferers to bleed from their noses and legs and others to ingest the running liquid. (Moving Image and Sound Archives)
Scatological-looking parasites invade a posh high rise in Cronenberg's *They Came from Within* (1976). (Moving Picture and Sound Archives)
An experimental skin-grafting experiment goes wildly out of control in *Rabid* (1977). (Copyright © 1977 New World Pictures)

theme, but in a somewhat different fashion. Scientist Patrick McGoohan's initially humane and potentially beneficial attempt at creating a drug to alleviate pain during pregnancy turns into a very different (and typically Cronenbergian) obsession with the possibilities of the drug's side effects being an evolutionary step in the development of man. The basically well-intentioned conspiracy gives rise to an alternate and utterly evil conspiracy in the hands of one of McGoohan's scanner sons (Michael Ironside).

On a tangential note, *Scanners* is the only film in Cronenberg's body of work prior to *Naked Lunch* (1991) to address the question of creativity, and it can—and perhaps should—be viewed as a kind of self-justification on the part of the filmmaker. Its inclusion of an artist character (Robert Silverman) whose work is the result of his need to channel the voices that come to him as a scanner certainly suggests this. That his work is at once bizarre, tortured, and deeply disturbing would also seem to link him with Cronenberg, whose obsessive film work provides a not dissimilar outlet and effect.

Cronenberg came very close to topping *Scanners* with his next project, *Videodrome*, his first film released by a major studio, Universal. A rich and characteristically disturbing work on the all-pervasive influence of television on society, *Videodrome* is everything the Paddy Chayefsky–Sidney Lumet film *Network* (1976) tried to be (they failed at it due to lack of nerve or imagination). Not short of either nerve or imagination, Cronenberg took careful aim at his target and went straight for the heart in a less preachy and far more unnerving manner. What Cronenberg included in his most outrageous horror-film plot yet was the one element the creators of *Network* overlooked—that a people seduced and altered by television are themselves guilty for succumbing to its blandishments in the first place.

Both *The Brood* and *Scanners* were comparatively warmer in tone than Cronenberg's earlier work. *Videodrome* at first seems a return to those earlier films, but only on the surface. James Woods's brilliantly played lead character is deliberately sleazy and opportunistic but undeniably real. What is most remarkable and daring about this is Cronenberg's insistence that we become Woods as the film progresses, and, like it or not, we do. What he experiences, we experience. His perceptions are grafted onto our own; as his ability to distinguish reality from fantasy crumbles, so does ours. This is the key to the film and the brilliance of Cronenberg's central conceit: We are forced into identifying with and sharing the experiences of a character we don't even like. That we don't like what Cronenberg makes us into is the cautionary truth behind the film and the most profound testament possible to his own (potentially dangerous) status as a singularly powerful filmmaker.

Plotwise, *Videodrome* is much of a piece with his other films—a misguided but well-intentioned conspiracy fosters a much less benign conspiracy. Other aspects of the film are clear outgrowths of its predecessors. As mentioned earlier, Woods's development of a vaginal opening in his stomach is a rethinking of the vampiric growth in *Rabid*. While the extremely unsettling ending with Woods

Samantha Eggar gives birth to one of her id creatures in *The Brood* (1979). (Copyright © 1979 New World Pictures)
Facing page: Best known for its grisly "exploding head" scene, Cronenberg's *Scanners* (1981) is probably the single most upbeat work in his oeuvre. (Copyright © 1981 Embassy Pictures)

shooting himself in the head as his mirrored TV image does the same, disgorging brains and blood from the shattered screen, is the darker side of the acceptance of transformation presented in *Scanners*. What really remains in the mind about the film, however, are its myriad Cronenberg touches, especially those concerning Professor O'Blivion's (Jack Creley) Cathode Ray Mission, where derelicts are treated to daily doses of TV "to help patch them back into the world's mixing board." The implications of a world so completely reliant on television are conveyed with startling aptness, and only slight exaggeration, through Cronenberg's most undervalued talent: the well-turned phrase. Such moments as the warning to Woods that the renegade cable TV channel of the title is dangerous "because it has something you do not—a philosophy" have a haunting quality because this is exactly what Cronenberg's own work has over that of most of his contemporaries. The weird fusion of the inanimate with the organic (a precursor to *The Fly*, 1986) is also enhanced by the dialogue, as when O'Blivion's daughter (Sonja Smits) "deprograms" Woods by removing a videocassette implanted in his vaginal opening, saying, "It always hurts when you take out the cassette," an appropriate summation of a

society so addicted to television that it has virtually become an organic extension of the medium.

If *Videodrome* flirted with the mainstream (a major feat for so bizarre and personal a film), *The Dead Zone* (1983) finally propelled Cronenberg into that stream. He did so, thankfully, without selling out, despite compromising to the extent of working from someone else's screenplay (Jeffrey Boam) and a Stephen King source novel. The worlds of Stephen King and David Cronenberg do not much intersect. But *The Dead Zone* does contain at least the germ of a connection between the two in its political conspiracy plotline, a variation on the director's ongoing obsession with scientific/political conspiracies. For all his repetitive style and overreliance on dialogue exchanges, King is a writer capable of creating believable and often quite likable characters. Since this is the area of Cronenberg's greatest weakness, there is an undeniable plus on the characterization side of the film.

Cronenberg's follow-up, *The Fly*, is a work that needs no excuses. This is one of the great modern horror films, and to some extent, it can be viewed as the film where the director finally got it all together. It is certainly the most human and touching of his works.

The Fly is even warmer in tone than *The Dead Zone*, but with no trade-offs. Fully as cerebral as Cronenberg's earlier works, the film still offers a far greater sense of its (and the director's) own humanity at the center. At first glance, this might seem the result of Charles Edward Pogue's screenplay, which Cronenberg altered only enough to justify taking a coscreenwriting credit. But the fact is that much of the film's humanity stemmed from Cronenberg's alterations.

Scarcely has a

project seemed less likely to succeed than this one. It is a radical rethinking of the rather silly (though much beloved) 1958 original, which boasted campy effects and even campier performances. Despite Vincent Price's (a supporting player in the original) talk-show claims that Cronenberg's film is more like what would have been done if the makers of the original had not been constrained by censorship, the basic concept of the 1958 film is essentially simpleminded and shallow. Cronenberg's remake—even shorn of its improved and far more graphic special effects—is anything but. It is a complex story about the nature of love and the ability of that love to withstand and weather even the most grotesque failure of the flesh. It matters not at all that the failure here is the result of a stupid mistake in a scientific experiment, presented in horror-film terms. The film's metaphoric failure of the flesh could be anything—from cancer to AIDS. Cronenberg's point is the amazing ability for constancy in love between two human beings, regardless of outer changes.

Cronenberg's next film, *Dead Ringers* (1988), is often viewed by admirers of his previous films as a step down, or even as a kind of selling out. There may be a grain of truth in the second assessment. Regardless of their individual merits, horror films are subject to a ludicrous snobbery by most critics and cineastes. Given this snobbery, the desire on the part of most genre filmmakers to break away eventually from doing work that is overtly in the horror-film vein is understandable. Cronenberg achieved this desire with *Dead Ringers*. But he did it very shrewdly, for while the film is not horrific in the usual sense and not in the least fantastic, its subject matter stayed well within the bounds of his previous work. That he lost some of his original fans in the process is part of the price any artist pays for personal and creative growth.

Taking his story from a real case and adapting it to suit his needs, Cronenberg returned to the questions of duality he had raised in *Scanners*, which involved two brothers—one good, one evil—who

even more disturbing by burying it—by making the twins' need to express their desires something they can achieve only by inverting those desires, by channeling them through the "proper vessel" of a shared woman (Geneviève Bujold).

In many respects, *Dead Ringers* is Cronenberg's most handsome film. Shining and glossy, it moves along at a languorous, almost hypnotic pace as it spirals us slowly into the twins' personal hell. At the same time, it also works as an extremely off-the-wall black comedy that slowly transforms itself into a

The near-final transformation of Jeff Goldblum into the titular insect in *The Fly* (1986), one of the great modern horror films and Cronenberg's most human and touching work. (Copyright © 1986 Twentieth Century-Fox) *Dead Ringers* (1988) with Geneviève Bujold and Jeremy Irons (playing a dual role) took Cronenberg's recurring theme of loss of identity to its horrifying conclusion. (Copyright © 1988 Twentieth Century-Fox)

ultimately merge into one. Here, his two characters (both played by Jeremy Irons) are even more closely aligned. They're twins, and it is only when they are together that they function as a whole person. Their penchant for taking on each other's personalities ("Don't forget, you haven't had an experience until we've both had it") is the interior conspiracy of their own minds, which ultimately destroys both of them as they merge, blend, and finally interchange. Done in almost stately style, *Dead Ringers* is a film built entirely on the terror of loss of identity taken to its most horrifying conclusion.

Apart from setting the film in Toronto rather than in New York City, Cronenberg's most notable departure from the facts of the actual case was his decision not to downplay or jettison (as has been suggested by some critics) the incestuously homosexual relationship between the twins. In fact, he made this relationship

grim—oddly touching—tragedy. The sickness of the humor—such as the twins' shared occupation as gynecologists—is pronounced. But it pales when placed alongside Cronenberg's next film.

At first glance, Cronenberg's decision to film William S. Burroughs's "unfilmable" novel *Naked Lunch* may have seemed a singularly bizarre and even wrongheaded notion. But before turning from science to art, Cronenberg first tried his hand at writing fiction, and to a large extent he has remained one of the most literary-minded of all contemporary filmmakers. While Burroughs's novel is indeed "unfilmable" ("It would cost hundreds of millions of dollars and be banned in every country on earth," Cronenberg has noted), the director had a very different and daring concept in mind. Rather than adapt the book in the usual sense, he opted to make a film about the writing of the novel. In the process, he made a film about what it's like to *be* William S. Burroughs.

Naked Lunch stands the idea behind *Dead Ringers* on its head. Where that film had largely eschewed the fantastic while retaining the horrific, *Naked Lunch* is built on the fantastic and relegates the horrific to a very minor—and almost wholly cerebral—position. In a brilliant stroke, Cronenberg cast one of the most limited actors of our generation, Peter Weller, in the role of Burroughs' alter ego, William Lee. This is probably the finest example in the history of film of a director actually cashing in on an actor's shortcomings, since the deadpan monotone of Burroughs himself seems to be second nature to Weller.

Naked Lunch is at its strongest in its examination (dissection, really) of the act of writing. "I gave up writing at the age of ten—too dangerous," explains Weller early in the film, only to find himself plunged into the act of writing against his will by his very nature later on. Circumstances—the accidental killing of his wife (Judy Davis)—make it necessary for him to assume the guise of a secret agent, one who must write endless reports. (The dangerous aspect of this is neatly conveyed when Weller trades the murder weapon for a typewriter.) Not only is he unable to escape his fate as a writer but the writing itself controls him, simply because it allows his true nature to reveal itself. The writing dictates his actions. He becomes homosexually inclined because the writing tells him to ("Homosexuality is the best all-around cover an agent can have"); he writes the novel without realizing he is doing it; and so on. This is a sharply double-edged sword. The writing exists on its own terms, but it also offers him a detached excuse for his sexual and artistic proclivities while serving as a release for his real self.

Writing—and, by extension, any act of creativity—is presented in the film as subversive,

cathartic, sexual, and inescapable. Whereas Cronenberg had presented art as a viable outlet for release in *Scanners*, in *Naked Lunch* he amplifies this theme by recognizing the fact that such release can lead to an inescapable trap for the artist. Weller's Burroughs would like to be a "normal" person, but this is not to be, because he is what he is—he has no choice.

Original, unsettling, and as dangerous and subversive as the writing it depicts, *Naked Lunch* is David Cronenberg's masterpiece. In some respects, it represents the director coming full circle, by arriving back where he started—with an art-film concept reminiscent of his earliest work as a filmmaker. But the difference between marginally professional sixty-five-minute experimental films and a big-budget Twentieth Century-Fox release with an impressive array of name actors is quite extreme. By following his own path in the horror and exploitation film world, Cronenberg has been able to achieve a level of personal filmmaking independence that few filmmakers can claim. How he will use that unique privilege is a question only he can answer—and undoubtedly will in continually surprising ways.

Filmography
1966: *Transfer** (director/writer); 1967: *From the Drain** (director/writer); 1969: *Stereo** (producer/director/writer); 1970: *Crimes of the Future** (producer/director/writer); 1972: *Secret Weapons*+ (director); 1976: *They Came from Within*, a.k.a. *The Parasite Murders* and *Shivers* (director/writer); *The Victim*+ (director), *The Lie Chair*+ (director), *The Italian Machine*+ (director/writer); 1977: *Rabid* (director/writer); 1979: *Fast Company* (director/cowriter), *The Brood* (director/writer); 1981: *Scanners* (director/writer); 1983: *Videodrome* (director/writer), *The Dead Zone* (director); 1986: *The Fly* (director/cowriter); 1988: *Dead Ringers* (coproducer/director/cowriter); 1991: *Naked Lunch* (director/writer); 1993: *M. Butterfly* (director).

　　*short film
　　+Canadian telefilm

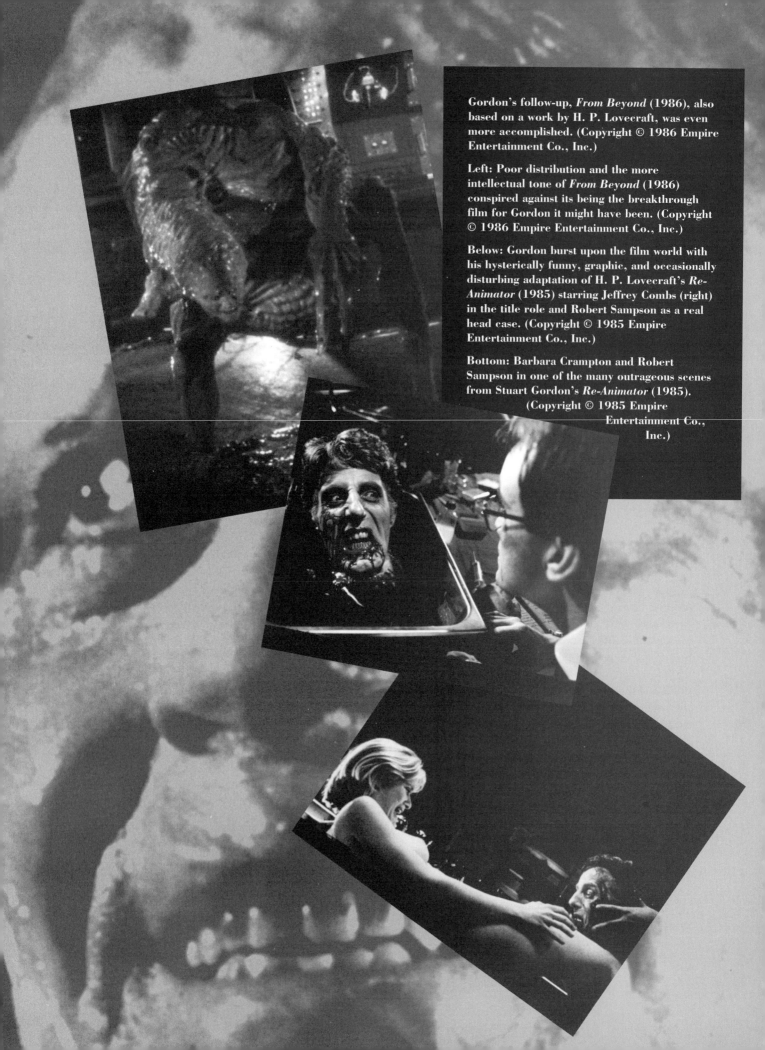

Gordon's follow-up, *From Beyond* (1986), also based on a work by H. P. Lovecraft, was even more accomplished. (Copyright © 1986 Empire Entertainment Co., Inc.)

Left: Poor distribution and the more intellectual tone of *From Beyond* (1986) conspired against its being the breakthrough film for Gordon it might have been. (Copyright © 1986 Empire Entertainment Co., Inc.)

Below: Gordon burst upon the film world with his hysterically funny, graphic, and occasionally disturbing adaptation of H. P. Lovecraft's *Re-Animator* (1985) starring Jeffrey Combs (right) in the title role and Robert Sampson as a real head case. (Copyright © 1985 Empire Entertainment Co., Inc.)

Bottom: Barbara Crampton and Robert Sampson in one of the many outrageous scenes from Stuart Gordon's *Re-Animator* (1985). (Copyright © 1985 Empire Entertainment Co., Inc.)

STUART GORDON

Soft-spoken, gently humorous, and a bit of a sentimentalist, the thoroughly American Stuart Gordon seems an unlikely candidate for creator of some of the most outrageously over-the-top, blood-splattered fearfilms ever made. Or is it so unlikely when we consider that these films, for all their buckets of blood, boast uncommonly human and likable characters, right alongside a gallery of lip-smacking villains of the Lionel Atwill/George Zucco school?

Equally surprising is Gordon's background of fifteen years as artistic director of Chicago's Organic Theatre (whose alumni also include Joe Mantegna and John Heard), where his forte was comedy. "We did a real eclectic bunch of shows," says Gordon, "including horror and science fiction." Yet, like James Whale before him, Gordon took to film with an almost uncanny knack, and, like Whale, his approach to filmmaking is theatrical in the best sense of that often-misunderstood term.

When Gordon burst upon the film world with his hysterically funny, graphic, and occasionally disturbing adaptation of H. P. Lovecraft's *Re-Animator* (1985), many viewers were convinced that here was a new and powerful fear filmmaking voice. In a time when David Cronenberg seemed the only major artist working in a genre otherwise enlivened by the odd Wes Craven or Tobe Hooper film, Gordon's *Re-Animator* was a badly needed transfusion of fresh blood. The film evidenced an unusual respect for dialogue, character, and story. The panache with which Gordon staged his scenes bore no resemblance to the meat-on-the-hoof slasher stuff currently pervading fearfilms. His characters were, amazingly, just that—characters—not just so many blood-squirting department store dummies waiting to be ventilated by an equally characterless madman. His villains were colorful and complex figures with a

penchant for well-turned phrases distinctively delivered. The film's story line was carefully structured so that the horrific and outrageous scenes worked in a progressive fashion, with each new scene more involved and effective than the last. What Gordon had done was to return the genre to the kind of storytelling where viewers genuinely found themselves interested in what would happen next.

This much about Gordon's debut film was fairly obvious. What was—and to a degree still is—less apparent was his innate sense of theater. Take the sequence where Herbert West (Jeffrey Combs) and Dan Cain (Bruce Abbott) pursue a murderously antisocial reanimated cat around a basement with, respectively, a croquet mallet and a baseball bat. Gordon makes good use of the basics of cinema in this scene, yet his effects remain primarily theatrical. The impact of this and most of the film's horror set pieces stem almost entirely from the lighting, the sound effects, the performances—pure theatercraft—all of which could be easily reproduced as "floor effects" on the stage. It is this approach that gives *Re-Animator* both its charm and its sense of immediacy—both quite absent from the elaborate animatronics and process work of Brian Yuzna's sequel, *Bride of Re-Animator* (1990).

In many respects, Gordon's follow-up film, *From Beyond* (1986), also based on a work by H. P. Lovecraft, was even more accomplished. One gets the feeling from watching the film that it is bigger in both intent and execution and more intrinsically cinematic, but this is an illusion created by the film's use of process-work effects depicting the story's centerpiece flying creatures from another dimension. Closer examination of the film reveals that it is actually more confined in its locations (the bulk of the action takes place in a single house) than *Re-Animator*, while the process work is used very sparingly. Despite a fairly broad range of mechanical bogeys, the impact of the film stems once again from the effectiveness of its "floor effects"—lighting, character, and performances.

Re-Animator was intended to be, and primarily is, a "fun film." Its thematic qualities extend to very little beyond its unflattering portrait of the Ronald Reagan-like character of Dean Halsey ("the world's last living Puritan") as an authority figure without a thought in his head and its similar view of the well-respected Dr. Hill as a symbol of the utter sickness lying just beneath the surface of the accepted norm. The same thematic qualities permeate From Beyond. The respected Dr. Pretorious (Ted Sorel) is motivated almost solely by his desire to rechannel his sexual impotency into ever-more-degenerate pursuits, while the authoritarian asylum director played with delicious malice by Carolyn Purdy-Gordon is set on locking mental cases away rather than dealing with them, and she likewise delights in the chance to lock away (and even torture) a rival (Barbara Crampton) who does not share her views.

More to the point, From Beyond pivots on the theme of sexual and intellectual repression. The unseen forces that come "from beyond" merely serve to tap into this aspect of human nature. A great deal of the resulting danger stems from the characters' basic lack (or supression) of knowledge of themselves. For anyone familiar with H. P. Lovecraft, this approach must be judged either as subversively anti-Lovecraftian or as an unmasking of Lovecraft's own subconscious subtext.

With From Beyond, Gordon more readily played the game by submitting the film to the MPAA for a rating and agreeing to some minor cuts in order to secure an R rating. Obviously, he was hoping this would be his breakthrough film. But poor distribution and the film's undeniably more intellectual tone (to say nothing of its lack of teenaged characters) conspired against him. The reviews were again

Left: Gordon showed us that dolls are not always cute and cuddly in Dolls (1987), a tribute to James Whale's The Old Dark House. (Copyright © 1986 Empire Entertainment Co., Inc.)
Right: Gordon developed Honey, I Shrunk the Kids (1989) for Disney as his first mainstream project, but he missed out on the opportunity to direct it. (Copyright © 1989 Buena Vista Distribution, Inc.)

enthusiastic and a growing Gordon cult audience took to the film, but it was not the breakthrough it might have been.

Judged from the standpoint of Gordon's understandable desire to cross over to a more mainstream audience, his follow-up film, the much maligned Dolls (1987), probably seemed a better idea at the time than it actually was. The film, an attempt at a kind of adult fairy tale, seemed designed to reach a broader audience, but it erred by being too strong for that audience yet not strong enough for the Gordon cultists. Weak distribution didn't help, either.

Gordon and screenwriter Ed Naha (himself a pretty savvy film historian specializing in the horror genre) essentially refashioned the film into a rethinking of and homage to James Whale's The Old Dark House. The setup is remarkably similar: Travelers stranded in the British countryside (England in this case, the Welsh mountains in Whale's) are forced to stay the night in a creepy old house that slowly reveals its secrets. Guy Rolfe's head of the household is very clearly patterned on Ernest Thesiger's Horace Femm in The Old Dark House, while Stephen Lee's refreshingly unheroic hero is even more obviously based on Charles Laughton's Sir William Porterhouse in the Whale film. Indeed, Lee's arrival on the scene with a pair of punk girls of dubious morality is almost identical to the arrival of

Laughton and Lilian Bond in the Whale film.

That said, *Dolls* is by no means just a knockoff of Whale's masterpiece. Rather, it pays tribute to *The Old Dark House* with significant alterations. Ultimately, Gordon's old dark house is sinister only to the sinister, dangerous only to the unregenerately jaded. As in Whale's film, the horrors of the house afford the visitors the chance for personal salvation by allowing them the means to shape their proper destinies. But Whale's house does not offer this chance deliberately. Gordon's does. Moreover, Whale's film is primarily concerned with the broad theme of accepting personal responsibility, whereas Gordon's film centers entirely on the responsibility to retain—or regain—a measure of one's innocence.

Gordon's next foray was *Daughter of Darkness* (1989), arguably another attempt at reaching a more mainstream audience—this time by means of television. Gordon himself expresses little fondness for the telefilm as it aired on the CBS network, but he claims that the uncut theatrical version released in Europe was much better. The director nurses a certain

fondness for the project, however, because it introduced him to Anthony Perkins (who plays a vampire in the film). Perkins turned out to be a keen admirer of *Re-Animator*. The friendship that formed between the two might have resulted in the realization of one of Gordon's most cherished notions: teaming Perkins with Gordon stock company counterpart Jeffrey Combs.

Unfortunately, Perkins's death has canceled this tantalizing prospect. Financial and distribution problems plagued Gordon's next project, *Robot Jox* (1991), and the timing of its release threw off any chances of success. Essentially a futuristic story paralleling the Cold War, it came out after the Cold War had ended. Gordon's own feeling is that the mere fact that the film (an elaborate special-effects extravaganza made on a bargain-basement budget) was even finished at all was in itself a miraculous achievement. And its subsequent finding of an audience on videotape clearly pleases him. The film, however, is simply not in the same league with his earlier work.

But his next project, *The Pit and the Pendulum* (1991), is. In fact, it may well be the best thing he has done so far. Certainly it is his most ambitious film. For a project made on such a restrictive budget, *The Pit and the Pendulum* boasts a fine sense of period detail (in part because producer Charles Band owns the Italian castle that is the film's primary setting) and many far more expensive films cannot lay claim to anywhere near its period feel. The film's characters seem actually to live in their costumes and surroundings.

Of course, period detail counts for very little unless it is allied with a story of sound dramatic substance and a strong cinematic style. *The Pit and the Pendulum* scores very highly in both departments. To begin with, it is Gordon's most thematically substantial—and political—film to date. In it, he uses the witchcraft trials of the Spanish Inquisition to comment on similar abuses of power today—in much the same way Arthur Miller used the vehicle of the Salem witch trials in his play *The Crucible* to comment upon the McCarthy witch-hunt era, and Ken Russell had used John Whiting's historical play *The Devils* for similar purposes. The most unsettling aspect of this is that Gordon's film is the least allegorical of the three because time has caught up with the concept, as witness the unnerving similarity between the ravings of Gordon's Grand Inquisitor, Torquemada (Lance Henricksen), and the speeches of Pat Buchanan and Pat Robertson at the 1992 Republican convention.

Gordon and screenwriter Dennis Paoli actually take the film's allegorical content a step further by creating leading characters, Maria (Rona De Ricci) and Antonio (Jonathan Fuller), who are indirectly guilty of helping to foster the witch-hunting insanity of their time. These characters not only turn a blind eye to the atrocities committed around them; they actually benefit from them. While it is clear that neither Maria nor Antonio subscribe to the policies and beliefs of the Inquisition, they are sufficiently hardened and pragmatic enough to make a buck out of the situation. It

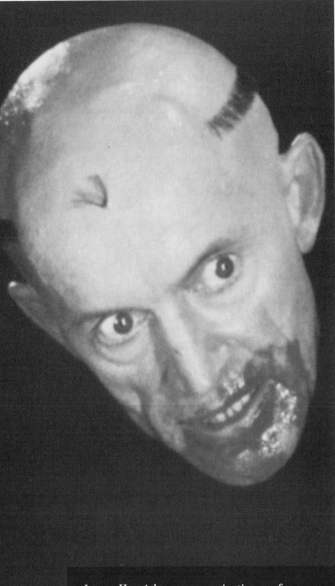

is only when the Inquisition touches them personally that they take serious notice of it. They are not stalwart freedom fighters and idealists. Rather, they are relatively simple people forced by circumstances into taking heroic measures. This approach has a great deal to do with the film's effectiveness, since it points up our own indirect guilt and complicity in accepting the status quo.

However, allegory, like period detail, will carry a film only so far. Unless it is interwoven with an involving, engaging and entertaining, story line, allegory quickly palls, and it may even alienate the viewer, who comes to feel that the drama unfolding is more sermon than entertainment. Fortunately, *The Pit and the Pendulum* is a typical Gordon film in that it offers a well-developed, systematically constructed story with complex, believable characters delivering well-honed and witty dialogue. Gordon's familiar stock company of character actors— Carolyn Purdy-Gordon (in an unusually sympathetic role), Jeffrey Combs, and Stephen Lee—is aided by Lance Henricksen in a riveting performance as Torquemada and guest star Oliver Reed (boasting a delightfully Chico Marxish stage Italian accent) as a cardinal sent by the Pope to stop the Inquisition. Mention should also be made of the contribution of veteran actress Frances Bay as the sympathetic witch, Esmeralda, who uses her powers to assist the imprisoned Maria, and who, at her execution, gets her own back on her tormenters in a wonderfully inventive manner.

The film's link to Ken Russell's *The Devils* (1971) is no accident ("What do you think Oliver Reed and I talked about on the set?" the director asks rhetorically.) Very much an admirer of Russell's film (and of Russell's work in general), Gordon finds comparisons between his film and Russell's high praise indeed—and well he might, since his low-budget genre effort is both similar in tone and effect to Russell's controversial classic. *The Pit and the Pendulum* is no simple knockoff of *The Devils*, however, but a combined homage to and variant on it. Cross-references and variations abound. Russell's film ends with a cinematic reference to Brueghel's painting *Triumph of Death;* Gordon's film runs its opening credits over a series of isolated images from the same painting. Russell's film (and the John Whiting play on which it is primarily based) is suffused with the blackest of black humor; so is Gordon's. How far removed are the scenes

Lance Henricksen gave a riveting performance as Torquemada in *The Pit and the Pendulum* (1991), the best work Gordon has done so far. (Copyright © 1991 Full Moon Entertainment, Inc.)
Inset, above: Financial and distribution problems plagued Gordon's futuristic Cold War extravaganza *Robot Jox* (1991), and the timing of its release following the collapse of the Soviet Union threw off any chances of success. (Copyright © Empire Entertainment Co., Inc.)
Inset, below: An adult fairy tale deemed too strong for the potentially broader audience it was trying to reach, yet not strong enough for the Gordon cultists—from *Dolls* (1987). (Copyright © 1986 Empire Entertainment Co., Inc.)

of Max Adrian in *The Devils* examining the possessed nuns' vomit for signs of the devil ("That's a carrot!") from the outrage of Stephen Lee's acerbic comment, upon finding that Maria's tongue has been cut out, that "We don't do tongues"? In fact, *The Pit and the Pendulum*'s most cinematically powerful sequence—where Torquemada prays to a statue of the Virgin Mary to drive his lust for Maria from his mind, only to have the statue turn into Maria—almost certainly owes its inspiration to the crucifixion fantasy in Russell's film where Christ on the cross is transformed into the love object of Sister Jeanne's (Vanessa Redgrave) romantic obsession.

It would be a mistake, however, to view *The Pit and the Pendulum* as a full-fledged reworking of *The Devils.* In the first place, Gordon never forgets that his film is primarily a horror movie, and that fact, quite rightly, takes precedence, so that the film is geared toward ever more complex and involving horror set pieces, culminating in the "pit and the pendulum" sequence of the title. Moreover, Gordon's film eschews the more overtly political aspects of Russell's film. This is probably for the best insofar as its impact as a horror film is concerned, but it does tend to allow the film to be viewed as something less than it is, and perhaps causes it to seem less sharp-edged than such other highly charged, politically minded horror films as Tobe Hooper's *The Texas Chainsaw Massacre 2* (1986) and Wes Craven's *The People Under the Stairs* (1991). Ultimately, however, this may prove to be one of *The Pit and the Pendulum*'s greatest strengths, for its more oblique approach in this regard may wear better with future audiences.

The most satisfying aspect of *The Pit and the Pendulum*, though, is its clear demonstration that Stuart Gordon is a evolving filmmaker of considerable power. The beautifully idyllic sequence where Esmeralda takes Maria out of her body to another plane of existence in order to escape the pain of torture ("It's real if you want it to be") is quite unlike anything else in Gordon's work so far. Similarly, the film's ending, while tinged with the bitter reality that there will be subsequent inquisitions, is the most positive in Gordon's work to date.

As of this writing, Gordon has completed a science-fiction film called *Fortress* (1993), starring Christopher Lambert as a man imprisoned because he and his wife have produced more than the one child allowed by their futuristic government. But its premise pales in comparison with the prospect of Gordon's proposed film adaptation of H. P. Lovecraft's *The Shadow Over Innsmouth.*

"I've been trying for a long time to get this made, and I haven't had a lot of success," Gordon notes. "It's a big movie. And one of his best stories, I think. It's a terrifying story. Dennis Paoli, Brian Yuzna, and I have worked out a screen treatment, but the problem is that the budget for this is considerable because you have to show this whole town full of monsters. It's a real challenging project, and the other thing is, it'll have to be shot on location. Brian and I have been up and down both coasts and we found one suitable town in Maine and another in Washington State. Originally, it was going to be Vestron that was going to fund it, but then they went belly-up, and we've been having a hard time finding someone to take their place."

Let's hope that replacement will not be long in coming.

Filmography
1985: *Re-Animator* (director); 1986: *From Beyond* (director); 1987: *Dolls* (director); 1989: *Honey, I Shrunk the Kids* (cowriter), *Daughter of Darkness* (director); 1991: *Robot Jox* (director), *The Pit and the Pendulum* (director); 1993: *Fortress* (director), *Body Snatchers* (cowriter); 1994: *Castle Freak* (director).

John (Jack) Brent lives in upstate New York, where he manages the graphics department of a weekly newspaper while pursuing his spare-time interests in publishing and filmmaking. In 1988, Jack began putting out a well-received magazine called *Phantasma*, a journal devoted to the serious study of science fiction, fantasy, and horror on the screen. The magazine is now on hiatus, Jack says, while he musters the financial resources to resume publishing. In the meantime, he is writing, directing, and coproducing a dramatic video feature for direct-to-video release. As an actor, Jack has appeared in fellow genre enthusiast Bruce G. Hallenbeck's feature film *Vampyre* (1991); as a writer, he contributed to John McCarty's *The Official Splatter Movie Guide*, Vols. 1 and 2 (St. Martin's Press).

Raymond G. Cabana, Jr., is a film historian, collector, and freelance writer. He published, coedited, and wrote for *Kaleidoscope*, a now-defunct magazine devoted to cinema history past and present, and is the coauthor of the critically acclaimed book *The Films of Peter Lorre* (Citadel Press). He has also contributed articles to such magazines as *Views & Reviews* and *American Classic Screen*. A noted authority on the great detective, Ray has been cited in *The World Encyclopedia of Sherlock Holmes and Dr. Watson, The Films of Sherlock Holmes* (Citadel Press), and *Holmes of the Movies*. In 1987, he provided rare motion pictures and memorabilia from his extensive collection to the Wistariahurst Museum of Holyoke, Massachusetts, for its one-hundredth anniversary celebration of Holmes's debut, and he did so again in 1990 when the Mark Twain House in Hartford, Connecticut, presented its own commemorative program of Holmesiana.

Michael J. Collins, Australian by birth, American by all other considerations, currently teaches filmmaking at Phillips Exeter Academy.

His essays and reviews have appeared in *Necrofile* and *The Journal of the Fantastic in the Arts.* Michael is also a videomaker whose award-winning experimental narratives have appeared in festivals, galleries, and on TV stations all over the world. He lives in New Hampshire with his wife, critic Kathleen Kirby, and is currently working on a book-length study of American subcultures, as well as on a new video.

Walter L. Gay is a lifelong horror enthusiast. His main fields of interest are British horror films, European terror and "trash" cinema, and domestic drive-in and grind-house horrors of days gone by. Walt's reviews have appeared in Chas. Balun's *Deep Red* magazine and in John McCarty's *The Official Splatter Movie Guide*, Vol. 2 (St. Martin's Press). He currently publishes a no-frills fanzine called *The Ghastly Ones*, and is engaged in an obsessive search for the missing seven minutes from *Last House on the Left.*

Bruce G. Hallenbeck is an author, screenwriter, and filmmaker. An expert on Hammer Horror, Bruce has contributed articles and reviews to such genre magazines as *Fangoria, Femmes Fatales, Little Shoppe of Horrors* (for which he does all the cover stories), *Black Oracle,* and *Monsterland,* as well as the books *The Modern Horror Film* (Citadel Press), John McCarty's *The Official Splatter Movie Guide*, Vol. 2 (St. Martin's Press), and *Dark Zones* (Warner Books). *Monster of the Northwoods,* his study of Sasquath, upstate New York's version of Big Foot, was recently published by North Country Books. Bruce also wrote and directed the feature film *Vampyre* (1991), now in distribution through Panorama Entertainment and Raedon Home Video, and *Fangs* (1992), a documentary on the vampire film, which is hosted by Veronica Carlson and is now in domestic release through Bruce's own label, Pagan Video, and internationally through Meridian Films.

Ken Hanke is a Florida-based freelance writer and independent filmmaker. His books include the critically acclaimed *Ken Russell's Films* (Scarecrow Press), *Charlie Chan at the Movies* (McFarland Publishing), and *A Critical Guide to Horror Film Series* (Garland Publishing). Ken is also a frequent contributor to *Films in Review* and *Filmfax*, and served as a "contributing splatterologist" for John McCarty's *The Official Splatter Movie Guide*, Vols. 1 and 2 (St. Martin's Press). Ken's most recent film, *A Dream Unbound,* is currently making the film festival circuit, and he is now at work on a new film, as well as two books, *Early Sound Features from Hollywood* (McFarland Publishing) and *Bob Hope: A Bio-Bibliography* (Greenwood Press).

The editor, **John McCarty,** was born in Albany, New York, in 1944. He has been a movie fan since he was five, and he started making his own films in his early teens. After graduating from high school in 1962, he attended Boston University, where he majored in film and began writing seriously on the subject. Following a stint in the Peace Corps, where he worked in educational television in Bogota, Colombia, John returned to the States and pursued a career as a broadcaster and advertising copywriter. His affection for the horror-film genre (and concern with what was happening to it) led to the writing of *Splatter Movies: Breaking the Last Taboo of the Screen* (St. Martin's Press). It has become a cult classic. He has written more than a dozen books on films and filmmakers in and out of the horror genre, including: John McCarty's *The Official Splatter Movie Guide*, Vols. 1 and 2; *Thrillers: Seven Decades of Classic Film Suspense* (Citadel Press); and *Hollywood Gangland: The Movies' Love Affair With the Mob* (St. Martin's Press). He lives in upstate New York with his wife, Cheryl, four crazy cats, and a neurotic dog.

Note: Page numbers in italics denote photo captions.

A

Aldrich, Robert, *81*, 82
Allen, Nancy, 152–54, *154*
Antonioni, Michelangelo, 86
Apache Woman, 55
Argento, Dario, 122, *126*, *128*, *129*, *131*, *132*, *134*
  career, 127–30, 132, 134–35
  filmography, 135
Arnold, Jack, *64*, *66*, *67*, *68*, *69*, *71*, *72*, 167
  career, 65, 67–73
  filmography, 73
Assault on Precinct 13, 169, 170, 174
Attack of the Crab Monsters, 55

B

Badham, John, 53
Barbeau, Adrienne, *124*, *138*, 140, 169, 170
Bat, The, 21–23, *21*, *24*, 26, 27
Bat Whispers, The, 20, 22–27, *23*, *26*, *27*
Bava, Mario, 127, 132, 134, 138, 139
Beast from 20,000 Fathoms, The, 65
Beast with a Million Eyes, The, 55
Becker, Harold, 53
Bergman, Ingmar, 137
Bertolucci, Barnardo, 127
Big City, The, 6
Big Trouble in Little China, 174
Bird with the Crystal Plumage, The, 127, 128, 129
Black Belly of the Tarantula, The, 128
Blackbird, The, 6
Black Cat, The, 109
Blob, The, 168
Blom, August, 11
Blood and Black Lace, 127, 139
Blood Feast, 4, 139
Blow Out, 153–54, *153*, *154*
Body Double, 147–48, 153, 154, *155*

Body Snatcher, The, 103
Boston Blackie, 78
Bride of Frankenstein, The, 29, 32–34, *32*, *33*, 72
Bride of Re-Animator, 187
Brides of Dracula, The, 89, 90–91
Brood, The, 177–80, *180*
Brooks, Mel, 102
Browning, Ricou, 67, 68
Browning, Tod, *3*, *4*, *5*, *7*, *8*, *9*, 29, 75
  career, 3–9
  filmography, 9
Bucket of Blood, A, 57
Buck Rogers, 168, *168*
Bug, 82, 83
Bujold, Geneviève, *150*, 151, 184, *184*
Burned Hand, The, 4

C

Cabinet of Dr. Caligari, 102
Cape Fear (1991), 95, 103
Capone, 59
Capra, Frank, 179
Carlson, Veronica, 87, 96–99, *96*
Carpenter, John, 157, *166*, *168*, *170*, *171*, *172*, *173*, 174
  career, 167–71, 173–75
  filmography, 175
Carrie, 140, 142, *147*, *150*, 151–52, 170
Castle, William, 53, *74*, *75*, *76*, *77*, *78*, *81*, *82*, 105
  career, 75, 77–83
  filmography, 83
Cat and the Canary, The, 15, 23
Cat Creeps, The, 23
Cat O'Nine Tails, The, 127–28, *134*
Cat People, 38, 40–43
Chance of a Lifetime, The, 78
Chaney, Lon, 5–6, *5*, *7*, 8, *8*, 9, *9*, 12, 13, *16*, 21, 22, *25*, 77
Chinatown, 105, 111, *114*
Christensen, Benjamin, *10*, *11*, *12*,

13, *15*, *16*, *17*, *19*
  career, 11–13, 15–19
  filmography, 19
Christine, *173*, 174
Church, The, 134
Clive, Colin, 29, *31*, *32*, 34, 86–87
Clouzot, Henri-Georges, *44*, *45*, *46*, *47*, *48*, *50*, *51*, *52*, 78–79
  career, 45–53
  filmography, 53
Clouzot, Vera, *44*, *50*, 52, *52*, 53
Code Name: Trixie. See *Crazies, The*
Colonel Bogey, 85
Combs, Jeremy, *186*, 187, 189, 191
Comedy of Terrors, The, 42
Corman, Roger, 53, *54*, *56*, *57*, *58*, *59*, *60*, *61*, *62*, 130
  career, 55–59, 61-62
  filmography, 62-63
Corsair, 27
Craven, Wes, *136*, *138*, *140*, *141*, *143*, *145*, 187, 192
  career, 137–45
  filmography, 145
Crawford, Joan, 81, 82, 101
Crazies, The (a.k.a. *Code Name: Trixie*), 117
Creature from the Black Lagoon, 67–68, *68*, 70, 73
Creature Walks Among Us, The, 70
Creepers. See *Phenomena*
Creeping Flesh, The, 101–2, *103*
Creepshow, 119–20, *124*
Creepshow 2, 116
Crescendo, 53
Crime Doctor, 78
Crime Does Not Pay, 41
Crimes of the Future, 177, *179*
Cronenberg, David, 72, *176*, *179*, *180*, *182*, *184*, 187
  career, 177–82, 184–85
  filmography, 185
Cry Baby Killer, The, 59
Cul-de-Sac, 105, 106, 111

Cunningham, Sean S., 137
Curse of Frankenstein, The, 85–87, *87, 89*, 95
Curse of the Demon, 37–38, *37*, 40, *40, 42*, 43
Curse of the Werewolf, The, 90, 92, 100–101
Curtis, Jamie Lee, *166*, 170, *170*
Cushing, Peter, 86–87, *87, 88,*, 89–91, *92*, 93, 95–96, 99–103, *99, 100, 103*

Dance of the Vampires. See *Fearless Vampire Killers, The*
Dario Argento's World of Horror, 134
Dark Half, The, 122, 123, *123*, 125
Dark Star, 168–69, *168*
Dark Tower, 101, 103
Darnborough, Anthony, 85, *86*
Daughter of Darkness, 189
Davis, Owen, 13
Dawn of the Dead, 118–19, *124*, 129
Day of the Dead, 120, 122, *124*
Day of the Triffids, The, 95
Day the World Ended, The, 56
Deadly Blessing, 136, 140, 145
Deadly Friend, 142–43, *143*
Dead Ringers, 182, 184, *184*, 185
Dead Zone, The, 181, *182*
Death Trap. See *Eaten Alive*
Deep Red, 128–29, *129*, 135
Demons, 131, 134
Deneuve, Catherine, 105–6, *107*
De Palma, Brian, 82, *147, 149, 150, 152, 153, 154, 155*
  career, 147–48, 151–55
  filmography, 155
Detour, 41
Devil Doll, The, 5, 9
Devils, The (Clouzot). See *Diabolique*
Devils, The (Russell), 191–92
Devil's Circus, The, 12, 17
Devil's Daughter, The. See *Sect, The*
Diabolique (a.k.a. *The Fiends* and *The Devils* and *Les Diaboliques*), *44*, 50–53, *50, 52*, 78-79, 82
Diary of Forbidden Dreams. See *What?*
Dickinson, Angie, 58, *152*, 154

Doctor and the Devils, The, 102–3
Dr. Butcher, M.D., 137
Dr. Jekyll and Mr. Hyde, 72, *72*
Doctors Don't Tell, 41
Dr. Strangelove, 168, *168*
Dr. Terror's House of Horrors, 98, 99
Dolls, 188–89, *188, 191*
Don't Torture a Duckling, 128
Dracula (Browning), *5, 6–8, 7, 9*, 24, 29, 42, 65, 67
Dracula (Melford), 6
Dracula Has Risen from the Grave, 96–99, *96, 100*
Dracula—Prince of Darkness, 91
Dressed to Kill, 147–48, 152–54, *152*
Dupont, E. A., 7, 45

Eaten Alive (a.k.a. *Starlight Slaughter* and *Horror Hotel Massacre* and *Death Trap*), 159–61
Eggshells, 158
Elephant Man, The, 102
Escape from New York, 170, *171*
E.T., 65, 161, 175
Everybody's Doing It, 4
Evil Dead, The, 145
Evil of Frankenstein, The, 87, 95–96, 98
Experiment Perilous, 40
Eyes of Mystery, The, 5

Faces of Death, 135
Fantômas, 11
Fast and the Furious, The, 55
Fear in the Night, 53
Fearless Vampire Killers, The (a.k.a. *Dance of the Vampires*), 105, 106, *107*, 109, *109*, 111
Feuillade, Louis, 11, 15, *16*, 17
Fiends, The. See *Diabolique*
Final Analysis, 53
Fisher, Terence, *84, 86, 87, 88, 89, 90, 91, 92*, 95, 142
  career, 85–87, 89–93
  filmography, 93
Five Guns West, 55
Flesh and the Fiends, The, 103
Florey, Robert, 29
Fly, The (1958), 182

Fly, The (1986), 181–82, *184*
Fog, The, 168, 170, *170*
Fortress, 192
Four Flies on Grey Velvet, 128, *132*
Four-Sided Triangle, 85
Francis, Freddie, *94, 96, 98, 99, 100, 103*
  career, 95–103
  filmography, 103
Frankenstein, 6, 8, 29–31, *30, 31*, 33, 42, 62, 65, 67, 68, 85–87
Frankenstein and the Monster from Hell, 84, 89
Frankenstein Created Woman, 87, 89, 142
Frankenstein Must Be Destroyed!, 87, 89, *92*
Frankenstein Unbound, 56, *58*, 61–62
Frantic, 111, 114
Freaks, 3, *3, 4*, 6, 8–9
Freddy's Nightmares, 165
Fresnay, Pierre, *45, 46*, 47–49
Friedkin, William, 49
From Beyond, 186, 187–88
From the Drain, 177
Frumkes, Roy, 137, 138
Fulci, Lucio, 128
Fun House, The (1972), 139
Funhouse, The (1981), *159*, 160–61
Fury, The, 150, 152

Gas-s-s-s, 59
Ghoul, The, 99
Gilligan's Island, 73
Gilling, John, 103
Girls in the Night, 65
Girly. See *Mumsy, Nanny, Sonny and Girly*
Glory, 95
Gordon, Stuart, *186, 188, 191*
  career, 187–92
  filmography, 192
Gorilla, The, 23
Great Garrick, The, 34
Greetings, 148
Griffith, D. W., 4, 5, 22

Haggard, Piers, 161
Hale, Creighton, *15*, 17
Halloween, 166, 167, *168*, 169-–70, 174
Hampton, Grayce, *20*, 26

Hansen, Gunner, 158, *158*
Haunted House, The, 10, 12, 13, 15, 16, 18
Haunted Palace, The, 56
Haunting, The, 38
Hawks, Howard, 169–71, *172,* 173–75
Häxan. See *Witchcraft Through the Ages*
Hay, Will, 85
Hell's Angels, 23, 29
Hemmings, David, 129, *129*
Henkel, Kim, 170–71
Hi, Mom!, 148
Hill in Korea, A, 95
Hills Have Eyes, The, 138, 139–41, 145
Hills Have Eyes, Part II, The, 140–41, *141*
Hitchcock, Alfred, 45, 47–53, 78, 81, *81,* 82, 95, 105, 127, 147, 148, 158, 169, 170
Homicidal, 78, 80, 82–83, 105
Honey, I Shrunk the Kids, 188
Hooper, Tobe, 101, *156, 157, 158, 159, 161, 163, 164,* 170–71, 187, 192
    career, 157–65
    filmography, 165
Horror Hotel Massacre. See *Eaten Alive*
Horror of Dracula, 88, 89–92
Hound of the Baskervilles, The, 91
House of Horror, The, 11, 17–19
House of Secrets, 53
House of Usher, 56, *60,* 130
House on Haunted Hill, 53, 74, 80, 82
Howling II, 140
Hubbard, Lucien, 19
Huston, John, 49, 95
Hysteria, 53, 95

Incredible Shrinking Man, The, 69, 70–72
Incredible Stranger, The, 41
Inferno, 127, 130, *134*
Innocents, The, 94
Intolerance, 5
Invaders from Mars (1953), 163–64
Invaders from Mars (1986), 163–65, *163*

Invasion of the Body Snatchers, 169, 175
Invisible Man, The, 28, 29, 32–33, 167
I Saw What You Did, 81, 82
Island of Terror, 92–93
Isle, Evan, 138
It Came from Outer Space, 64, 65, 67–70, *67, 68,* 167
I Walked with a Zombie, 36, 39, 40, 43, 143

Janos, Victor, 139
Jaws, 69
Jenny Lamour. See *Quai des Orfèvres*
Jim Bludso, 5
Joanou, Phil, 53
John Carpenter's Body Bags, 165
John Nesbitt's Passing Parade, 41
Journey's End, 29
Judex, 11
Jury of Fate, The, 5

K Karloff, Boris, 8, 29, 30, *30, 31, 33,* 34, 35, 57, 58, 62, 85, 90
King Kong, 68
Kneale, Nigel, 169, 174, 175
Knife in the Water, 105
Knightriders, 119
Kubrick, Stanley, 72
Kurosawa, Akira, 110

L Lang, Fritz, 7
L'Assassin Habite au 21, 46–47
Last House on Dead End Street, 139
Last House on the Left, 81, 137–40, *138, 142,* 145
Last House on the Left, Part II. See *Twitch of the Death Nerve*
La Terreur des Batignolles, 45
Laughton, Charles, *35,* 188-89
La Verité (a.k.a. *The Truth), 51*
Leatherface: The Texas Chainsaw Massacre III, 165
Le Corbeau (a.k.a. *The Raven), 45, 46,* 47–49, *48,* 53
Lee, Christopher, 86, *88,* 90, *90,* 91,

96–99, *98,* 102
Lee, Stephen, 188–89, 191, 192
Legend of the Werewolf, 100–101
Legion of Death, The, 5
Leni, Paul, 15
Leone, Sergio, 127
Leopard Man, The, 36, 43
Les Diaboliques. See *Diabolique*
Les Vampires, 11
Lewis, Herschell Gordon, 4
Liberty, 12
Lifeforce, 161, 163, 164
Lincoln, Fred, 137
Little Shop of Horrors, The, 57, 57, 58, 62
Litvak, Anatole, 45
Living Head, The, 4
Lodger, The, 47
London After Midnight, 6, 7, 8, *9*
Lourie, Eugene, 65
Lugosi, Bela, *5,* 6, 7, 8, 9, 25, 29, 75, 90
Lumet, Sidney, 180
Lynch, David, 102

M Macabre, 53, 75, 79–80, 82
Macbeth (1948), 110
Macbeth (1971), 19, 105, 110–11, *113*
Machine Gun Kelly, 56
Malden, Karl, 127–28, *134*
Malice, 53
Maniac, 53
Man Who Could Cheat Death, The, 88
Mark of the Vampire, 7, 8, 9
Martin, 117–18, *121*
Masque of the Red Death, The, 130
M. Butterfly, 177
Melford, George, 6
Memoirs of an Invisible Man, 167
Menzies, William Cameron, 164
Milland, Ray, 55–56, *59*
Miracles for Sale, 9
Moby Dick, 95
Mockery, 12, 16
Monkey Shines, 122–23, *123*
Monster, The, 13, 21–22, *25,* 77
Monster from the Ocean Floor, The, 55
Monster on the Campus, 72, 72
Morris, Chester, 24–27, *26, 27,* 78

Mouse That Roared, The, 72
Mr. Sardonicus, 78, 80–81
Mummy, The (original), 91
Mummy, The (1959 remake), 90, 91–92
Mumsy, Nanny, Sonny and Girly (a.k.a. Girly), 101
Murder à la Mod, 148
Murnau, F. W., 6–7
Mysterious Island, The, 19
Mysterious X, The, 11

Naked Lunch, 176, 180, 184–85
Network, 180
Neumann, Kurt, 33
New House on the Left, 138
Newman, Joseph M., 70
Nick Carter—Master Detective, 41
"Night Call," 41
Nightmare, 53, 95
Nightmare on Elm Street, A, 140, 141–42, 146, 165
Night Must Fall, 95
Night of Revenge, 11
Night of the Living Dead, 70, 117, 118, 120, 159, 169
Not of This Earth (1957), 57, 61
Not of This Earth (1988), 61

O'Bannon, Dan, 168
Obsession, 150, 151
Old Dark House, The (1932), 29–32, 35, 188–89, 188
Old Dark House, The (1963), 77
Once Upon a Time in the West, 127
One Exciting Night, 22
One More River, 29
Opera (a.k.a. Terror at the Opera), 126, 127, 129, 134
Out of the Past, 43
Outside the Law, 6

Paranoiac, 53, 95, 96
People Under the Stairs, The, 144–45, 145, 192
Pete Smith Specialties, 41
Phantom of the Opera, The (1925), 42, 148, 149

Phantom of the Opera, The (1962), 91, 92
Phantom of the Paradise, 148, 149, 151
Phantom Raiders, 41
Phenomena (a.k.a. Creepers), 132, 135
Pirates, 111, 114
Pit and the Pendulum, The (1961), 53, 59
Pit and the Pendulum, The (1991), 190–92, 191
Polanski, Roman, 19, 75, 83, 104, 107, 109, 110, 113, 114, 115
    career, 105–6, 109–11, 114
    filmography, 114–15
Poltergeist, 101, 161–64, 161
Premature Burial, The, 53, 59
Preminger, Otto, 49
Price, Vincent, 57, 58, 59, 60, 61, 62, 80, 82, 182
Prince of Darkness, 169, 174, 174
Project X, 82, 83
Psycho, 47, 50–53, 78, 80, 81, 82-83, 99, 105, 147, 158, 170
Psychopath, The, 95, 100

Quai des Orfèvres (a.k.a. Jenny Lamour), 47, 48, 49
Quartermass II, 175

Rabid, 177–80, 179
Raimi, Sam, 145
Rains, Claude, 29, 32–33, 167
Raising Cain, 147, 147
Raven, The (1943, Clouzot).
    See Le Corbeau
Raven, The (1963), 57
Re-Animator, 186, 187–89
Rear Window, 148, 169
Reed, Oliver, 90, 92, 95, 96, 161, 178, 179, 191
Reflections of Murder, 53
Reitman, Ivan, 177
Remember Last Night?, 29
Reptile, The, 99
Repulsion, 105–6, 107
Revenge, 5
Revenge of Frankenstein, The, 87, 88,

89, 95
Revenge of the Creature, 68–70, 68
Rio Bravo, 169
Robot Jox, 189, 191
Robson, Mark, 41, 42, 109–10
Romero, George A., 70, 116, 120, 121, 123, 124, 129, 134, 134, 157–59, 169, 170
    career, 117–20, 122–23, 125
    filmography, 125
Room at the Top, 95
Rosemary's Baby, 16, 19, 75, 83, 105, 109, 110, 110
Russell, Ken, 190–92

St. Valentine's Day Massacre, The, 59
Salem's Lot, 160
Scanners, 177, 179–82, 179, 180, 184, 185
Scorpian with Two Tails, 128
Scorsese, Martin, 95, 103
Scream of Fear, 53
Sect, The (a.k.a. The Devil's Daughter), 134
Serling, Rod, 41
Serpent and the Rainbow, The, 143, 143, 145
Seven Deaths in the Cat's Eye, 128
Seven Footprints to Satan, 15–19, 15, 16
Seven Keys to Baldpate, 13, 23
Seventh Victim, The, 109–10
Shanks, 83
Sherwood, John, 70
Ship That Died, The, 41
Shocker, 143–44, 143
Show, The, 3
Show Boat, 29
Siegel, Don, 169
Signoret, Simone, 50, 52, 53
Simon, Simone, 38, 42, 43
Sisters, 148, 149, 151, 153
Skull, The, 99, 101–2
Soavi, Michele, 134
So Long at the Fair, 85, 86
Someone's Watching Me, 169
Sons and Lovers, 95
Sorcerer, 49
Space Children, The, 72
Spielberg, Steven, 65, 69, 161–64

Spontaneous Combustion, 157, 165
Stage Fright, 134
Starlight Slaughter. See Eaten Alive
Starman, 175
Stereo, 177, *179*
Strait-Jacket, 81, *81*, 82
Stranger in Our House, 140
Suspiria, 130, *132, 134*
Swamp Thing, *138*, 140, 142, 145
Swamp Women, 55

T Tale of Two Cities, A, 41
Tales From the Crypt, 99, *100*
Tales of Terror, 57
Tales That Will Rip Your
    Heart Out, 137
Tales That Witness Madness,
    99, *103*
Tarantula, 69–70, 72
Tenant, The, 105, 111, *115*
Tenebrae (a.k.a. Unsane), *126*, 130,
    132
Terror, The, 23
Terror at the Opera. See Opera
Tess, *104*, 105, 106, 111, 114
Texas Chainsaw Massacre, The, *156*,
    157–61, *157, 158*, 164–65, 171
Texas Chainsaw Massacre 2, The,
    160, 164–65, *164*, 192
They All Come Out, 41
They Came from Within, 177–80, *179*
They Live, 166, 169, 174–75
Thing, The (1951), 65, *67*, 170–71,
    172, 173, 174
The Thing (1982), 167, 170–71, *172*,
    173–74
13 Ghosts, 80
Thirteenth Letter, The, 49
This Island Earth, 70, *71*
Thunderball, 67
Tingler, The, 53, 77, 80, 82
Todd, Thelma, *10, 15, 16*, 17, 19, 27
Together, 137
Tomb of Legeia, *61*
Torture Garden, 99
Tourneur, Jacques, *36, 37, 38, 39,
    40, 42*, 143
  career, 37–38, 40–43
  filmography, 43
Tourneur, Maurice, 19, 40–41
Transfer, 177
Treasure of the Sierra Madre, The, 49

Tremors, 70
Trip, The, 59
Trog, 101
Truth, The. See La Verité
Twin Peaks, 144
Twitch of the Death Nerve (a.k.a. Last
    House on the Left, Part II), 138
Two and Two Make Six, 95
Two Evil Eyes, 122, 134–35, *134*
Two Faces of Dr. Jekyll, The, 92
Two Men and a Wardrobe, 111
2001: A Space Odyssey, 72, 168, *168*

U Ulmer, Edgar G., 109
Undertaker and His Pals,
    The, 139
Underwood, Ron, 70
Unholy Three, The, 5, 6, 9
Unknown, The, 3, 6
Unsane. See Tenebrae

V Vengeance, 95
Venom, 161
Vertigo, 47, 51, 53, 148
Videodrome, 178, 180–81,
    182
Virgin Spring, The, 137

W Wages of Fear, The, 47, 49,
    51
War Gods of the Deep, 42
Wasp Woman, The, 55
Waterloo Bridge, 29
Welles, Orson, 110
West, Roland, *20, 21, 22, 23, 24, 25,
    26, 27*
  career, 21–27
  filmography, 27
West of Zanzibar, 3, 8
Whale, James, 6, *28, 30, 31, 32, 33,
    35*, 65, 67, 72, 77, 86, 167,
    187–89, *188*
  career, 29–34
  filmography, 35
What? (a.k.a. Diary of Forbidden
    Dreams), 105, 111
Whatever Happened to Baby Jane?,
    81, 82
Where East Is East, 6
Whistler, The, 78
Whoopee!, 23
Wicked Darling, The, 5

Wild Angels, The, 59
Williams, Grant, *69*, 70–72
Wise, Robert, 38, 41, 103
Witchcraft Through the Ages (a.k.a.
    Häxan), 11–12, 13, 15, 19, *19*
Wolf Man, The, 42
Woods, James, 178, 180–81, *182*

X X—The Man with X-Ray
    Eyes, *54*, 55–56
X the Unknown, 93, 163